Communications in Computer and Information Science 599

Commenced Publication in 2007
Founding and Former Series Editors:
Alfredo Cuzzocrea, Dominik Ślęzak, and Xiaokang Yang

More information about this series at http://www.springer.com/series/7899

Leszek A. Maciaszek · Joaquim Filipe (Eds.)

Evaluation of Novel Approaches to Software Engineering

10th International Conference, ENASE 2015
Barcelona, Spain, April 29–30, 2015
Revised Selected Papers

 Springer

Editors

Leszek A. Maciaszek
Institute of Business Informatics
Wrocław University of Economics
Wrocław
Poland

and

Department of Computing
Macquarie University
Sydney
Australia

Joaquim Filipe
Institute for Systems and Technologies
  of Information, Control and
  Communication (INSTICC)
Setúbal
Portugal

and

Department of Systems and Informatics
Instituto Politécnico de Setúbal (IPS)
Setúbal
Portugal

ISSN 1865-0929   ISSN 1865-0937 (electronic)
Communications in Computer and Information Science
ISBN 978-3-319-30242-3   ISBN 978-3-319-30243-0 (eBook)
DOI 10.1007/978-3-319-30243-0

Library of Congress Control Number: 2015955869

Printed on acid-free paper

This Springer imprint is published by SpringerNature
The registered company is Springer International Publishing AG Switzerland

Preface

The present book includes extended and revised versions of a set of selected papers from the 10th International Conference on Evaluation of Novel Approaches to Software Engineering (ENASE 2015), held in Barcelona, Spain, during 29–30 April, 2015, which was sponsored by the Institute for Systems and Technologies of Information, Control and Communication (INSTICC) and technically co-sponsored by the IEEE Computer Society and IEEE Computer Society's Technical Council on Software Engineering (TCSE).

The mission of ENASE (Evaluation of Novel Approaches to Software Engineering) is to be a prime international forum in which to discuss and publish research findings and IT industry experiences with relation to the evaluation of novel approaches to software engineering. The conference recognizes the necessary changes in systems and software thinking due to contemporary shifts of computing paradigms to e-services, cloud computing, mobile connectivity, business processes, and societal participation.

By comparing novel approaches with established traditional practices and by evaluating them against systems and software quality criteria, ENASE conferences advance knowledge and research in software engineering, including and emphasizing service-oriented, business-process driven, and ubiquitous mobile computing. ENASE aims at identifying the most hopeful trends and proposing new directions for consideration by researchers and practitioners involved in large-scale systems and software development, integration, deployment, delivery, maintenance, and evolution.

ENASE 2015 received 74 submissions, from 33 countries in all continents, of which 40 % were orally presented and 16 % presented as posters, and their authors were invited to submit extended versions of their papers for this book. In order to evaluate each submission, double-blind reviewing was performed by the Program Committee. Finally, only the best 10 papers were included in this book.

We would like to highlight that ENASE 2015 also had four plenary keynote lectures, given by internationally distinguished researchers, namely: George Giaglis (Athens University of Economics and Business, Greece), Witold Staniszkis (Rodan Development, Poland), Martin Mocker (MIT, USA and Reutlingen University, Germany), and Nuria Oliver (Telefonica Research, Spain). We must acknowledge the invaluable contribution of all keynote speakers who, as renowned researchers in their areas, have presented cutting-edge work, thus contributing to the scientific content of the conference.

We especially thank the authors, whose research and development efforts are recorded here. The knowledge and diligence of the reviewers were essential to ensure the quality of the papers presented at the conference and published in this book. Finally, a special thanks to all members of the INSTICC team, whose involvement was fundamental for organizing a smooth and successful conference.

April 2015

Joaquim Filipe
Leszek A. Maciaszek

Organization

Conference Chair

Joaquim Filipe   Polytechnic Institute of Setúbal/INSTICC, Portugal

Program Chair

Leszek A. Maciaszek   Wroclaw University of Economics, Poland and
Macquarie University, Sydney, Australia

Program Committee

Marco Aiello	University of Groningen, The Netherlands
Mehmet Aksit	University of Twente, The Netherlands
Guglielmo de Angelis	CNR - IASI, Italy
Costin Badica	University of Craiova, Romania
Paul Bailes	The University of Queensland, Australia
Ayse Basar Bener	Ryerson University, Canada
Jan Blech	RMIT University, Australia
Carlos Canal	University of Malaga, Spain
Shiping Chen	CSIRO, Australia, Australia
William Cheng-Chung Chu	Tunghai University, Taiwan
Rem Collier	University College Dublin, Ireland
Rebeca Cortazar	University of Deusto, Spain
Massimo Cossentino	National Research Council, Italy
Bernard Coulette	Université Toulouse Jean Jaurès, France
Mads Dam	KTH - Royal Institute of Technology, Sweden
Maya Daneva	University of Twente, The Netherlands
Mariangiola Dezani	Università di Torino, Italy
Tadashi Dohi	Hiroshima University, Japan
Mahmoud Elish	King Fahd University of Petroleum and Minerals, Saudi Arabia
Angelina Espinoza	Universidad Autónoma Metropolitana, Iztapalapa (UAM-I), Spain
Vladimir Estivill-Castro	Griffith University, Australia
Joerg Evermann	Memorial University of Newfoundland, Canada
Maria João Ferreira	Universidade Portucalense, Portugal
Stéphane Galland	Université de Technologie de Belfort Montbéliard, France

Ronald H. Perrott	Oxford e-Research Centre, UK
Dana Petcu	West University of Timisoara, Romania
Marcelo Pimenta	UFRGS, Brazil
Naveen Prakash	MRCE, India
Adam Przybylek	Gdansk University of Technology, Poland
Elke Pulvermueller	University of Osnabrück, Germany
Lukasz Radlinski	West Pomeranian University of Technology, Poland
Philippe Roose	LIUPPA/IUT de Bayonne/UPPA, France
Antonio Ruiz-Cortés	University of Seville, Spain
Krzysztof Sacha	Warsaw University of Technology, Poland
Camille Salinesi	University Paris 1 - Pantheon Sorbonne, France
Markus Schatten	University of Zagreb, Croatia
Fabio A. Schreiber	Politecnico di Milano, Italy
Marcin Sikorski	Gdansk University of Technology, Poland
Josep Silva	Universidad Politécnica de Valencia, Spain
Ioana Sora	Politehnica University of Timisoara, Romania
Andreas Speck	Christian-Albrechts-Universität Kiel, Germany
Miroslaw Staron	University of Gothenburg, Sweden
Armando Stellato	University of Rome, Tor Vergata, Italy
Jakub Swacha	University of Szczecin, Poland
Bedir Tekinerdogan	Wageningen University, The Netherlands
Stephanie Teufel	University of Fribourg, Switzerland
Rainer Unland	University of Duisburg-Essen, Germany
Olegas Vasilecas	Vilnius Gediminas Technical University, Lithuania
Krzysztof Wecel	Poznan University of Economics, Poland
Bernhard Westfechtel	University of Bayreuth, Germany
Martin Wirsing	Ludwig-Maximilians-Universität München, Germany
Igor Wojnicki	AGH University of Science and Technology, Poland
Dinghao Wu	The Pennsylvania State University, USA
Kang Zhang	The University of Texas at Dallas, USA
Alfred Zimmermann	Reutlingen University, Germany

Additional Reviewers

Raul Barbosa	University of Coimbra, Portugal
Felice Cardone	Università di Torino, Italy
Ferruccio Damiani	Università Degli Studi di Torino, Italy
Octavio Martín-Díaz	Universidad de Sevilla, Spain
Henry Muccini	University of L'Aquila, Italy
Gianluca Palermo	Politecnico di Milano, Italy
Manuel Resinas	Universidad de Sevilla, Spain
José Miguel Cañete Valdeón	Universidad de Sevilla, Spain
Chen Wang	CSIRO ICT Centre, Australia

Invited Speakers

George Giaglis	Athens University of Economics and Business, Greece
Witold Staniszkis	Rodan Development, Poland
Martin Mocker	MIT, USA and Reutlingen University, Germany
Nuria Oliver	Telefonica Research, Spain

Contents

On Generating Test Cases from EDT Specifications

R. Venkatesh, Ulka Shrotri, Amey Zare, and Supriya Agrawal[✉]

Tata Research Development and Design Centre, Pune, India
{r.venky,ulka.s,amey.zare,supriya.agrawal1}@tcs.com

Abstract. In an earlier work we presented a cost-effective approach to generate test cases that cover functional requirements of reactive systems. The approach involved specifying requirements in EDT (Expressive Decision Tables) and generating test cases from them using RGRaF, a Row-Guided Random algorithm with Fuzzing.

In this paper we propose DRAFT, a novel Dependency driven Random Algorithm with Fuzzing at Time boundaries, to improve requirement coverage. DRAFT is an enhancement over RGRaF in its ability to exploit dependencies between requirements. To compare DRAFT and other test case generation approaches - manual, pure random and RGRaF, we conducted experiments on four real-world applications. The experiments indicated that DRAFT achieves better coverage than RGRaF and its variants. When compared with the manual approach, our test cases subsumed all manual test cases and achieved up to 60 % reduction in effort.

Keywords: Reactive systems · Functional test generation · Random test case generation

1 Introduction

Our earlier work presented Expressive Decision Tables Based Testing (EBT), a cost-effective method to automatically generate functional test cases for reactive systems [1,2]. Test generation in EBT is done by *EDT-Test*, a tool that targets coverage of requirements and their interactions. There is a need to automate functional test case generation as it is an intellectually demanding and critical task that has a strong impact on the effectiveness and efficiency of the entire testing process [3]. For large and complex reactive software, it is hard even for domain experts to envision all interactions between requirements. Hence, it becomes very difficult to manually write functional test cases that cover all requirements and the interactions among them.

A formal specification of the requirements is necessary to generate test cases with expected results. Therefore, any method to generate these test cases automatically must have three attributes: (a) an easy-to-use formal notation to specify requirements, from a practitioner's point of view, (b) a scalable

© Springer International Publishing Switzerland 2016
L.A. Maciaszek and J. Filipe (Eds.): ENASE 2015, CCIS 599, pp. 1–20, 2016.
DOI: 10.1007/978-3-319-30243-0_1

test-generation algorithm, and (c) coverage criteria that map to requirements. EBT had these attributes and included an easy-to-use tabular notation, EDT, and the tool, *EDT-Test*.

Traditionally, Random Test case Generation (RTG) [4] and Model-Based Testing (MBT) [5] have been used for test case generation. We now describe some advantages of EBT over MBT and RTG, when compared on the three attributes.

Formal Notation: Although MBT is implemented by several tools [6–9], it is not widely adopted by practitioners as requirements need to be specified in the formal languages supported by the tools. Often, these languages demand a strong mathematical background from the user and require the user to design the state space of the problem even if it is not part of the requirements [10]. This makes MBT effort-intensive and adversely affects the overall cost of the approach. In fact, very little is known about the cost-effectiveness of MBT [11]. To reduce this specification complexity and effort, EBT uses EDT as the formal language. EDT has been shown to be more efficient and effective for specifying functional requirements of reactive systems [2], than state-based formalisms such as Statecharts [9] and Software Cost Reduction (SCR) [12]. In an EDT specification, rows correspond to requirements that are described in a natural language.
RTG generates input sequences using input signals and their types and does not use any formal specification of a system. As a result, though RTG is the easiest to use, it cannot generate expected output along with the generated input sequence. Therefore, additional efforts are required to check the validity of the input sequences and its expected output whereas EBT generates expected results also.
Test-generation Algorithm: As stated earlier, RTG generates input sequences randomly using only input signals and their types. MBT tools use a combination of random generation and constraint solving to generate test cases, neither of which scale up to industry-size applications [13,14]. EBT includes RGRaF algorithm (pronounced as R-graph) that combines Row-Guided Random input generation with Fuzzing at time boundaries. RGRaF generates expected results and scales up better than constraint solving and random algorithms.
Coverage Criteria: The syntactic structure of languages supported by MBT is very different from the original requirements description resulting in no direct mapping from specifications to requirements. Hence, the coverages targeted by these tools, such as state and transition coverage, do not directly map to the requirements [15]. Coverage criteria targeted by RTG is based on the values taken by individual input events leading to a large number of redundant test cases. EBT targets requirement and requirement interaction coverage, which correspond to coverage of requirements and interaction between requirements.

In summary, existing methods have the following restraints: (a) they are effort intensive - they either require specifications in a formal language or need expected results to be determined, (b) the algorithms implemented by them do not scale to industry-size applications, and (c) the generated test cases do not map directly to requirements. EBT was conceived to overcome these limitations. RGRaF, however, sometimes fails to cover all requirements of a large system. We present a new algorithm DRAFT, an improvement over RGRaF that exploits dependencies between requirements to achieve better coverage. *EDT-Test* has been enhanced to include DRAFT.

To evaluate EBT and its algorithms, we conducted experiments by running *EDT-Test* on 13 real-world software modules of four projects from automotive domain. For this paper, three of the projects are same as in our previous work [1] and a new project is included. We conducted fresh experiments for all the four projects. We specified requirements of all 13 modules in EDT and generated test cases using *EDT-Test*. To evaluate the scalability of our algorithms we first compare RGRaF with: (a) a pure random test case generation algorithm and (b) RGRaF without fuzzing. Next we compare the coverages achieved by DRAFT and RGRaF. As manually created test cases and effort data for these case studies were available with us, we also assessed the cost-effectiveness of EBT for them. Our findings clearly show that RGRaF scales better than pure random test case generation and RGRaF without fuzzing. However, DRAFT fares better than RGRaF on most of the examples. The findings also showed that EBT is more cost-effective than manual testing. Additionally, the case studies revealed a bug in a production code and uncovered several missing requirements showing the usefulness of EBT.

We have not compared our algorithms with model-checking or constraint solving because it does not scale up on real-world applications [14]. We validated this through an experiment in which we took a realistic example, smaller than the ones in our case studies, translated it to the C language and ran the constraint solving tool Autogen [16] on that example. We observed that Autogen was not able to generate any test cases whereas *EDT-Test* covered all requirements. Based on the findings of this experiment, we decided not to compare *EDT-Test* against any constraint solving based tools.

The main contribution of this paper is a cost-effective method, EBT, to generate functional test cases. This is achieved by the following:

- Using EDT as a specification language to reduce the effort required in specifying requirements.
- Extending EDT with constructs that enable easy modeling of the environment.
- A row-guided random algorithm (RGRaF) that also adds fuzzing at time boundaries to scale up test generation.
- An enhancement (DRAFT) to RGRaF that exploits dependencies between requirements to achieve better coverage.
- Targeting two test coverage criteria, row and row-interaction coverage, to ensure that all requirements and interactions between requirements are tested adequately.

The organization of the paper is as follows. Section 2 discusses the related work. We explain the EDT Notation in brief in Sect. 3. The coverage criteria for *EDT-Test*, row and row-interaction, are described in Sect. 4. Section 5 describes the algorithms RGRaF and DRAFT in detail. We present extensions to EDT in Sect. 6 and describe the observations and findings of the experiments conducted in Sect. 7. Finally, Sect. 8 concludes the paper.

2   Related Work

The relevant work in this area can be classified based on the source specification language, the technique employed and the targeted coverage criteria.

Generating test cases from specifications has received a lot of attention with tools that have a variety of input languages. There are tools based on languages such as Software Cost Reduction method (SCR) [12], Statecharts [17], Z [18], Spec# [19], and Lustre [20]. These languages require test engineers to specify the requirements of the system under test (SUT) in the form of mathematical expressions or state diagrams, which takes a lot of effort. Tahat et al. [15] have proposed an approach to generate test cases from requirements given in textual and SDL format, but they do not have any data to show the benefits of their approach nor have they evaluated their approach for cost-effectiveness. To the best of our knowledge, there has been no work that compares the effort required to specify requirements in a formal language and generate test cases using a tool for industry examples. EBT reduces the effort required for specification by choosing a compact and easy to use notation, EDT [2].

Additionally, all the aforementioned tools target a coverage criterion that is natural to the formal language being used. Thus, if the language is Statecharts based then state and transition coverage criteria are targeted, and in the case of Z, pre-/post-operation relations are considered as coverage criteria. As a result, these coverage criteria do not always achieve requirements coverage. In contrast, *EDT-Test* generates test cases to achieve row and row-interaction coverage giving direct mapping to requirements coverage as EDT rows map directly to requirements.

Several tools employ a constraint solver or a model-checker to generate test cases. These include Java Path Finder [21], Autogen [16], KLEE [22] and Pex [23]. The scalability of constraint solvers [13,14] continues to limit the applicability of these techniques and there are still some challenges that need to be overcome for its wider adoption [24]. Random testing [25] has also been studied extensively as an alternative to systematic testing as it is very easy to generate a large number of test cases randomly. Theoretical studies indicate that random testing is as effective as systematic testing [26,27]. On the other hand, empirical studies [28,29] have shown that pure random testing achieves less code coverage than systematic test generation. Unlike existing methods, EBT implements a row-guided random technique with fuzzing at time boundaries to achieve scalability and coverage.

3   EDT Notation

EDT [2] is a tabular notation to formally specify requirements of reactive systems. This notation is designed in a manner that makes it easy to understand and use, and yet keeps it formal enough to enable automated test case generation. It provides a uniform notation to specify both – state-based and sequence-based requirements, leading to compact specifications of reactive systems.

An EDT specification consists of one or more table(s) where the column headers specify the input and output signal names, and the rows specify relationships between patterns of input and output signal values or events. We illustrate EDT through partial requirements of the *Alarm* module of a real world automotive application, which are described below:

1. If *Ignition* and *Alarm* are *Off*, and *PanicSw* is pressed and released twice within 3 s, then *Alarm* should be *On* for 30 s, and *Flash* should blink 30 times with a gap of 500 ms between each *On* and *Off* and should have *No_Req* after that.
2. If *Alarm* is *On* and *PanicSw* is pressed for more than 3 s and then released (called as *long press*), then the *Flash* should be *No_Req* and *Alarm* should be *Off*.
3. If *Ignition* becomes *On*, then *Flash* should be *No_Req* and *Alarm* should be *Off*.

Table 1 specifies the above requirements using EDT, in which each row maps directly to one of the requirements. The column headers specify three input signals: *Ignition*, *PanicSw* and *Alarm*, and two output signals: *Flash* and *Alarm*. Its is worth noting that *Alarm* is an input and output (I/O) signal. The pattern expressions in each input cell specify the sequence of input value(s) that will match the requirements of that cell. The pattern expressions in an output cell specify the sequence of signal value(s) that will be output when the requirements of all the input cells in that row are matched. The pattern language itself is regular, as EDT supports a discrete timed model, and can be recognized by a discrete timed automaton [30]. The pattern *Off* given in the first row for columns corresponding to the signals *Ignition* and *Alarm* matches when the environment sends the value *Off* to the system. The compactness of EDT is illustrated by the pattern '{{*Press;Release*}{=2}}{<3s}' which is detected when the values

Table 1. EDT for alarm feature.

Sno	In Ignition	In Alarm	In PanicSw	Out Alarm	Out Flash
1	Off	Off	{{Press;Release}{=2}} {<3s}	On{=30s}; Off	{On{=500ms};Off{=500ms}} {=30};No_Req
2		On	Press{>3s};Release	Off	No_Req
3	On			Off	No_Req

Press followed by *Release* are received twice within three seconds for the signal *PanicSw*. The output pattern in the first row corresponding to the signal *Flash* specifies that the values *On* followed by *Off* should be output with a gap of 500 ms, and this pattern should be repeated 30 times.

4   Coverage Criteria

To effectively test the system specified using EDT, we propose two coverage criteria – row coverage and row-interaction coverage, which are described below:

4.1   Requirement/Row Coverage

An EDT row is covered when it is matched in at least one generated test case. Complete row coverage is said to be achieved when all rows in the EDT are covered. The intuition behind row coverage is that an individual requirement can often be mapped to one or more EDT row(s) and hence row coverage implies requirements coverage.

Table 2 illustrates a test case corresponding to EDT specification shown in Table 1. The default values of input signals *Ignition* and *Alarm* are considered to be *Off*. When *PanicSw* values are generated as *Press* followed by *Release* twice within three seconds, that is at time 1500 milliseconds (ms) in Table 2, Row 1 is matched and hence the expected output of *Alarm* is *On* and the flashing pattern is '*On followed by Off*'.

4.2   Requirement-Interaction/ Row-Interaction Coverage

Requirements, as specified in EDT, can have the following two types of interactions between them:

- I/O row-interaction: (r_1, r_2) is said to be a I/O row-interaction if r_1 outputs a value that is used by r_2.
- O/O row-interaction: (r_1, r_2) is said to be a O/O row-interaction if both r_1 and r_2 output values for the same signal at the same time.

Row-interaction is covered when a test case captures either of the aforementioned interactions between rows.

In the example mentioned in Table 1, because of the common I/O signal *Alarm*, there are three I/O row-interactions: $(1, 2), (2, 1)$ and $(3, 1)$. This is because the output *On* to *Alarm* in Row 1 is used by Row 2 and the output *Off* to *Alarm* in Rows 2 and 3 is used by Row 1. The input sequence shown in the test case in Table 2 covers the row-interaction $(1, 2)$.

In Table 1, Rows 1 and 3 form an O/O row-interaction $(1, 3)$ as both these rows can potentially affect the output value of the same signal *Flash* at the same time. Consider the input sequence shown in Table 3. At time 1500 ms, the output pattern for *Flash* will start because Row 1 is matched. However, at time 2000 ms

Table 2. Test Case for Row and I/O row-interaction coverage.

Time(ms)	Input Signals	Remarks
0	PanicSw=Press	
500	PanicSw=Release	
1000	PanicSw=Press	
1500	PanicSw=Release	Row 1 output starts
2000	PanicSw=Press	
5500	PanicSw=Release	Row 2 output starts

Table 3. Test Case for O/O row-interaction coverage.

Time(ms)	Input Signals	Remarks
0	PanicSw=Press	
500	PanicSw=Release	
1000	PanicSw=Press	
1500	PanicSw=Release	Row 1 output starts
2000	Ignition=On	Row 3 output starts

the output of *Flash* is changed to *No_Req*, although the previous output pattern is still going on. This happens because Row 3 is matched due to the occurrence of *Ignition = On*. When such input sequence is generated in a test case, it is said to have covered O/O row-interaction $(1, 3)$.

5   RGRaF and DRAFT Algorithms

We now present the algorithms RGRaF and DRAFT that are used to generate test cases with expected output from EDT specifications. A test case consists of a timed sequence of input values and corresponding expected output values. Each element of the sequence is a tuple of the form $(signalname, value, time, category)$ where, *signalname* is an input signal, *value* is a valid value for that signal, *time* is the time when the *value* arrives, and *category* indicates if the signal is an input, output or I/O signal. The sequence is arranged in increasing order of time. The test case generation algorithms that generate a set of these sequences consists of four main steps; Automata construction, Input sequence generation (InpGen), Expected output sequence generation (ExpGen) and fuzzing at time-boundaries (Fuzz).

5.1   RGRaF: Row-Guided Random Algorithm with Fuzzing

RGRaF begins by building a discrete timed automaton corresponding to the regular expression in each cell, using known techniques. It then invokes InpGen, which selects a random sequence of rows and then systematically expands each row in the sequence to produce a sequence of inputs that may match that row. This input sequence is passed on to ExpGen, which executes the timed automaton of each cell for each input to determine the rows that match. When a row matches, ExpGen modifies the input sequence by adding outputs generated by the matched row, thus creating the final test sequence. To increase the probability of time related requirements getting covered, ExpGen invokes Fuzz, a function that randomly fuzzes the time of inputs at the time(τ) of the nearest potential time-out event. This execution of InpGen and ExpGen is repeated till either all rows and row-interactions are covered or the number of row sequences generated by InpGen exceeds a given threshold (Sample Size), S. We refer to the number of row sequences generated as *test cases tried*. The generated test cases are always a subset of the *test cases tried*. The steps involved in RGRAF are described in detail below:

RGRaF InpGen( )	*DRAFT InpGen( )*
$R_s := [\,]$	$R_s := [\,]$
Populate R_s randomly	Select a r_u such that $r_u \in U_r$
$I_s := \varnothing$	$R_s := R_s . r_u$
For each r in R_s	While (i $\leq M$)
$\quad I_r := Expand(r)$	$\quad$ Select r such that there is a high probability that
$\quad I_s := I_s . I_r$	$\quad$ some r'$\in R_s$ depends on r
End For	$\quad R_s := R_s . r$
return I_s	$\quad$ i := i+1
	End while
	$I_s := \varnothing$
	For each r in R_s
	$\quad I_r := Expand(r)$
	$\quad I_s := I_s . I_r$
	End For
	return I_s

Fig. 1. InpGen( ).

InpGen for RGRaF: This function (Fig. 1) first creates a sequence of rows R_s by randomly selecting some EDT rows, with uncovered rows having a higher probability of selection. It then invokes the function *Expand*, which generates an input sequence for each cell of each row r in R_s, by selecting an element from the language specified by that cell's regular expression. The sequences of all the cells of a row are merged, maintaining time ordering, to get an input sequence I_r for the row. Each I_r is appended to I_s to get a combined input sequence for all the rows in R_s. Note that the expansion of each row proceeds independent of the other rows in the sequence and does not take into account any value for I/O variable that may be generated by a previous row. As a result, the actual rows matching the generated sequence of inputs could be different from the rows in R_s. This systematic expansion of rows ensures the generation of input patterns that need repetition. The probability of such repeated pattern getting generated will be low if input generation is purely random.

ExpGen: This function (Fig. 2) takes I_s as input, which consists of inputs yet to be processed. Each input in I_s is processed by taking a *step* of each row r, of the EDT table T. A *step* of a row consists of taking a transition in the automaton of each cell in that row. Once a step is taken a row matches if all its automata are in their final state, with at least one of them having reached the final state due to the current signal. When a row matches, tuples with *category* output or I/O corresponding to the output O_p of that row are merged ($\oplus$) with the input sequence I_s maintaining its time ordering and the matched row is added to the set of matched/covered rows M_r. If the current row matched due to outputs generated by a previously matched row r_i, then the pair $\langle r_i, r \rangle$ is added to the matched/covered interactions M_i. Any I/O signal produced by a matched row is processed in the next step. If an automaton is in a state that has an outgoing time-out transition it is said to be in a time-out state. Of all the automata in a time-out state ExpGen returns the smallest time τ_{min} at which a time-out transition may occur.

Fuzz: As in standard discrete timed automata each transition of a cell's automaton is either labeled by a signal value or is a *time-out* transition of the form $\langle c, op, n \rangle$ where c is a clock variable, op is one of the operators $\{<, \leq, >, \geq\}$ and n is a positive integer representing time. Timing constraints modeled as *time-out* transitions are one of the reasons why model-based approaches to test generation

$ExpGen(I_s)$	$RGRaF/DRAFT\ Algorithm$
For each r in table T	U_r := Set of all uncovered rows
$\quad \tau := ExecuteAutomata$(r,first($I_s$))	U_p := Set of all uncovered row-interactions
$\quad$ If (r matches)	i := 0
$\quad\quad I_s := I_s \oplus O_p$ of r	For each cell in each r
$\quad\quad M_r := M_r \cup r$	$\quad Build$ its timed automaton
$\quad$ End If	End For
$\quad$ For all rows r_i that produce some input of r	While(i $\leq$ S and ($U_r \neq \varnothing$ or $U_p \neq \varnothing$))
$\quad\quad M_i := M_i \cup \{\langle r_i, r \rangle\}$	$\quad I_s :=$ RGRaF/DRAFT InpGen( )
$\quad\quad$ End If	$\quad$ While ($I_s \neq \varnothing$)
$\quad \tau_{min} := \min (\tau_{min}, \tau)$	$\quad\quad (M_r, M_i, \tau) :=$ ExpGen(I_s)
End For	$\quad\quad U_r := U_r$ - M_r
Return (M_r, M_i, τ_{min})	$\quad\quad U_p := U_p$ - M_i
	$\quad\quad I_s := I_s \rightarrow$ Next
	$\quad\quad$ Fuzz: Randomly change time of first(I_s)
	$\quad\quad$ to before or after τ
	$\quad$ End While
	$\quad$ i := i+1
	End While

Fig. 2. ExpGen( ) and RGRaF/DRAFT Algorithm.

do not scale up to industry size code. Random algorithms too are unable to cover time-based requirements. To address this issue, at the end of each step, we randomly change the time of inputs occurring around the nearest time τ, at which a time-out may occur. The generated scenario is altered by randomly changing the time of some inputs that occur either - (a) at a time $t < \tau$ to a time $t' > \tau$ or (b) at a time $t > \tau$ to a time $t' < \tau$.

We call the above alteration *fuzzing* at time boundaries. Consider the scenario presented in Table 2. After processing the input at 1500 ms, the nearest time-out will occur at 3000 ms due to the PanicSw pattern in Row 1 of the example given in Table 1. At this point, the algorithm could randomly choose to fuzz the scenario by changing the time of the input at 2000 ms to 3500 ms or it could change the time of the input occurring at 5500 ms to 2500 ms. If fuzzing is not performed, the scenario will be generated only at the 3000 ms that is the time-out. Hence, fuzzing helps in generating scenarios with different time around τ and thus helps in covering complex time-based scenarios. All these steps are repeated until full row coverage and row-interaction coverage is achieved (i.e., $U_r = \varnothing \wedge U_p = \varnothing$), or the number of test cases tried exceeds the Sample Size S.

5.2 DRAFT: Dependency Driven Random Algorithm with Fuzzing at Time Boundaries

DRAFT (Fig. 2) uses row dependencies to generate test cases and differs from RGRaF only in the manner by which it selects R_s in InpGen. Details of InpGen of DRAFT are as follows.

InpGen for DRAFT: DRAFT populates a sequence of rows R_s, as shown in Fig. 1, based on the dependencies of rows on each other. A row r is said to be dependent on a row r_d if output of r_d is consumed as an input by r. DRAFT first selects a row r_u from the set of uncovered rows U_r, and appends r_u to R_s. Next, another row r is selected such that there is a high probability that some row in R_s depends on it. r is appended to R_s. The process of selecting and appending rows in R_s is repeated till R_s reaches a given maximum size(M). This size limit of R_s is taken as an input from user. Once R_s is populated, the remainder of InpGen functions similar to InpGen of RGRaF.

6   Extensions to EDT

For the generated test cases to be useful they should not have any input combinations that will never be generated by the environment. To eliminate such invalid combinations, the environment constraints need to be specified. We have extended the EDT notation with a special output column RejectFlag to support easy modeling of the environment constraints as required for testing. Similarly, we have also added a special column ErrorFlag to support specification of properties. These two extensions are described in detail below.

6.1 Modeling Environment Constraints

In reactive systems, there could be several combination(s) of input(s) that can never occur in the actual run of the system. For instance, in a car, the left and right indicator switches cannot be *On* simultaneously. We provide a special output column, *RejectFlag* to model such environment constraints. These constraints are specified as an EDT row with a *Reject* output value to the *RejectFlag* column. Sample EDT row specifying an environment constraint is illustrated in Table 4.

If a test case generated by the Input Sequence Generator matches the row in Table 4, then that test case is rejected. So *RejectFlag* is actually used to eliminate test cases for all the combinations that cannot happen in the functioning of real-world reactive systems.

Table 4. Specification for environment constraints.

Sno	In LeftSw	In RightSw	Out RejectFlag
1	On	On	Reject

6.2 Property Checking

The requirements of real-world reactive systems generally contain certain safety-critical requirements that should never be violated during any execution of the system. These can be seen as properties of the system. For example, 'when a vehicle is moving at a considerable speed (say, >20 kmph), all doors should be locked', is one such requirement. It is often easier to express such requirements as a system property. This property should not be violated by other requirements that alter either the vehicle speed or door lock/unlock status. To specify such properties, we provide a special output column, *ErrorFlag*.

An example of specifying system properties is illustrated in Table 5. As RGRaF generates test cases for row coverage, to cover the row in Table 5, a test case will be generated that matches this row. Once the row is matched, ExpGen will generate 'Error' as the expected output of that test case. This test case is a counter-example to the given property. So this special output signal is actually used to detect and report error for all the signal combinations that are possible in real-world reactive systems but should not occur due to pre-defined system properties.

Table 5. Specification for property checking.

Sno	In VehicleSpeed	In DoorStatus	Out ErrorFlag
1	> 20	Unlocked	Error

7   Experiments: Results and Observations

We conducted case studies on four different real-world projects to evaluate the practical usefulness and cost-effectiveness of EBT, and answer the following four questions:

1. Can formal specification based methods for test generation take lesser efforts than writing test cases test cases manually?
2. Can they achieve better row and row-interaction coverage than manually written test cases?
3. Does fuzzing at time boundaries help in generating better test cases on real-world systems?
4. Does DRAFT achieve better coverage than RGRaF and do both achieve better coverage than pure random generation on real-world projects?

To investigate the aforementioned questions we needed real-world projects which have - (a) documented requirements in a natural language, (b) manually written test cases and, (c) detailed data of effort spent in writing these test cases. We identified four projects from the automotive domain and carved out case studies from these projects such that each case-study was fairly big and was representative of a real-world reactive system.

Brief description of the conducted case studies followed by details of the comparisons are given below.

Case Study 1 was from Body Control component of an automotive original equipment manufacturer (OEM). It consisted of a single sub-system named Integrated-FAT that had three modules – Flasher, Alarm and Trunk Back Door. Each module was further divided into sub-modules and requirements of sub-module were available. We modeled these requirements in EDT and generated test cases for each module as well for the sub-system level.

Case Study 2 was from another automotive OEM. We conducted experiments on four modules – Power Lift Gate (PLG), Power Closure Decision (PCD) and Panic Alarm from Body Control component, and also for Blower Control module from Climate Control component. For all these modules and a sub-system (Integrated-PLG+PCD) that merged PLG and PCD, we generated test cases in MATLAB [31] compatible format.

Case Study 3 was from Engine Control component of an automotive tier one supplier. We generated test cases, in CoverageMaster winAMS [32] compatible format for three modules - TF Switch Open, TF Switch Low and RD Switch Operation.

Case Study 4 was from Body Control component of second automotive OEM. It consisted of a single feature named Voltage Range Monitor(VRM). We generated test cases for VRM feature to evaluate the condition, decision and modified condition/decision coverage(MCDC) of test cases. For this case study, the effort data for manual test cases was not available.

For doing a comparative evaluation of coverage, we generated test cases using RGRaF, it's variants and DRAFT for all the case studies. For the first three case studies, we have already presented the experimental results for RGRaF and it's variants in our previous paper [1]. However, some of these experimental results have changed due to recent enhancements in *EDT-Test* implementation and thus we had to generate test cases for these case studies again.

7.1   Comparison of RGRaF, DRAFT and Pure Random

To compare RGRaF, DRAFT and pure random test case generation we executed these algorithms on all the modules and sub-systems of the selected case studies. We used the same `Sample Size` for all the algorithms. Pure random algorithm generated random input sequences with a random time assigned to each tuple in the input sequence. Each input sequence was of a random length. Once an input sequence was generated, the rest of the algorithm was similar to RGRaF and involved execution of automata and retained only those sequences that covered a new row or a row-interaction.

Tables 6, 7 and 8 present the results of these experiments. RGRaF, when compared with pure random algorithm, achieved equal or higher row coverage and row-interaction coverage in 12 out of 13 modules. Moreover, RGRaF achieved 100 % row coverage for 7 modules whereas the pure random variant achieved 100 % row coverage in only 4 modules. DRAFT, on the other hand, achieved 100 % row coverage for 9 modules and achieved equal or better row coverage than RGRAF on the remaining four modules. During these experiments, we observed that pure random test generation was achieving lesser row and row-interaction coverage for larger sub-systems/modules/systems. For instance, in Alarm module, which had 822 rows, DRAFT covered 694 rows and RGRaF covered 628 rows whereas pure random could cover only 573 rows (Table 7). For the same module RGRAF covered 1126 row interactions, whereas

Table 6. Comparison of test cases tried when 100 % rows covered.

Case Study	Feature Name	No. of EDT Rows	#Test Cases Tried			
			DRAFT	RGRaF	RGRaF Without Fuzz	Pure Random With Fuzz
Study 1	Trunk Back Door	86	107	103	226	10K(53)
Study 2	Blower Control	101	101	96	112	10k(97)
	PLG	52	1329	2154	8456	10K(40)
	PCD	16	30	30	223	30
	PLG + PCD	68	57925	80749	200K(65)	200K(59)
Study 3	TF Switch Open	14	3	856	10K(0)	3759
	TF Switch Low	14	275	642	229	702
	RD Sw Operation	31	22901	50K(30)	79	20216
Study 4	VRM	256	2646	10K(253)	10K(255)	10K(0)

*The numbers written in brackets indicate the number of rows covered when 100 % row coverage is not achieved.

Table 7. Comparison of rows covered when all rows are not covered.

Case Study	Feature Name	No. of EDT Rows	#Rows covered			
			DRAFT	RGRaF	RGRaF Without Fuzz	Pure Random With Fuzz
Study 1	Alarm	822	694	628	592	573
	Flasher	146	144	140	128	96
	Integrated-FAT	1052	936	934	843	427
Study 2	Panic Alarm	262	259	259	259	244

random covered only 303 interactions(Table 8). Due to lack of time we did not measure row interactions covered by DRAFT for any of the modules.

An analysis revealed that our algorithms performed better in cases where size of input domain was large and in cases where to cover a row, an input with a specific value had to be generated within a specific time. This is illustrated by the example in Table 1. To cover Row 1 of this example the Panic Switch has to be pressed and released twice within three seconds. The probability of this happening in pure random generation is very low. When we generated test cases for this example using RGRaF and pure random, RGRaF needed to try only 6 test cases to cover all rows and row-interactions, whereas the pure random algorithm

Table 8. Comparison for row-interaction coverage.

Case Study	Feature Name	No. of EDT Rows	#Row-Interactions Covered		
			RGRaF	RGRaF Without Fuzz	Pure Random With Fuzz
Study 1	Alarm	822	1126	1094	303
	Trunk Back Door	86	63	63	28
	Flasher	146	541	561	365
	Integrated-FAT	1052	2076	1180	1180
Study 2	Panic Alarm	262	967	961	597
	Blower Control	101	264	257	224
	PLG	52	360	353	285
	PCD	16	5	5	5
	PLG + PCD	68	359	331	265
Study 3	TF Switch Open	14	22	0	22
	TF Switch Low	14	23	23	23
	RD Sw Operation	31	46	46	46
Study 4	VRM	256	427	369	0

needed to try 663. We also observed that pure random with fuzzing algorithm generated many row sequences that contained invalid input combinations, and hence the number of test cases tried by this algorithm are more than the others.

7.2   Impact of Fuzzing on Test Case Generation

To evaluate the contribution of fuzzing we ran RGRaF with and without fuzzing on all the modules. To fuzz, at the end of each step of all automata, the next input was optionally chosen. If the chosen input had a time less than the nearest time-out τ, then the time of the input was modified to a value higher than τ else it was changed to a time less than τ.

Tables 6, 7 and 8 present the results of the comparison. Fuzzing at time boundaries helped in 10 modules because these had complex time-based requirements. For these modules, RGRaF achieved higher row and row-interaction coverage as compared to RGRaF without fuzzing. This demonstrates that fuzzing of timings of inputs helps in increasing row and row-interaction coverage, especially in the presence of time-based requirements. A thorough analysis revealed that fuzzing helped in cases having time constraints associated with I/O signals, as explained in Sect. 5, because these I/O signals' time constraints were not taken into account while expanding rows. As fuzzing helped in RGRaF, we assume that with DRAFT also, fuzzing has helped in achieving better coverage.

An exception has been the module RD Sw Operation, for which RGRAF without fuzzing tried far fewer test cases (79) than the other algorithms to cover all rows. This could be because the module has only two inputs with Boolean type and no timing constraints on the inputs.

7.3   Comparison with Manual Testing

For the first three case studies, manually created test cases with the corresponding efforts data were available to us. These test cases were created by respective application development teams consisting of test engineers and domain experts whereas, the team that created EDT specifications and generated test cases using *EDT-Test* did not have automotive domain knowledge.

Table 9 presents a summary of our findings of a comparison between EBT and manual test case generation for effort required. In the case of EBT the effort is split into the person hours taken to specify requirements in EDT and the time taken by RGRaF to generate test cases. We have not compared the two methods for coverage because no coverage data was available for the manual test cases. Instead we asked the domain experts from the project teams to manually compare and analyze the two sets of test cases.

The findings reveal that on an average EBT required up to 60 % less effort for test case creation. In all the modules, EBT not only generated all the test cases present in the manual sets, but also generated many additional interesting scenarios. These additional scenarios should have been part of the manual test cases, according to the domain experts. In two modules, Flasher and PLG, EBT test cases needed more effort compared to manual ones primarily because, these

Table 9. Comparison of EBT with manual approach.

Case Study	Feature Name	No. of EDT Rows	Test Case Generation Using EBT			Manual Test Case Generation [person hours]	Efforts savings by EBT
			EDT Creation [person hours]	EDT-Test Execution	Total Efforts [person hours]		
Case Study 1	Alarm	822	13	95 mins	14.5	38.5	33 %
	Trunk Back Door	86	7	2 mins	7	10	
	Flasher	146	18.5	32 mins	19	12	
	Integrated-FAT	1052	0	6.5 hours	6.5	-NA-	–
Case Study 2	Panic Alarm	262	40	5 mins	40	80	44.8 %
	Blower Control	101	5	12 mins	5	18	
	PLG	52	12.5	1.5 mins	12.5	6	
	PCD	16	1	1 second	1	2	
	PLG + PCD	68	0	30 mins	0.5	-NA-	–
Case Study 3	TF Switch Open	14	0.75	1 min	0.75	9	62.5 %
	TF Switch Low	14	1.25	1.75 mins	1.25	9	
	RD Sw Operation	31	10	1.5 mins	10	14	

modules required an understanding of complex domain functionality that the manual test case writers already had.

Analysis of some key findings from all the experiments is presented as follows:

- In *Case study 1*, for the Trunk Back Door module, EBT generated cases covered 40 more row-interactions and in the case of Flasher it covered 346 more row-interactions than the manually written test cases.
- In *Case Study 1*, Integrated-FAT module clearly showed scalability of our algorithm. It had approximately 1000 requirements and 98 signals. Due to the complexity of the requirements, it was hard for the testers to visualize all the requirements' combinations. Hence, the manually created test cases covered only module level requirements and interactions between modules were not adequately covered. EBT test cases subsumed all the manually created ones and generated many more valid and necessary requirements combinations as confirmed by the domain experts and the project team.
- In *Case Study 2* EBT test cases, when run on the model, detected a bug in a post-production sub-system, Integrated-PLG + PCD. We detected this bug by specifying properties of the sub-system using the *ErrorFlag* in EDT specifications, as explained in the Sect. 6. In case of Panic Alarm module, three missing requirements were uncovered when EBT generated test cases were executed on corresponding MATLAB models.
- In *Case Study 3*, EBT generated test cases achieved 100 % condition and decision coverage when executed on C code using CoverageMaster winAMS. This is interesting because EBT does not explicitly target code coverage.
- In *Case Study 4*, EBT generated test cases achieved superior condition, decision and MCDC coverage when compared with manual test cases, as shown in Table 10. EBT generated test cases were executed on VRM feature's MATLAB models for coverage evaluation.

Table 10. Coverage comparison for case study 4.

Coverage criteria	EBT	Manual
Condition	88 %	76 %
Decision	100 %	98 %
MCDC	75 %	52 %

The overall analysis of our experiments demonstrates that, on real-world projects, EBT is more cost-effective and generates better test cases than manual test cases. It also shows that DRAFT performs better than other algorithms including RGRaF, RGRaF without fuzzing and pure random. However, there are some threats to validity of our experiments as given in the next section.

7.4 Threats to Validity

The threats to the validity of our findings are described as follows:

- Random test data generation is parameterized by the number of random inputs to be generated, whereas DRAFT and RGRaF are parameterized by the maximum number of rows to be used to generate inputs. This makes any comparison between the two unfair. For the experiments, the number of inputs to be generated by the random algorithm was taken as twice that of the number of rows to be generated by the other algorithms. This was based on an analysis of EDTs used for the experiments, which revealed that on an average there are two inputs per row.
- Although DRAFT performed better than RGRaF on most examples, in some cases it was only marginally better. More experiments will have to be conducted to arrive at a clear conclusion.
- All the systems we selected are from the automotive domain and although we expect the findings to carry over to reactive systems from other domains, explicit experiments will have to be conducted to confirm it.
- To assess the quality of the generated test cases we relied on the judgment of domain experts. A more objective study that determines the number of defects detected by *EDT-Test* will have to be conducted to ascertain its effectiveness. However, getting defect data is not easy and we were not able to get it for all the systems we considered, making it difficult to conduct an experiment.

8 Conclusions and Future Work

From the experiments we conclude that:

- It is possible to have a formal specification based method and yet, reduce testing efforts up to 60 %. This requires an appropriate choice of notation.

- Test case generation algorithms based on random generation of events can generate scenarios that are found to be useful and interesting by test engineers and domain experts.
- Fuzzing at time boundaries helps improve coverage when timing requirements are present in the specification.
- Using row dependencies for input sequence helps in further increasing coverage of complex specifications. Even for simple specifications for which all rows can be covered by both RGRaF and DRAFT, exploiting row dependencies helps in reducing the number of test cases tried.

Our previous algorithm RGRaF faced scalability issues in generating test cases for applications having large and complex time-based requirements. We have improved the scalability in test generation by means of DRAFT algorithm. Going forward, we aim to improve the scalability of our approach for even larger reactive systems. Further, we plan to evaluate the effectiveness of various coverage criteria in finding bugs in the system under test, and enhance the criteria to enable coverage of long sequences of requirements' interaction. Although the experiments were performed on applications from the automotive domain, we expect similar benefits on reactive systems belonging to other domains as well.

References

1. Venkatesh, R., Shrotri, U., Zare, A., Agrawal, S.: Cost-effective functional testing of reactive software. In: Evaluation of Novel Approaches to Software Engineering. SCITEPRESS (2015)
2. Venkatesh, R., Shrotri, U., Krishna, G.M., Agrawal, S.: EDT: a specification notation for reactive systems. In: Proceedings of the Conference on Design, Automation &Test in Europe, p. 215.European Design and Automation Association (2014)
3. Anand, S., Burke, E.K., Chen, T.Y., Clark, J., Cohen, M.B., Grieskamp, W., Harman, M., Harrold, M.J., Mcminn, P.: An orchestrated survey of methodologies for automated software test case generation. J. Syst. Softw. **86**, 1978–2001 (2013)
4. Arcuri, A., Iqbal, M.Z., Briand, L.: Black-box system testing of real-time embedded systems using random and search-based testing. In: Petrenko, A., Simão, A., Maldonado, J.C. (eds.) ICTSS 2010. LNCS, vol. 6435, pp. 95–110. Springer, Heidelberg (2010)
5. Dalal, S.R., Jain, A., Karunanithi, N., Leaton, J., Lott, C.M., Patton, G.C., Horowitz, B.M.: Model-based testing in practice. In: Proceedings of the 21st International Conference on Software Engineering, pp. 285–294. ACM (1999)
6. Reactis: Reactis. (http://www.reactive-systems.com/model-based-testing-simulink.html). Accessed 29 October 2015
7. Peranandam, P., Raviram, S., Satpathy, M., Yeolekar, A., Gadkari, A., Ramesh, S.: An integrated test generation tool for enhanced coverage of simulink/stateflow models. In: 2012 Design, Automation & Test in Europe Conference & Exhibition (DATE), pp. 308–311. IEEE (2012)
8. Wang, J., Li, H., Lv, T., Wang, T., Li, X.: Functional test generation guided by steady-state probabilities of abstract design. In: Proceedings of the Conference on Design, Automation & Test in Europe, p. 321. European Design and Automation Association (2014)

9. Harel, D., Lachover, H., Naamad, A., Pnueli, A., Politi, M., Sherman, R., Shtull-Trauring, A., Trakhtenbrot, M.: Statemate: A working environment for the development of complex reactive systems. IEEE Trans. Softw. Eng. **16**, 403–414 (1990)
10. Thyssen, J., Hummel, B.: Behavioral specification of reactive systems using stream-based I/O tables. Softw. Syst. Model. **12**, 265–283 (2013)
11. Briand, L.: Software verification - a scalable, model-driven, empirically grounded approach. In: Tveito, A., Bruaset, A.M., Lysne, O. (eds.) Simula Research Laboratory, pp. 415–442. Springer, Heidelberg (2010)
12. Heitmeyer, C., Kirby, J., Labaw, B., Bharadwaj, R.: SCR: A toolset for specifying and analyzing software requirements. In: Hu, A.J., Vardi, M.Y. (eds.) CAV 1998. LNCS, vol. 1427, pp. 526–531. Springer, Heidelberg (1998)
13. Cadar, C., Sen, K.: Symbolic execution for software testing: Three decades later. Commun. ACM **56**, 82–90 (2013)
14. Păsăreanu, C.S., Rungta, N.: Symbolic pathfinder: Symbolic execution of java bytecode. In: Proceedings of the IEEE/ACM International Conference on Automated Software Engineering, ASE 2010, pp. 179–180. ACM, New York (2010)
15. Tahat, L.H., Vaysburg, B., Korel, B., Bader, A.J.: Requirement-based automated black-box test generation. In: 25th Annual International Computer Software and Applications Conference COMPSAC 2001, pp. 489–495. IEEE (2001)
16. Bokil, P., Darke, P., Shrotri, U., Venkatesh, R.: Automatic test data generation for C programs. In: Third IEEE International Conference on Secure Software Integration and Reliability Improvement SSIRI 2009, pp. 359–368. IEEE (2009)
17. Offutt, J., Liu, S., Abdurazik, A., Ammann, P.: Generating test data from state-based specifications. Softw. Test. Verification Reliab. **13**, 25–53 (2003)
18. Cristiá, M., Albertengo, P., Frydman, C., Plüss, B., Monetti, P.R.: Tool support for the test template framework. Softw. Test. Verification Reliab. **24**, 3–37 (2014)
19. Veanes, M., Campbell, C., Grieskamp, W., Schulte, W., Tillmann, N., Nachmanson, L.: Model-based testing of object-oriented reactive systems with spec explorer. In: Hierons, R.M., Bowen, J.P., Harman, M. (eds.) FORTEST. LNCS, vol. 4949, pp. 39–76. Springer, Heidelberg (2008)
20. Raymond, P., Nicollin, X., Halbwachs, N., Weber, D.: Automatic testing of reactive systems. In: Proceedings of the 19th IEEE Real-Time Systems Symposium, pp. 200–209. IEEE (1998)
21. Brat, G., Havelund, K., Park, S., Visser, W.: Java pathfinder - second generation of a java model checker. In: Proceedings of the Workshop on Advances in Verification (2000)
22. Cadar, C., Dunbar, D., Engler, D.R.: Klee: Unassisted and automatic generation of high-coverage tests for complex systems programs. In: OSDI, vol. 8, pp. 209–224 (2008)
23. Tillmann, N., de Halleux, J.: Pex–white box test generation for.NET. In: Beckert, B., Hähnle, R. (eds.) TAP 2008. LNCS, vol. 4966, pp. 134–153. Springer, Heidelberg (2008)
24. Cadar, C., Godefroid, P., Khurshid, S., Păsăreanu, C.S., Sen, K., Tillmann, N., Visser, W.: Symbolic execution for software testing in practice: Preliminary assessment. In: Proceedings of the 33rd International Conference on Software Engineering ICSE 2011, pp. 1066–1071. ACM, New York (2011)
25. Hamlet, R.: Random Testing. Wiley, New York (2002)
26. Duran, J.W., Ntafos, S.C.: An evaluation of random testing. IEEE Trans. Softw. Eng. **10**, 438–444 (1984)
27. Chen, T.Y., Kuo, F.C., Merkel, R.G., Tse, T.: Adaptive random testing: The ART of test case diversity. J. Syst. Softw. **83**(1), 60–66 (2010). SI: Top Scholars

28. Ferguson, R., Korel, B.: The chaining approach for software test data generation. ACM Trans. Softw. Eng. Methodol. **5**, 63–86 (1996)
29. Marinov, D., Andoni, A., Daniliuc, D., Khurshid, S., Rinard, M.: An evaluation of exhaustive testing for data structures. Technical report, MIT Computer Science and Artificial Intelligence Laboratory Report MIT -LCS-TR-921 (2003)
30. Bowman, H., Gomez, R.: Discrete timed automata. In: Concurrency Theory, pp. 377–395. Springer, London (2006)
31. Mathworks: Matlab. (http://www.mathworks.in/products/matlab/). Accessed 29 October 2015
32. winAMS, C.: Coveragemaster winams. (http://www.gaio.com/product/dev_tools/pdt07_winams.html). Accessed 29 October 2015

A Process Support with Which to Identify Interactions Between Quality Characteristics

Gabriel Alberto García-Mireles[1(✉)], Mª Ángeles Moraga[2],
Félix García[2], and Mario Piattini[2]

[1] Departamento de Matemáticas,
Universidad de Sonora, Hermosillo, Sonora, Mexico
mireles@mat.uson.mx
[2] Instituto de Tecnologías y Sistemas de Información,
Universidad de Castilla-La Mancha, Ciudad Real, Spain
{MariaAngeles.Moraga,Felix.Garcia,
Mario.Piattini}@uclm.es

Abstract. Achieving a balance between the quality characteristics that need to be addressed during the development of a software product may determine the success of a software project. However, few software organizations deal with interactions between the quality characteristics that could be present in a software project. In order to support organizations, we have developed a process framework, SQIMF, which can be used to manage this type of interactions. In this work we describe one of the SQIMF processes - that which is employed to monitor product quality requirements - in order to support software organizations as regards identifying interactions between quality requirements, in addition to characterizing them and identifying relevant contextual factors. An exploratory case study was conducted in order to initiate the validation of the proposed process, as the result of which we found interactions between usability and security during the inception phase of a software project.

Keywords: Software product quality · Interaction between quality characteristics · Process for monitoring quality characteristics interactions · Interaction between quality requirements · SQIMF framework

1 Introduction

One of the main goals of software engineering is to deliver high-quality software products and systems. The identification and specification of both functional and non-functional requirements (NFRs) are important activities as regards establishing a baseline that can be used to assess software quality. Quality requirements, as a subset of the NFRs [1], are closely related to both making decisions about selecting implementation technologies and driving the process used to design software architecture [2]. However, dealing with quality requirements during software development is difficult because they are hard to define, they are described vaguely, and they might influence each other [3]. Software developers might therefore select a design option that compromises some requirements in order to achieve others [3].

© Springer International Publishing Switzerland 2016
L.A. Maciaszek and J. Filipe (Eds.): ENASE 2015, CCIS 599, pp. 21–39, 2016.
DOI: 10.1007/978-3-319-30243-0_2

The interaction between requirements is described as a situation in which the satisfaction of one requirement may influence the satisfaction of another [4]. In this work, we are interested in the interactions between quality requirements, particularly the negative interactions, or the conflict between quality requirements. For instance, negative interactions between usability and security requirements could occur when the implementation of a means to provide access to a software system requires the users to memorize long strings of illegible data.

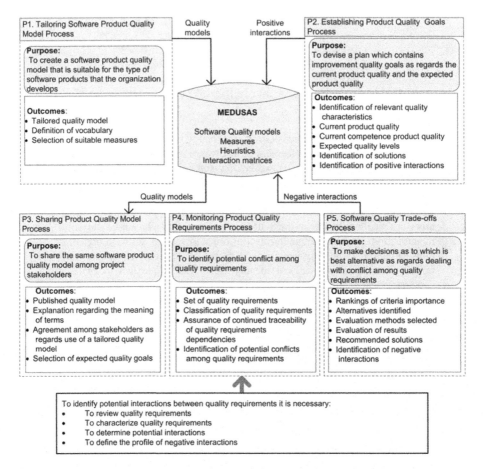

Fig. 1. SQIMF framework.

There is a need to develop methods which support the goals of eliciting and analyzing customers' quality requirements, including negotiation approaches with which to resolve conflicting interactions [5]. In industrial practice, software organizations that overlook conflicting interactions between quality requirements may confront issues related to increasing development costs and decreasing stakeholder satisfaction [3, 6]. The poor management of interactions between quality requirements could also be considered a causal factor in the failure of some projects [7–9].

Several methods with which to deal with interactions between quality requirements have been proposed, particularly negotiation approaches and prioritization methods [10]. However, the goals of these approaches and their application scope cover only specific processes as those described in ISO/IEC 12207 [10]. Interactions between quality requirements are relevant to other stages of the software development life-cycle, such as software architecture and software testing [2]. Software organizations therefore require methodological support in order to address the identification and documentation of interactions between quality requirements and the resolution of negative ones. This support should cover all the stages of the software development life cycle.

In order to provide a possible solution to the issue of managing interactions between quality requirements throughout the software development life cycle, we take into account two essential ideas; first, that the software process influences the quality of a software product, and second, that a product quality model, such as ISO/IEC 25010, can be used to generalize the quality requirements through the different processes of software development (Table 1 depicts the main quality terms used in this paper). We implemented the first idea by reviewing several process models and the literature concerning improvement initiatives. As a result, we found that few process models explicitly address quality characteristics [11, 12] and that they mention quality characteristics in processes related to eliciting and analyzing quality requirements [12]. The second idea was based on the ISO/IEC 25010, since it can be used to specify, measure and evaluate software product quality throughout the stages of the software development life cycle.

Table 1. Definition of some quality-related terms.

Term	Definition
Quality requirement	A requirement that a quality attribute which is present in software [13]
Quality characteristic	Category of software quality attributes that have a bearing on software quality [13]
Quality model	Defined set of characteristics, and the relationships between them, that provides a framework in which to specify quality requirements and evaluate quality [13]
Target quality goals	A description of relevant quality characteristics and their respective expected values that an organization is attempting to attain in a software product
Interaction model	A matrix-based description of interactions between quality characteristics that shows the influences of one quality characteristic on the others
Attribute	Inherent property or characteristic of an entity that can be distinguished quantitatively or qualitatively by humans or by automated means [13]

The main goal of this research, which uses process support as a basis, is to provide a process that can be used to monitor interactions between quality requirements when considering the quality characteristics described in ISO/IEC 25010. This process is part of the Software Quality Interaction Management Framework (SQIMF) (Fig. 1) which was presented in Garcia-Mireles et al. [14]. In this paper we detailed the process 'P4.

Monitoring product quality requirements' (P4 process in Fig. 1) and described the approach used to identify interactions between quality characteristics. The activity 'A2. Check potential interactions between quality requirements', which is a part of this process, was validated by conducting an exploratory case study. As an additional proposal, we included a process with which to carry out trade-offs when negative interactions occur (P5 in Fig. 1).

The paper has seven sections. Section 2 shows an overview of the main approaches used to deal with interactions between quality requirements and depicts an overview of the SQIMF. The process with which to manage interactions between quality requirements is presented in Sect. 3 while Sect. 4 presents both the exploratory case study design and its main outcomes. Section 5 presents a discussion of the results and threats to validity, while a summary of the process used to resolve conflicting interactions is provided in Sect. 6. Finally, our conclusions and future work are addressed in Sect. 7.

2   Related Work

Software requirements analysis and requirements negotiation are the main activities within the analysis stage of software development process during which stakeholders may discover conflicting interactions between quality requirements. According to Dahlstedt and Persson's notion of interaction [6], the conflicting interactions between quality requirements occur when one quality requirement constrains the design or coding options of another quality requirement. In general terms, the conflicting interactions are resolved by employing trade-off methods.

Barney et al. [15] carried out a mapping study in order to identify approaches with which to perform trade-offs. They found a variety of methods, such as the Analytical Hierarchy Process, the Architectural Trade-off Method, Quality Function Deployment and algorithmic approaches, among others. As a conclusion, they pointed out that the field is immature and more research is needed to address software quality tradeoffs. The articles that [15] had categorized into both the requirements and process stage were then reviewed in order to classify them as regards their goals and the main process that the methods contained therein support. As a result, the methods were classified as either prioritization approaches if they seek only to assign a weight to each quality characteristic or negotiation approaches when the method provides a means that stakeholders can use to discuss their alternatives [10]. In addition, we found that methods with which to carry out trade-offs can be used in several processes, including those related to quality assurance.

Several methods are based on the modeling approach. For instance, the Non-Functional Requirements Framework [16] considers requirements to be goals, and more particularly quality requirements to be softgoals. Software developers should build a graph in order to describe the potential interactions between goals and the extent to which design mechanisms and components contribute to achieving those goals. Other researchers rely on both ontologies and literature surveys to model interactions between quality characteristics. The catalog of conflicting interactions can be used to identify potential interactions in new software projects [17, 18].

Our proposal for dealing with interactions is process-based. In order for a software process to contribute toward improving product quality, it should include appropriate practices [19]. Traditional software process models (such as CMMI [20], or ISO/IEC 12207 [21]) currently lack the appropriate support needed to improve product quality when it is assessed with a product quality model [12]. Indeed, there is a lack of mechanisms with which to integrate the methods required to support quality characteristics [22]. These facts and the need to support the management of interactions between quality requirements are some of the reasons why we were motivated to develop the SQIMF framework [14].

The SQIMF framework provides a set of five processes that together contribute toward identifying and documenting interactions in addition to resolving the conflicting interactions which occur during the software development process [14]. The ISO/IEC 25010 [13] product quality model was used to derive specific quality models for usability, maintainability and security. These specific models were then used to identify potential interactions between quality characteristics. The interactions identified in literature surveys were documented in interactions models, which describe the kind of relationship between quality characteristics (e.g. positive, negative, and independent) [23]. The SQIMF framework also includes a process that software organizations can use to review the practices that may be included in a particular software project in order to improve a product quality characteristic. These types of proposals are based on a mapping between practices targeted toward improving a particular quality characteristic and a software process model (please see, for example, [24]).

The processes included in the SQIMF framework can be applied at both project and organization level. At organizational level, there are two processes whose respective main goals are tailoring the product quality model to the settings in which software organizations develops software and developing an improvement initiative in order to introduce practices with which to enhance the desired product quality characteristics. At project level, three processes are aimed at: promoting a strategy which ensures that all project team members understand the quality terms, seeking interactions between quality requirements and resolving negative interactions through the use of trade-off studies. However, the processes are described only in terms of purpose and outcomes [14]. In this paper we describe two processes related to the identification of interactions between quality characteristics (P4. Monitoring interactions between quality requirements process) and the resolution of negative interactions (P5. Software quality trade-offs process). The first process (P4) also includes the design and outcomes of an exploratory case study.

3 Process for Monitoring Interaction Between Quality Requirements

We use the SPEM 2.0 notation [25] and the EPF composer version 1.5 (https://eclipse.org/epf/) to describe the process employed to monitor interactions between quality requirements (Fig. 2). The process description includes the process objectives, work products (inputs and outputs), roles, activities and an activity diagram.

The monitoring quality requirements process relies on the interaction model to uncover potential negative interactions (or conflicts) between quality requirements. Several conditions may have a tendency to lead to the appearance of interactions between quality requirements, such as clashes among stakeholders' quality requirements, the selection (or design) of software components based on quality requirements, and strict targeted values for quality requirements. When a conflict between quality requirements is identified it should be described in the interaction profile for further analysis. The main outcome of this process is the interaction profile, but it is also possible to update quality requirements and the interaction model.

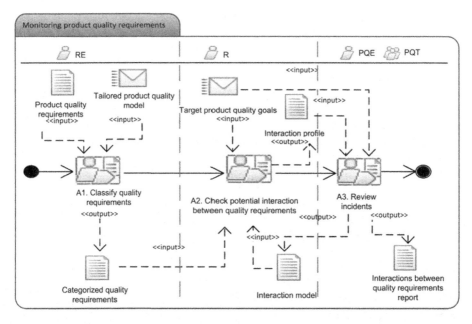

Fig. 2. Activity diagram used to monitor product quality requirements process.

3.1   Process Objectives

The objectives of the monitoring quality requirements process are the following:

- A review of the consistency of quality requirements with target quality values.
- A verification of the potential interactions between quality requirements by means of the quality characteristics.
- An update of the appropriate interaction model using the interactions discovered.

3.2   Inputs and Outputs

The work products required in this process are: product quality requirements and related product components, a tailored product quality model, target product quality goals, and an interaction model. The output artifacts are: a prioritized list of quality requirements, an interaction profile and a summative report containing the interactions found.

3.3   Roles

The roles participating in this process are presented in Table 2.

Table 2. Roles participating in the process.

Role name	Description
Product Quality Team (PQT)	A group of participants who have a diversity of quality interests in a particular software product. They can describe quality goals and apply appropriate methods to introduce and assess product quality
Product Quality Expert (PQE)	A participant who has the knowledge needed to adapt a product quality model in the context of organizational needs
Requirements Engineer (RE)	A participant responsible for eliciting, analyzing, specifying and validating requirements who can also categorize quality requirements using a product quality model
Reviewer (R)	A role responsible for detecting potential interactions between categorized quality requirements which can also create an interaction profile when a negative interaction is discovered

3.4   Activities

There are three main activities in this process: classify quality requirements, check potential interaction between quality requirements and review incidents. While the project is in progress, the activities classify quality requirements and check potential interactions that can be carried out when the process allows review sessions. We suggest that the last activity be performed when the project is at the closing stage in order to evaluate the impact of the conflicting interactions and the degree to which alternatives have resolved the problem.

- A1. Classify quality requirements activity. With regard to the tailored quality model, the RE classifies the product quality requirements. If each review session addresses changes that must be made as regards quality requirements, this activity needs to be carried out in order to update the classification of quality requirements.
- A2. Check potential interactions between quality requirements activity. Categorizing quality requirements in their respective quality characteristic allows the reviewer to identify potential interactions between quality requirements since the interaction model includes data about interactions between quality characteristics. If an interaction is identified, the Reviewer therefore needs to describe it in the interaction profile template.
- A3. Review incidents. PQE and PQT review the interaction profile reported in the software project. The analysis focuses on the characteristics of the reported

Table 3. Terms related to contextual factors.

Term	Description
Contextual factor	An aspect from the environment that influences either the way in which software is developed or the resulting software product
Contextual facet	A coherent set of contextual factors
Product facet	This includes contextual factors such as maturity, quality, size, system type, customization and programming language [26]
Process facet	This describes the work-flow of the development. It includes activities, work-flows, and artifacts [26]
People facet	This includes aspects related to project participants' skills and experience in addition to the assigned (project/organization) positions' jobs and roles
Organizational facet	This includes the organizational structure, organizational unit, certification, and distribution [26]
Market facet	This represents the customers and competitors. The market facet includes number of customers, market segments, strategy and constraints [26]

interactions in order to evaluate its impact on both the software project and the artifacts of the SQIMF framework (e.g., interaction model). The actions derived from this review are documented and stored in the organization's knowledge base.

4 Exploratory Case Study

4.1 Case Study Design

In order to validate the activity 'A2. Identify potential interactions between quality requirements' which is a part of the process 'P4. Monitoring quality requirements', we decided to conduct an exploratory case study. The purpose of the study was to understand how practitioners identify interactions between quality requirements and how they can be described. The study was conducted at a small software firm that we named Company A, and which was selected opportunistically since we needed an organization that was aware of how software quality can be implemented in software projects.

Company A is currently certified as a testing laboratory with the ISO/IEC 17025 standard. The company provides consulting services based on software process improvement initiatives or using the ISO/IEC 25010 to enhance product quality. Two people from Company A participated in the interviews.

We performed the case study by breaking down the activities into two groups. The first group of activities focused on the design of materials required to characterize the contextual factors that needed to be taken into account. The second group of activities was carried out a week after the first part of the study. Its main purpose was to identify and describe the profile of an interaction in a current project.

In the first part of the case study, we developed an interaction profile template whose goal was to characterize an interaction between quality requirements. The lists of factors employed to describe an interaction were extracted from Robinson et al. [4], while the context facets [26] were used to identify factors that contribute to the occurrence of an interaction. Table 3 describes the factors used in the interaction profile template.

The first version of the interaction profile template was reviewed by two researchers. Minor details concerning the interpretation of the factors were found, which were resolved by improving their explanations. The corrected version of the template was used to support semi-structured interviews.

The managing director and the quality leader, both of whom were employees at company A, were informed about the aims of this study and the need to record interview sessions. They agreed to an audio recording and also to filling in the templates and questionnaires. Both interviewees had been working with process improvement initiatives and enhancing product quality with ISO/IEC 25010 for more than four years. The main data source was based on their experience of working in the quality assurance field.

The data collection procedures required notes to be taken during the interview sessions. The notes were verified with audio files. The interactions between the quality characteristics identified by both interviewees were compared in order to gather suitable evidence for this research. Data triangulation was applied to data regarding contextual factors in order to identify relevant contextual factor for this company.

The second part of the exploratory case study was focused on the application of the activity 'A2. Check potential interactions between quality requirements' to a software project being developed by the company. The purpose of this was to understand the extent to which it would be feasible to use the process, including the artifacts, in industrial settings. A questionnaire was developed in order to obtain information about the feasibility of using the process.

4.2 Interviews Results

Company A decided to apply the process for monitoring interactions among quality requirements in a new project they were working on. The software to be delivered was a web application which supports an organization as regards providing web information content for a target audience that includes the visually impaired. The exploratory case study was conducted at the conception stage of this web project.

The interaction profile includes a section that addresses the interaction model. In this case, it was developed in order to determine the type of relationships between security and usability sub-characteristics. The interviewees used their own experience and the features of the software project under study as a basis on which to establish the type of interaction. For instance, Table 4 shows an interaction model between security and usability filled in by one of the interviewees.

Positive interactions are marked with the sign (+) while negative interactions are marked with (-). The sign (O) is used when the interviewee does not have sufficient information to ensure that there is an influence between the quality sub-characteristics

Table 4. Interaction model filled in by an interviewee.

Product usability → Security	Appropriateness recognozability	Learnability	Operability	User error protection	User interface aesthetics	Accesibility
Autenthicity	O	O	-	O	O	-
Confidentiality	O	O	O	O	O	O
Conformance	O	O	O	O	O	O
Attack detection	O	O	O	O	O	O
Availability	O	O	O	+	O	O
Integrity	O	O	O	O	O	O
Non-repudiation	O	O	O	O	O	O
Traceability	O	O	O	O	O	O

under review. In this case study, the interviewees reported positive interactions between availability and user error protection. They also reported two negative interactions between the pairs authenticity – operability and authenticity – accessibility.

After identifying an interaction between quality requirements, the next step was to characterize the relevant factors that foster it. The interviewees used the contextual facets to report factors related to the product and process facet.

The main factors within the product facet are quality and application type. Quality refers to usability and security requirements that the project should address. The needs of a particular set of targeted users constrain both the design and implementation options of security mechanisms, since they are visually impaired people. In addition, the application type influences the security mechanisms that can be implemented. Moreover, the characteristics of the screen sizes and interaction mechanisms also need to be considered when designing the web application.

With regard to the process facet, one of the interviewees suggested that the review of software increments at the end of a software development process iteration might be an appropriate means to identify potential interactions between quality requirements. The executable version of software can be used to evaluate the quality requirements. In the light of the testing results, the customer can make decisions concerning how quality requirements were achieved. The use of this review approach allows both the software firm and its customers to negotiate negative interactions between quality requirements. Although the study was focused on identifying interactions between quality requirements, the interviewee also requested methods, tools or practices that support the management or resolution of negative interactions. He also suggested that software developers need training if they are to manage conflicting interactions.

With regard to the organizational facet, Company A works by means of projects. For this web application the team consisted of four team members. However, these factors were not relevant as regards describing an interaction. With regard to the market facet, the interviewees did not consider that any of its factors might contribute to the occurrence of an interaction. In the case of the person facet, the interviewees did not consider that people's knowledge and skills were potential influencing factors. However, since the interviewees provide consulting to improve software quality, their knowledge may be a relevant contextual factor as regards identifying interactions.

The interviewees determined a negative interaction between accessibility and authenticity. They found particularly difficult to provide access support for all types of users, including those suffering from blindness. As an argument they commented that "a common approach employed to register users in a web system is that of using CAPTCHAs, but they distort a label as regards differentiating between a real user and a bot." However, this mechanism requires an in-depth study in the context of this web application owing to the profile of intended users.

In summary, the negative interaction only occurs with a particular group of users when the application should display appropriate information (resources) for each type of user. This signifies that the quality requirements for a web application are the main contextual factors that contribute to the occurrence of a negative interaction.

The interviewees additionally highlighted positive interactions between a pair of quality characteristics. They reported that integrity (security) has a positive influence on user error protection (usability). The rationale for this relation is that the security mechanisms implemented ensure that only the user with modification access can change data records. This interaction relies on their previous experience in developing and assessing systems.

The interaction profile template was therefore a feasible instrument with which to characterize a negative interaction between quality characteristics. The interaction model serves as a guideline to determine the type of interaction between quality characteristics. The main contextual facets that were relevant for Company A in the project under study were both the product and process facets. However, the person facet needs to be studied in great depth in order to determine to what extent the participants' skills contribute toward identifying and characterizing negative interactions.

The second part of the exploratory case study was focused on studying the feasibility of using the monitoring quality requirements process in a software firm. Our main goal was to characterize the interactions between quality requirements. We developed guidelines for the use of the interaction profile template and the activity diagram. After the participant had finished the tasks in the process, we asked him to answer a questionnaire developed to understand the suitability of the process.

With regard to the template for the interaction profile, the participant was clearly able to fill in identification data: project id, date, reviewer, type of software and artifacts analyzed. With regard to the interaction model, it can serve to identify both positive and negative perceived interactions between quality sub-characteristics. When the participant filled in the factors that characterized the interaction, his responses were based mainly on his previous experiences in developing software and assessing software quality. Since the project under study was at a conception stage, this may explain why there are few references to specific means or requirements used to describe the interaction and its potential impact. Table 5 shows paraphrased responses for relevant factors.

The analysis of the questionnaire filled in by the participant showed that process objectives, roles, descriptions and work products are clearly described. However, the process tasks and the interactions profile could be improved to support the identification of interactions. With regard to the understandability of process elements, the

Table 5. Responses to diverse factors used to describe an interaction profile.

Factor	Response
Basis Which quality requirements are involved in an interaction? Do the contextual factors have an influence on a given quality requirement?	In this project, adding security requirements may have a negative influence on accessibility and operability since the software features are only available to certain types of users
Criterion Which reasons are considered to lead to these interactions?	New security components affect system structure.
Establish the degree of the interaction What is the scope of the interaction between quality requirements? What features, components or users' categories are involved?	Application type and target users might impact on the degree of interaction between quality characteristics.
	The stakeholder's experience in the security field may influence the quality of security requirements.
	The expert's knowledge can be used to establish a security mechanism to reduce the influence of highly secure mechanisms on accessibility or operability.
Probability of occurrence What is the probability of a conflicting interaction occurring?	The interactions occur during the software development under the constraints considered.
Impact of the interaction What is the effect of the interaction on the software project? For instance: Catastrophic, inconvenient, system failure, system reboot, unsatisfied users.	The main effect: Application does not meet basic quality requirements. Unsatisfied users and application cannot be delivered to target users.
Type of interaction What is the type of this interaction? It is a perceived interaction when it is described at requirements level. It is an implementation interaction when it is based on the analysis of implementation means	Perceived interaction
Context What contextual factors influence the interaction between quality characteristics?	Main contextual factors: Application users and application type.

questionnaire answers depicted that process objectives, description of roles, work products and templates are easy of understand. The process elements of the tasks should, however, be improved.

When asked to state the extent to which process objectives are easy to apply, the participant marked the disagree option. The comments written in the instrument showed that there is a lack of information with which to understand how the interactions can be identified when software quality measures and indicators are used. With regard to this last comment, the experience of previous software quality assessment can be used to identify interactions between quality characteristics. Moreover, the quality goals should be linked to specific practices in order to evaluate whether the practices contribute toward resolving negative interactions.

5   Results and Discussion

The exploratory case study has provided evidence about the potential usefulness of the SQIMF. The interaction matrix and the characterization of interactions using the contextual facets were relevant as regards establishing a profile of the conflicting interactions between security and usability.

The interaction matrix was provided in order to determine the type of relationships that occur between the sub-characteristics of usability and security. The case study participants found it easy to fill in the matrix. One reason for this is that this company is focusing on evaluating the quality of software products from the process and product perspective. Although they could be considered expert practitioners in the field of software quality, this case study was the first time that they had addressed the topic of interactions between quality characteristics.

Several studies have reported interactions between software quality characteristics, including security and usability [1], but few empirical studies address the interaction issues by taking into account the sub-characteristic which belongs to each quality characteristic. This is therefore an important finding to be considered when dealing with interactions.

The purpose of the interaction profile is to characterize the interaction between quality characteristics using the contextual facets. The evidence gathered through this case study showed that the relevant factors that influence the interaction between usability and security requirements are the user's quality needs, user's profiles, and the type of application. The type of application is a factor that determines the type of quality attributes to be addressed in a software project [3, 27]. With regard to the process facet, the interviewees believed that a customer can participate in evaluating software increments. At the end of each iteration, the customer can review the software execution in order to identify any conflicts with the initially established quality requirements.

The interviewees did not consider the remaining context facets, such as people, organization, and market, to be factors that identify conflicting interactions between quality requirements. One reason for this is that the project was at its conception stage and the final set of requirements to be addressed in the software project had not as yet been specified. The identification of interactions is therefore based on the interviewees' perceptions and the main factors were the stakeholders' quality needs and product type.

The exploratory case study has shown that the process for monitoring product quality requirements can help in the identification of interactions between quality requirements and that it can be used in the conception stage of a software project. The activity 'A2. Check potential interaction between quality requirements' is useful as regards identifying and characterizing conflicting interactions between quality requirements. However, the tasks related to this activity need some refinement for use in industrial projects. Furthermore, it is necessary to validate the other activities in this process: A1. Classify quality requirements and A3. Review incidents.

In order to mitigate the effects of threats to validity, we followed the guidelines of Runeson et al. [28]. As regards the external validity, the exploratory case study carried out cannot be generalized to other companies. Nevertheless the characterization of the organization and the outcomes related to conflicting interactions between usability and security can provide useful insights into the development of a theory with which to characterize interactions at the conception stage of a software product. Moreover, we identified interactions between quality sub-characteristics that can be generalized to their respective quality characteristics considering the hierarchical structure of the quality models. This result is thus consistent with reports of conflicting interactions between usability and security [1, 8].

The research was kept under control through the application of the template approach, because it allows the design of instruments and the a priori establishment of how the instruments can contribute to the research [28]. Furthermore, in order to improve the reliability of the artifacts designed, all of them were checked by two researchers. Moreover, we used findings obtained from different sources to apply data triangulation when identifying evidence [28].

Since this was the first time that Company A had worked with interactions between quality requirements, the first part of the case study addressed the contextual factors. These were commented on with the interviewee in order to clarify the terms.

With this action, we thus attempted to mitigate the effects of construct validity. In addition, the guidelines used in the case study included descriptions in order to support participants when filling in the templates. However, it was not possible to interview the participants about whether these materials were useful as regards identifying interactions between quality characteristics.

6 Towards Resolving Negative Interactions Between Quality Characteristics

We propose that the software quality trade-off process (Fig. 3) can be used to resolve conflicting interactions between quality characteristics. The purpose of the software quality trade-off process is to make decisions concerning the best resolution alternative when conflicting interactions between quality requirements appear during software development. The process employs a rationalistic approach based on criteria defined in order to evaluate the potential resolution alternatives, and also considers the appropriate

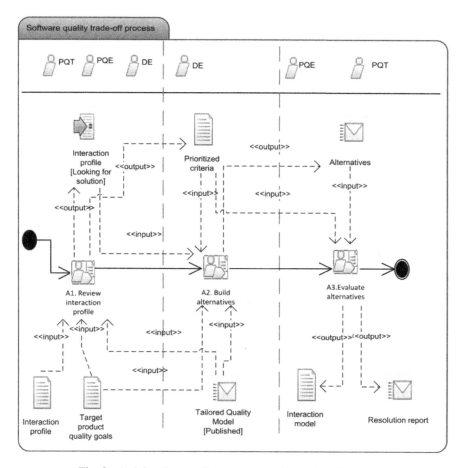

Fig. 3. Activity diagram for software quality trade-offs process.

methods with which to analyze the alternatives used to resolve conflicting interactions between quality characteristics.

The process starts when an interaction profile is created and the software development team wishes to resolve the conflicting interaction that has been discovered. The main outcome of executing this process is a set of solution alternatives that are then evaluated in order to recommend that which satisfies the decision criteria. Furthermore, as a result of applying this process the interaction model can be updated.

6.1 Process Objectives

The software quality trade-off process can be used to attain the following:

- A systematic approach can be applied to analyze conflicting interactions and to provide a recommended solution.

- The set of alternatives can be built using appropriate methods.
- Both the recommended solution and the interaction profile can be used to update the interaction model.

6.2 Inputs and Outputs

The work products required in this process are: tailored product quality model (published), target product quality goals and interaction profile. Moreover, the interaction model is an input to be updated during the implementation of this process. The process outcomes are the following work products: the decision to carry out a further analysis of the interaction profile, the prioritized criteria used to assess alternatives, the set of alternatives and the resolution report. The interaction profile can additionally be updated during the implementation of this process.

6.3 Roles

Table 6 depicts the roles that participate in this process.

Table 6. Roles participating in the software quality trade-off process.

Role	Description
Product Quality Team (PQT)	Described in Table 2.
Product Quality Expert (PQE)	Described in Table 2.
Discipline Expert (DE)	This role has the knowledge and skills needed to deal with product quality characteristics in the context of the process under study. The role's responsibilities include the construction of alternatives with which to resolve a conflicting interaction in addition to selecting and applying methods with which to analyze proposed alternatives.

6.4 Activities

The process consists of three activities: review interaction profile, build alternatives and evaluate alternatives. These are described in the following paragraphs.

- A1. Review interaction profile. The PQE and the PQT review the interaction profile in order to determine further activities as regards conflicting interactions between quality requirements. The review is enriched with the DE´s opinions with regard to the specific quality characteristics and process under study. The outcome of the review is a decision concerning the relevance of additional activities in order to recommend a solution.
- A2. Build alternatives. The DE builds a set of potential alternatives with which to resolve the interactions that have arisen between quality requirements in the context

of the software process in which they emerge. The methods used to assess alternatives are additionally documented and used to determine the extent to which each alternative achieves the assessment criteria previously established.

- A3. Evaluate alternatives. The PQE and the PQT roles review alternatives and the results of the assessment methods. The alternatives are assessed by considering the assessment quality criteria and procedures established to carry out the assessment. The resolution report should include the means used to resolve the conflicting interaction and how the selected means could be implemented in the software project. The interaction model is also updated with the interaction profile information and with the recommended solution.

7 Conclusions

Software organizations need appropriate support to manage interactions between quality requirements. In order to support them, in this paper we have described a process with which to monitor interactions between quality requirements. An exploratory case study has also been conducted to validate the activity 'A2. Check potential interactions between quality requirements'. This resulted in the main contextual factors that contribute to the identification and characterization of an interaction. Furthermore, we have presented a summary of a process that can be used to resolve conflicting interactions.

Although we prepared a template and guideline to support the exploratory case study participants as regards understanding interactions and contextual factors, we found that interactions between quality requirements were reported as a perceived interaction because the project under study was at the conception stage. However, without explicit reference to the potential impact of the interaction on the software project it is difficult to understand to what extent it may influence software development activities or project success. The identification of perceived interaction is a first step toward understanding and characterizing an objective interaction, but it is necessary to include other approaches in order to uncover the real impact of the interaction on the software project. For instance, a risk-based technique would provide information about the impact of the interactions.

With regard to the validation of the monitoring product quality requirements process, the results showed that it can be used for a software organization which deals with product quality, but some tasks should be improved. With regard to the artifacts used in the exploratory case study, the participants stated that the interaction profile is easy to use and apply. They also suggested taking into account indicators and measures of software product quality in order to establish a mechanism with which to identify interactions between quality characteristics.

As future work, it will be necessary to validate the process used to monitor interactions between quality characteristics in other stages of the software development life cycle and also to consider both other organizational contexts and application domains. A software tool currently provides information about interactions between quality characteristics, but it needs to be improved so as to address the information used to characterize an interaction. The process employed to resolve negative interactions should also be validated by means of empirical studies.

Acknowledgements. This work has been funded by the VILMA and INGENIOSO projects (Consejería de Educación, Ciencia y Cultura - Junta de Comunidades de Castilla La Mancha) and Fondo Europeo de Desarrollo Regional FEDER, Ref.: PEII11-0316-2878 and Ref. PEII11-0025-9533) and GEODAS-BC project (TIN2012-37493-C03-01 funded by the Spanish Ministerio de Economía y Competitividad and by FEDER (Fondo Europeo de Desarrollo Regional).

References

1. Mairiza, D., Zowghi, D., Nurmuliani, N.: Towards a catalogue of conflicts among non-functional requirements. In: 5th International Conference on Evaluation of Novel Approaches to Software Engineering, ENASE 2010, pp. 20–29 (2010)
2. Ameller, D., Ayala, C., Cabot, J., Franch, X.: Non-functional requirements in architectural decision making. IEEE Softw. **30**, 61–67 (2013)
3. Chen, L., Babar, M.A., Nuseibeh, B.: Characterizing architecturally significant requirements. IEEE Softw. **30**, 38–45 (2013)
4. Robinson, W.N., Pawlowski, S.D., Volkov, V.: Requirements interaction management. ACM Comput. Surv. **35**, 132–190 (2003)
5. Loucopoulos, P., Sun, J., Zhao, L., Heidari, F.: A systematic classification and analysis of NFRs. In: 19th Americas Conference on Information Systems, AMCIS 2013 - Hyperconnected World: Anything, Anywhere, Anytime, pp. 208–217, Chicago, IL, USA (2013)
6. Dahlstedt, A., Persson, A.: Requirements interdependencies: state of the art and future challenges. In: Aurum, A., Wohlin, C. (eds.) Requirements engineering, pp. 95–116. Springer, Berlin Heidelberg (2005)
7. Boehm, B., In, H.: Identifying quality-requirement conflicts. IEEE Softw. **13**, 25–36 (1996)
8. Theofanos, M.F., Pfleeger, S.L.: Guest Editors' introduction: shouldn't all security be usable? IEEE Secur. Priv. **9**, 12–17 (2011)
9. Thakurta, R.: A framework for prioritization of quality requirements for inclusion in a software project. Softw. Qual. J. **21**, 573–597 (2013)
10. García-Mireles, G.A., Moraga, M.Á., Garcia, F., Piattini, M.: Methods for supporting management of interactions between quality characteristics. In: Filipe, J., Maciaszek, L. (Eds.) 9th International Conference on Evaluation of Novel Approaches to Software Engineering, pp. 93–100. INSTICC, Lisboa (2014)
11. Unterkalmsteiner, M., et al.: Evaluation and measurement of software process improvement—a systematic literature review. IEEE Trans. Softw. Eng. **38**, 398–424 (2012)
12. García-Mireles, G.A., Moraga, M.Á., García, F., Piattini, M.: Towards the harmonization of process and product oriented software quality approaches. In: Winkler, D., O'Connor, R.V., Messnarz, R. (eds.) EuroSPI 2012. CCIS, vol. 301, pp. 133–144. Springer, Heidelberg (2012)
13. ISO, ISO/IEC FCD 25010: Systems and software engineering - system and software product quality requirements and evaluation (SQauRE) - System and software quality models (2010)

14. García-Mireles, G.A., Moraga, M.Á., García, F., Piattini, M.: A framework to support software quality trade-offs from a process-based perspective. In: McCaffery, F., O'Connor, R.V., Messnarz, R. (eds.) EuroSPI 2013. CCIS, vol. 364, pp. 96–107. Springer, Heidelberg (2013)
15. Barney, S., Petersen, K., Svahnberg, M., Aurum, A., Barney, H.: Software quality trade-offs: a systematic map. Inf. Softw. Technol. **54**, 651–662 (2012)
16. Chung, L., Nixon, B.A., Yu, E., Mylopoulos, J.: Non-Functional Requirements in Software Engineering. Kluwer Academic Publisher, Dordrecht (2000)
17. Al Balushi, T.H., Sampaio, P.R.F., Loucopoulos, P.: Eliciting and prioritizing quality requirements supported by ontologies: a case study using the ElicitO framework and tool. Expert Syst. **30**, 129–151 (2013)
18. Mairiza, D., Zowghi, D.: An ontological framework to manage the relative conflicts between security and usability requirements. In: 3rd international workshop on managing requirements knowledge, MaRK2010, pp. 1–6 (2010)
19. Allen, J., Kitchenham, B., Konrad, M.: Theme Q. The relationships between processes and product qualities. In: Forrester, E., (ed.). vol. pp. 19–28. Software Engineering Institute, Carnegie Mellon. (2006)
20. CMMI, P.T. CMMI for Development, Version 1.3 (CMU/SEI-2010-TR-033) (2010). cited 2012, http://www.sei.cmu.edu/library/abstracts/reports/10tr033.cfm
21. ISO: ISO/IEC 12207 Systems and software engineering — Software life cycle processes (2008)
22. Chiam, Y.K., Staples, M., Ye, X., Zhu, L.: Applying a selection method to choose Quality Attribute Techniques. Inf. Softw. Technol. **55**, 1419–1436 (2013)
23. García-Mireles, G.A., Moraga, M.Á., Garcia, F., Piattini, M.: Identificación de interacciones entre las características de calidad del software. In: XVIII Jornadas de Ingeniería del Software y Bases de Datos JISBD2013, pp. 141–154. Universidad Complutense de Madrid, Madrid, España (2013)
24. García-Mireles, G.A., Moraga, M.Á., Garcia, F., Piattini, M.: The influence of process quality on product usability: a systematic review. CLEI Electron. J. **16**, 1–13 (2013). http://www.clei.org/cleiej/paper.php?id=278
25. OMG, Software & Systems Process Engineering Metamodel specification (SPEM) Version 2.0 (2008)
26. Petersen, K., Wohlin, C.: Context in industrial software engineering research. In: 3rd International Symposium on Empirical Software Engineering and Measurement ESEM 2009., IEEE, Editor, pp. 401–404. Lake Buena Vista, FL, USA (2009)
27. Berntsson Svensson, R., et al.: Quality requirements in industrial practice-an extended interview study at eleven companies. IEEE Trans. Softw. Eng. **38**, 923–935 (2012)
28. Runeson, P., Höst, M., Rainer, A., Regnell, B.: Case Study Research in Software Engineering: Guidelines and Examples. Case Study Research in Software Engineering: Guidelines and Examples. John Wiley and Sons (2012)

A Method to Identify Talented Aspiring Designers in Use of Personas with Personality

Farshid Anvari[(✉)] and Deborah Richards

Department of Computing, Macquarie University, Sydney, Australia
farshid.anvari@acm.org, deborah.richards@mq.edu.au

Abstract. Personnel engaged in developing applications using User-Centred Design (UCD) techniques need to have special abilities and training to design products that meet the needs of users. Persona, an archetypical user, is used for design of applications. Persona with personality is deemed to better represent a user as personality provides a richer profile and affects the way users interact with technology. This paper presents a novel technique to identify talented aspiring designers in use of persona with personality. We authored four personas with different personality traits. Thirty-three participants completed a spatial ability test, answered personality trait questionnaires and performed a design activity. Our assessment of design artefacts indicate that participants who score high in imagination personality factor and spatial ability tests are talented designers in the use of personas with personality within UCD methodologies. The implication of our study is that the talented designers can be identified and utilised more productively.

Keywords: User-Centred Design · Holistic persona · Scenario · Personality traits · Big-Five Factors · Imagination · Spatial ability

1 Introduction

User-Centred Design (UCD) methodologies consider the goals of the users as the primary requirement for developing software application [1], are increasingly used in software engineering practices and processes [2]. Personas, archetypical users, are tools used within UCD methodologies for software applications or product design and communication with stakeholders and scenarios are the actions carried out by the personas interacting with the applications [3]. Personas support the design of the application by focusing on target users and facilitating communication with stakeholders regarding the scope and final outcomes [3]. To improve the usability and accessibility of the application, and hence reduce cognitive load on the users, and for better communication with stakeholders, Anvari and Tran [4] proposed Holistic Persona, a persona with five dimensions: Factual, Personality, Intelligence, Knowledge and Cognitive Process. In this paper we explore the use of Holistic Persona in UCD, focusing on the personality dimension as the literature stresses the role that personality plays in differentiating individuals [5, 6] and as a factor that affects the way users interact with technology [7].

© Springer International Publishing Switzerland 2016
L.A. Maciaszek and J. Filipe (Eds.): ENASE 2015, CCIS 599, pp. 40–61, 2016.
DOI: 10.1007/978-3-319-30243-0_3

To understand the usefulness of Holistic Persona with personality as a design method, we sought to investigate the features of designers that may influence their design performance using the method. The relationship between performance in creative professions and personality has been studied by a number of researchers e.g. [8, 9]. It has been found that professionals who have been successful in domains such as architecture, engineering and programming are good in spatial ability [10]. Based on this prior research, we sought to identify if there was a specific link between design, spatial ability and personality within software engineering and UCD methodologies. To contribute to this understanding, we measure the performance of software engineering students in a spatial ability test and use an established psychometric test to determine their personality traits. In this paper we also report on our investigation of the effect of the personality dimension of the Holistic Persona on the participants' preferences and conceptual designs and the design rubric to assess the design artefact. The next section presents a literature review covering the concept of persona and previous work on intelligence, personality traits and spatial ability. Section 3 presents the research questions, methodology and design of the rubric. The results appear in Sect. 4 with specific discussion of personality traits, spatial ability and design ability in Sect. 5. Sections 6 and 7 present further discussion (includings threats to the experiment settings, and measures to mitigate these), conclusion and plans for future research.

2   Literature Review

Personas are authored using photographs, sketches, factual information gathered by market research, such as demographics, profession, hobbies and interests, etc. [3]. Long [11] reported a higher level of empathy toward personas with photos of real people compared with illustrated personas.

Intelligence is the ability to solve problems. Gardner [12] listed seven intelligences: linguistic, logical-mathematical, spatial, musical, bodily-kinaesthetic, interpersonal and intrapersonal. Persons with innate ability or giftedness have high talent in one or more domains; with little tutoring, they can understand the abstract concepts, ask deep questions, reflect on various interpretations of the problems [13] and can transfer their knowledge from similar domains [14]. Plucker et al. [15, p 156] based on a number of peer reviewed journals defined creativity as "the interplay between ability and process by which an individual or group produces an outcome or product that is both novel and useful as defined within some social context". In a longitudinal study of mechanical engineering students, Field [16] found that their performance in design subjects was more related with their intuition and spatial ability and less related with their logical and mathematical ability.

Relationships between personality, creativity and academic performance were studied by a number of researchers. The Big-Five Factors (BFF) of personality is widely used to understand the structure of personality [9, 17–19]. Two models of the BFF of personality that are used by researchers are Trait Descriptive Adjective (TDA) by Goldberg [5] and NEO Personality Inventory, Revised (NEO PI-R) by Costa and McCrae [20]. Both models use similar terms to describe the five factors [5]. According to Goldberg [5] the BFF are: (1) Extraversion, (2) Agreeableness,

(3) Conscientiousness, (4) Emotional Stability and (5) Imagination or Intellect. Creative scientists are more likely to have personality traits of extraversion and openness to experience [8] and academics are more likely to be agreeable, conscientious and open to experience [21]. Silvia [22] suggested that Plasticity (Extraversion and Imagination) is more strongly related to creativity than Stability (Agreeableness, Conscientiousness and Emotional Stability). McCrae [23] in a study of 268 men found that openness to experience and divergent thinking, a psychometric investigation of the creativity, were correlated. Poropat [9] in a meta-analysis of students' measures of academic performance measured by grade point average found that secondary and tertiary students' performances were related to consciousness and intelligence.

The importance of spatial ability in science and engineering are studied by many researchers. Shea et al. [24] in a longitudinal study of 563 students in late 1970 s using Scholastic Assessment Test and spatial ability tests found that those who scored better in a spatial ability test had selected careers in Science, Technology, Engineering or Mathematics. Wai et al. [25] drawing a random sample from the population of 400,000 students, who were longitudinally studied for 11 years, found that among those who chose careers in science, technology or mathematics scored high in spatial ability during their adolescence. Charyton et al. [26] in a study of engineering students found that their score in a Creative Engineering Design Assessment, a test for measurement of creativity in engineering, is related to their performance in Purdue Spatial Visualization Test of Rotation. Ault and John [27] surveyed the literature across the USA with the result that students doing four year engineering courses generally scored about 75 % in the Spatial Rotation of Visualisation test. Anvari et al. [14] found that students with high spatial ability had lower cognitive load while performing 3D computer graphics drawing and were better able to transfer knowledge from one domain to another similar domain.

Researchers and educators often use assessment tools to monitor students' progress in design courses. For example, McMartin et al. [28] developed a rubric consisting of seven criteria to measure undergraduate engineering design capability in a scenario based assignment, where the students were assessed based on how they would solve a realistic problem rather than providing a solution.

Blooms taxonomy revolves around the knowledge that a participant has and cognitive process to use the knowledge [29]. In designing a rubric for assessing the design produced by engineering students, Bailey and Szabo [30] specified the design objectives that were going to be measured and listed key criteria of an assessment strategy to suit their requirements, two of the key criteria considered were: (1) the rubric assesses processes and (2) the rubric criteria are linked to different levels of Bloom's taxonomy [29]. Zowghi [31] used Blooms taxonomy to assess Requirements Engineering students' gain in knowledge which most students achieved to Comprehension level or above.

Analytic and holistic rubrics use different approaches for the assessment of design work; in an analytic scoring rubric each criterion is scored on a different descriptive scale but in a holistic scoring rubric the scoring is allocated on a single descriptive scale considering all criteria [32].

3   Research Questions & Methodology

Based on the studies of Furnham and Bachtiar [8], Poropat [9], Anvari et al. [14], Field [16], Shea et al. [24], Charyton et al. [26] we find that both personality traits and spatial ability are important in cognitively demanding tasks such as creativity and design within the software engineering field. Hence in this paper we address the research question:

Can we use a spatial ability test and self-assessment of personality traits to identify talented aspiring designers who can produce a design that matches Holistic Persona's needs considering her personality?

This question attempts to discover innate capabilities of a participant as a UCD designer. We conducted an empirical study to obtain data to allow us to answer the above research question as well as other research questions that were part of a larger study concerning the influence of the Holistic Persona on the designer and the relation between the designer's and persona's personality traits. In the study we investigated two factors of the personality, extraversion and emotional stability. This study also contributes to our understanding of the personality traits and abilities required for recognising personality in a persona and being a talented designer in the use of personas with personality. Some of our findings for other questions are reported elsewhere [33].

Before the study commenced, we provided a brief introduction to UCD methodologies, an example of a persona, a conceptual design and a scenario; these materials were for educational purposes only. Participants were then asked to give consent if they wished to continue. The 75-min study consisted of six parts: demographics questionnaires, self-assessed personality traits, assessing four Holistic Personas, a design task for one of the randomly assigned personas, post design questionnaires and a spatial ability test. The parts that are relevant to this paper are described briefly in the following subsections.

3.1   Demographic Questions

Demographic questionnaires consisted of questions about the participant's gender, birth year, occupation, interest in design, level of competence in the English language, country in which they spent their youth and the courses they are studying or have studied. The demographic data was used for analysis of the results.

3.2   Self-Assessed Personality Trait

Participants rated their own personalities using Goldberg's 50 question Trait Descriptive Adjectives (TDA) on a 5-point Likert scale. The test is adopted from the literature [5] and the International Personality Item Pool [34]. The bi-polar answers to the self-assessment questions on a 5 point likert scale are added together after reverse scoring the negative questions [5] to provide results in the range of 10-50. The resultant data is treated as interval-level data, converted to percentages and analysed using R statistical packages [35].

3.3   Assessment of Holistic Persona

Participants rated four Holistic Personas (Table 1) using on a 7-point Likert scale. The test is adopted from literature [6]. The bi-polar answers to the assessment questions on a 7 point likert scale are added together after reverse scoring the negative questions [6] to provide results in the range of 2–14. The participants were also asked to indicate their liking of the Holistic Persona and whether they thought the Holistic Persona is a real person The resultant data is treated as interval-level data, converted to percentages and analysed using R statistical packages [35].

3.4   Design Task

Participants performed a design session of 15 min duration with a Holistic Persona that was assigned randomly yet evenly from a set of four Holistic Personas that were authored to be very similar to one another in all dimensions except in the personality dimension. Two personality factors were varied as shown in Table 1 (see Appendix I for an example of a Holistic Persona, Doris).

Table 1. Holistic personas and their personality traits.

Persona for assessment	Persona for design	Extraversion	Emotional Stability
Jane	Doris	Extravert	stable
Jean	Katie	Extravert	unstable
Jade	Minty	Introvert	stable
June	Eliza	Introvert	unstable

Participants wrote their conceptual design for a software application or product of their choice that would help the assigned Holistic Persona and a scenario about how the Holistic Persona would use the software application or product.

3.5   Spatial Ability Test

Participants performed a 20-item Purdue Visualization of Rotation Test. This activity was timed. The test consisted of 20 questions; each question showed an object in a position and the participant needed to mentally rotate the object to a new position; there were 5 choices representing how the object looks in the new position, one of which is correct. One mark was given for the correct answer and there was no penalty for the wrong answer. Participants' total score at 10 min was selected as the measure of their performance in the spatial ability test [36].

3.6   Rubric for Evaluation of the Design

Rubric, a descriptive scoring scheme, as an assessment tool assists in consistent subjective assessment of a written work; the work is divided into categories and a score is allocated to each category by considering the description of the characteristics of the responses within each category [37]. In designing the rubric the revised Blooms [29] taxonomy was researched and the success of other researchers who developed rubric for assessment of design was investigated.

The design rubric used for this paper consists of five parts for numeric scoring:

1. Abstract Design (5 marks): The design can be either an application that is a diary, a calendar, a recommender or a specialized forum; or an abstract design with sufficient description that is possible to visualise how the application works.
2. Design scenario (3 marks): A design scenario shows how the Holistic Persona interacts with the application.
3. Factual information and reminder (2 marks): The participant is expected to refer to the Holistic Persona by her name and the application reminds her about applying skin lotion while intending to walk in the sun, carrying eye glasses for certain appointments, and alerting her to her allergies while ordering food.
4. Weight issues (2 marks): As overweight is the main issue the Holistic Persona is facing, the application is expected to suggest on food, exercise or weight.
5. Suitability to Holistic Persona (3 marks): Expressions that reflect consideration given to the Holistic Persona as a person while explaining the design and scenario.

In our study, one of the main issues that the Holistic Persona is facing is that she is overweight. Part four gives credit to the design that addresses weight issue by concentrating on food, exercise or anyway in which it can help Holistic Persona to reduce her weight. Holistic Persona does not have any issues with other activities such as managing her musical interests or her studies; hence addressing other interests or aspects of her life in the design attracts credit for abstract design (part 1) only. If a participant indicates that her/his design is to help the Holistic Persona to deal with weight or forgetfulness issues either immediately or in the long term s/he gets credit for connectedness in suitability of the design to Holistic Persona (part 5). An example of connectedness would be to provide the Holistic Persona a confidence building tool with the intention that she can take part in sporting activity.

The rubric was reviewed independently by an experienced designer Hien Minh Thi Tran, the second author, Professor Deborah Richards and another academic Associate Professor Michael Hitchens. Adjustments were made to the rubric to resolve any discrepancies.

4   Analysis of Results

To answer the questions in the larger study, participants had received one of four personalities to design for, hence the designs were varied. This section reports the results for the variations in participants' designs, personalities, abilities and preferences.

4.1   Participants

This paper presents data from 41 participants who completed some or all of the relevant activities of the study for this paper; they are termed as sample population (Table 2, item 5). They completed demographics, self-assessment of personality and one or more of Holistic Persona assessment, design artefact, design questionnaire, post design questionnaire and spatial ability test. The thirty-three participants who completed the design activity for a Holistic Persona are referred as aspiring UCD designers (Table 2, item 2). The data from aspiring UCD designers are used for statistical evaluations of conceptual design (Sect. 5).

Table 2. Participants in the study.

Item	Activities completed	Number of participants
1	Completed ratings of Holistic Personas	38
2	Completed or attempted design activity for Holistic Persona (aspiring UCD designers)	33
3	Completed post design questionnaire	32
4	Completed self-assessment of personality, design and spatial ability test	32
5	Total number of participated in the study – completed all or some of the activities (sample population)	41

The majority of the participants in sample population (73 %) were studying a second year Software Engineering subject within the IT Department. They were invited to participate in this research during their tutorial session to gain understanding of HCI design through exposure to the UCD methodologies and tools, without receiving any course credit. Other participants were postgraduate students and professionals (Financial Analyst, Artist, Hydraulic Engineer, Human Resources Manager, Chef and two unknowns).

In the sample population, for the question about gender, 78 % of the participants selected male, 17 % of the sample population selected female and 5 % of the sample population selected other. 93 % of the sample population spoke and wrote in English for more than three years; 7 % of the sample population wrote and spoke English for 1–3 years. 80 % of the sample population had lived in Australia or New Zealand or UK or the USA during their youth. Hence participants had different backgrounds.

Most of the sample population finished the study, including the introductory session, within 70 min. All participants were thanked for their participation in the study and those who gave an email address received a copy of their results for spatial ability and personality tests. None of the participants received any financial benefit. The results from the study presented in this section cover the following topics:

1. Participants' assessment of Holistic Personas personality (Sect. 4.2).
2. Effect of Holistic Persona on conceptual design (Sect. 4.3).
3. Participants' preferences for a Holistic Persona (Sect. 4.4).

4.2 Participants' Assessment of Holistic Personas' Personalities

The Holistic Persona was assessed by the sample population to ensure that the authored personality dimension is as intended. The objective of analysis in this section is: *Does the sample population recognize the personality dimension of a Holistic Persona as intended?*

The statistic for this analysis, the number of participants who have completed ratings of Holistic Personas, is data from 38 participants (Table 2, item 1). The mean values (in percentages) of the rating given to each Holistic Persona (Sect. 3.3) by the participants are presented in Table 3.

Table 3. Mean Values of Holistic Personas' Personality Factors Rated by the Participants.

Holistic Persona	Ex %	Ag %	Cn %	ES %	Im %	Holistic Persona represents a real person %
Jane	75**	73	75*	77*	70**	61*
Jean	61	43+	52	31	56	58*
Jade	40	73	73	74*	68*	72*
June	16 **	57*	57	31 +	41+	61 +

Note: ** $p < .01$; * $p < 0.05$; + $p < 0.1$
Legend: Ex – extraversion; Ag – agreeableness; Cn – conscientiousness; ES – emotional stability; Im – imagination.

From Table 3 Jade has been rated similarly to Jane in all factors except extraversion. June is rated similarly to Jean in all factors except extraversion. Also Table 3 shows that Jane and Jade are rated high for emotionally stability (77 % and 74 %) and Jean and June are rated low for emotionally stability (both 31 %). These results confirm to the design of the personas, as listed in Table 1. Due to inter relationship between the five factors [38], even though the other personality traits agreeableness, consciousness and imagination are authored similarly for the personas, the sample population rated these factors differently. As shown in Table 3 these differences don't affect the overall results. Table 3 also shows that the participants in the study considered that the Holistic Personas resemble a real person (Jane 61 %, Jean 58 %, Jade 72 %, June 61 %). Hence, the participants clearly saw the authored personas' personalities as intended (Table 1) and they resemble a real person.

4.3 Perceived Effect of Holistic Persona on Conceptual Design

Participants' awareness of the personality of the Holistic persona and the resultant effect that the personality had on their design was measured by design and post design questionnaires. This section presents the relevant questionnaire and the statistical calculations of their answers. Following statements were made in post design survey questionnaire related to awareness of personality dimension of the Holistic Persona assigned for the design activity. The aspiring UCD designers' responses are presented in Table 4.

1. The personality of the Holistic Persona positively influenced the scenario writing/design activity.
2. I would like to do another scenario writing/design activity with the same Holistic Persona or a persona that has similar personality again.
3. To meet the Holistic Persona's needs, I added features to the design which otherwise I would not have added.

Analysis of answers to the above questions (Table 4) indicate that the participants were aware of the personality dimension of the Holistic Persona: 79 % of them reported that the holistic persona's personality influenced their design activity (57 % positively and 22 % negatively); 78 % of them reported that they would like to design for a Holistic Persona with a different personality than the one they were given.

Table 4. Participants' perception of Holistic Persona.

No	Statements about Holistic Persona	Participants' Responses (%)		
		Agree	Neutral	Disagree
1	Her personality positively influenced design activity	57	22	22
2	Would like to do another session with her	22		78
3	Extra Features Added	57		43

Table 4 indicates that 57 % of the aspiring UCD designers took the personality of the Holistic Persona into consideration and provided conceptual designs that are tailored to the personality of the Holistic Persona. Table 6 presents a sample of quotes from participants while they were engaged in the conceptual design task. Based on the above analysis it can be deduced that the participants felt that the Holistic Persona's personality affected their conceptual design of the software application.

4.4   Preferred Holistic Persona

The participants spent some time with each Holistic Persona while they were rating the persona and designed for one Holistic Persona. Hence they may have formed a preference for a persona that they would like to work with. Table 5 shows the answers the participants provided to the question: Which Holistic Persona is the preferred one?

Table 5. Choice of Holistic Persona for a future design activity.

Holistic Persona	Percentage of participants select (%)
Jane	18.9
Jean	5.4
Jade	27.0
June	5.4
I cannot remember the name	43.2

Table 5 shows that 45.9 % of the participants who answered post design questionnaire prefer to design for a Holistic Persona that is emotionally stable (Table 1); 18.9 % of them selected Jane (extrovert and emotionally stable) and 27.0 % of them selected Jade (introvert and emotionally stable). 43.2 % of the participants couldn't remember the name of their preferred Holistic Persona. Hence the majority of the participants (56.8 %) had a preference for a particular Holistic Persona.

5 Personality Traits, Spatial Ability and Design Ability

This section addresses the research question: *Can we use a spatial ability test and self-assessment of personality traits to identify talented aspiring designers who can produce a design that matches Holistic Persona's needs considering her personality?*

From Table 2, data from 33 participants were complete, their scores for conceptual design, spatial ability and personalities were analysed and the results are presented.

Table 6. Design comments about personality of the persona.

Id	Holistic Persona assigned	Design comments
1029	Doris (Extravert/Emotionally stable)	"…*The virtual diary allows for entries based on various user designed topics or sub topics, weather that be health food ideas or new music that they enjoyed, or information relating to her social activities. The reminder application will utilize multiple parts of a phones system (assuming that such a social girl would have a relatively advanced phone). …*"
1024	Katie (Extravert/Emotionally unstable)	"… *I think this person need some kind of personal coach that will just ping or notify her of various reminders and set goals for her to do each day and she can fill these out like a survey and the coach will say some words of encouragement …*"
1036	Minty (Introvert/Emotionally stable)	"*Minty could possibly benefit from an app that recommended local social events. This would encourage Minty to socialize more with the people she is already comfortable around and continue to engage her social skills in new, yet familiar environments. …*".
1031	Eliza Introvert/Emotionally unstable	"*i feel like she would not be willing to listen if I recommended a health and fitness program … possibly go and see a counsellor to help work through her self-doubt. Software is not what this girl needs. She needs human contact…*"

(*Continued*)

Table 6. (*Continued*)

Id	Holistic Persona assigned	Design comments
1023	Eliza (Introvert/Emotionally unstable)	"*An anonymous, public forum of message board where discussion is encouraged. -This would allow Eliza to find groups of people with similar interests, issues, and ideas to discuss and socialize with reduced pressure from her introverted personality (since the application is online and anonymous). -When she would otherwise be under too much social anxiety or has been previously rejected in face-to-face conversations, an online forum would allow group discussion and input from other users who are much more likely to empathize. This can also boost self-esteem from the support other users are likely to provide….*"

5.1   Imagination Personality Traits and Design Performance

Table 7 presents the breakdown of the sample populations according to their performance in design based on the rubric (Sect. 3.6). The sample population was divided into groups based on their scores in imagination personality factor and spatial ability. In Sect. 5.2, the groups are compared with one another based on the influence that the abilities have on their performance in design. The influence is described using effect size, the Pearson's correlation coefficient, r, computed from the t-test [35]. Table 8 shows partial correlation (r) of the five factors of personality with the participant's performance in design. Field et al. [35] lists the description of effect size as small when $r = 0.1$, medium when $r = 0.3$ and large when $r = 0.5$.

Table 7. Performance in design.

No	Performance in design (%)	Participant (%)
1	85–100	31
2	75–84	15
3	65–74	6
4	50–64	24
5	Less than 50	24

Our sample population indicates that there is a medium sized relationship between imagination personality factor and performance in design and it is significant ($r = 0.37$, $p = 0.049$) having a shared variability of 14 %.

5.2   Dividing Performance into Four Quadrants

Since in our sample population, imagination personality factor is the only personality factor correlated with design performance, our further analysis concerning performance in design is restricted to the imagination personality factor and spatial ability.

Table 8. Partial correlation of the performance in design with personality factors study.

BFF	pcor (r)	r^2	t-value*	p (> |t|)	Effect size
Ext	−0.01	0.00	−0.07	0.95	Nil
Agr	0.07	0.00	0.36	0.72	Nil
Cn	−0.16	0.02	−0.86	0.40	Nil
ES	0.09	0.01	−0.47	0.64	Nil
Img	**0.37**	**0.14**	**2.1**	**0.049**	**Medium**

Legend: Ext – extraversion; Agr – agreeableness; Cn – conscientiousness; ES – emotional stability; Img – imagination; df – degrees of freedom; pcor – partial correlation; p – probability. *(df = 27)

Figure 1 shows a scatter plot of the participants' performance in the spatial ability test at 10 min versus their imagination personality factor; the points are labelled with their performance in design. Figure 1 shows a group of participants in the top right hand corner who mostly have performed well in design. Using the area of the plot covered by this group as a guide, the figure is divided into four quadrants. The first quadrant (Q1) is bounded by those participants who scored 75 % or greater in spatial ability [27] and the imagination personality factor; in most Australian universities 75 % or greater is used to award the grade of Distinction. Table 9 shows that 27 % participants are in Q1.

Table 9. Quadrant population.

No	Quadrant	Participant (%)
1	Quadrant 1 (Q1)	27
2	Quadrant 2 (Q2)	15
3	Quadrant 3 (Q3)	31
4	Quadrant 4 (Q4)	27

The second quadrant (Q2) is bounded by those participants whose score in spatial ability is less than 75 % but their score in the imagination personality factor is equal to or above 75 %. Table 9 shows that 15 % of participants are in Q2. The third quadrant (Q3) represents those participants whose score in spatial ability is equal to or above 75 % but their score in the imagination personality factor is below 75 %. Table 9 shows that 31 % of participants are in Q3. The fourth quadrant (Q4) is bounded by those participants whose scores in spatial ability and the imagination personality factor are below 75 %. Table 9 shows that 27 % of participants are in Q4. Figure 1 shows that most participants in the first quadrant scored highly for their performance in design with the mean value of 84.1 (Table 10).

5.3   Five Scenarios to Study Results in Four Quadrants

The participants' data were analysed using five scenarios (Table 10). In each scenario the performance in design was studied for two groups. The five scenarios are listed below:

1. Effect of high imagination and spatial ability: performance of the group whose score in both imagination personality factor and spatial ability are high (Q1) compared with the rest of the sample population (Q2, Q3 & Q4);
2. Effect of imagination: difference in performance in design for the group of participants whose score in the imagination personality factor is high (Q1 & Q2) versus other participants (Q3 & Q4);
3. Effect of spatial ability - high imagination: difference in performance in design for the group of participants who scored high in both imagination personality trait and spatial ability (Q1) versus the participants who only scored high in imagination personality trait (Q2);
4. Effect of spatial ability: difference in performance in design for the group of participants whose score in spatial ability is high (Q1 & Q3) versus group of other participants (Q2 & Q4);
5. Effect of imagination - high spatial ability: difference in performance in design for the group of participants who scored high in both spatial ability and imagination personality factor (Q1) versus the participants who only scored high in spatial ability (Q3).

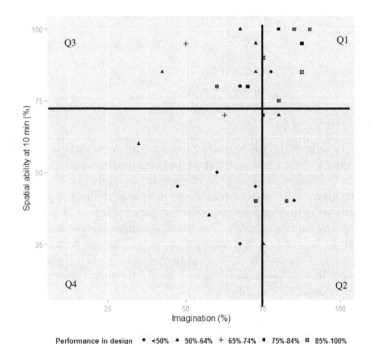

Fig. 1. Participants' performance in design.

Table 10. Analysis of participants' performance in design under five scenarios.

SNo	Quadrants (Q)	Mean %	SE %	Median %	Welch tsst t-test				Effect Size (r)
					t-test	df	P	Reject H0	
1	Q1 (SImg =>75 % & SpAb =>75 %)	84.1	6.3	90.0	-3.3	16	0.002	True	0.6 Large
	Q2, Q3 & Q4	59.1	4.3	58.5					
2	SImg =>75 % Q1 & Q2	76.5	5.8	85.0	-2.4	28	0.011	True	0.4 Medium
	SImg < 75 % Q3 & Q4	58.1	4.9	57.0					
3	Q1 (SpAb =>75 %)	84.1	6.3	90.0	1.84	7	0.053	False	0.6 Large
	Q2 (SpAb < 75 %)	62.8	9.7	60.0					
4	SpAb =>75 % Q1 & Q3	74.2	4.8	80.0	-2.61	28	0.007	True	0.4 Medium
	SpAb < 75 % Q2 & Q4	54.6	5.7	57.0					
5	Q1 (SImg =>75 %)	84.1	6.3	90.0	2.13	17	0.024	True	0.5 Large
	Q3 (SImg < 75 %)	65.3	6.2	68.0					

Note: H0 – Hypothesis – True difference in mean is zero – Reject H0 at 5 % confidence
H1 – Alternate Hypothesis – True difference in mean is greater than zero
Legend: SNo – senario number; Q – quadrant; SE – standard error; df – degrees of freedom;
p – probablity; SImg – score in imagination personality factor;
SpAb – score in spatial ability; Welch tsst t-test – Welch two sample single tail t-test;

5.4   Comparison of the Results in Four Quadrants

Table 10 shows Mean (m), Standard Error (SE) and Median for each group of participants. The two groups in each scenario are compared using Welch two sample single tail t-test and the effect size (r) between the two samples are described using the Pearson's correlation coefficient, r computed from the t-test [35].The null hypothesis (H0) is that all groups are drawn from the same population, hence the difference in means of the different groups is zero, the alternate hypothesis (H1) is that the difference in mean is greater than zero. Figure 2 shows five box plots of participants' performance in UCD conceptual design for each of the five scenarios listed in Table 10:

- Scenario 1 shows that the participants who scored high in both spatial ability and imagination personality factor performed significantly higher in design (m = 84.1, SE = 6.3) compared with the other participants' performance in design (m = 59.1, SE = 4.3). The Welch two sample single tail t-test indicates that the difference in the means of the two samples is significant at 5 % (t = − 3.3, df = 16, p < 0.05) and the Pearson's correlation coefficient shows the effect size is large.
- Scenario 2 (Table 10 and Fig. 2) shows that the participants who scored high in the imagination personality factor performed significantly better in design (m = 76.5, SE = 5.8) compared with the other participants' performance (m = 58.1, SE = 4.9), (t = − 2.4, df = 28, p < 0.05) and the Pearson's correlation coefficient shows the effect size is medium.
- Scenario 3 (Table 10) shows that the participants who scored high in both imagination personality factor and spatial ability (m = 84.1, SE = 6.3) did not perform significantly better than the participants who only scored high in imagination personality factor (m = 62.8, SE = 9.7). The Welch two sample single tail t-test indicates that the difference in the means of the two samples is not significant (t = 1.84, df = 7, p > 0.05). However the Pearson's correlation coefficient shows the effect size is large.

- Scenario 4 (Table 10) shows that participants who scored high in the spatial ability test performed significantly better than those whose spatial ability score was not high (t = − 2.61, df = 28, p < 0.05). The Pearson's correlation coefficient shows the effect size is medium.
- Scenario 5 (Table 10), shows that the participants who scored high in imagination personality factor and spatial ability performed significantly better in design (m = 84.1, SE = 6.3) compared with the participants who scored high in spatial ability but scored low in imagination personality factor (m = 65.3, SE = 6.2) (t = 2.13, df = 17, p < 0.05). The Pearson's correlation coefficient shows the effect size is large.

From Table 8, imagination personality factor is related to performance in design (r = 0.37, p = 0.049) and, Table 10 shows the combined effect of imagination personality factor and spatial ability significantly influence performance in design (t = − 2.4, df = 28, p < 0.05). In the sample population, the correlation between performance in design and other personality factors such as agreeableness, extraversion and emotional stability is inconclusive.

Hence the results indicate that participants whose score of imagination personality factor and spatial ability test places them in first quadrant (Q1) have better chance of performing well in design.

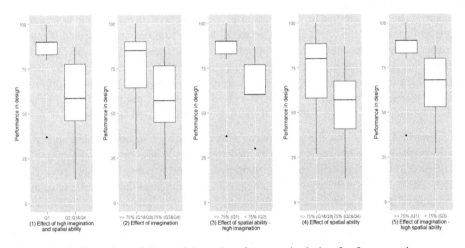

Fig. 2. Box plots of the participants' performance in design for five scenarios.

6 Discussion

For the design activity, the participants were required to read the description of the Holistic Persona (Appendix I), understand her requirements and prepare a design work within fifteen minutes. The range of designs including the level of detail and quality was varied. A quantitative analysis of results was considered for final assessment, as it would not be prone to subjectivity and variability.

6.1 Variability in Study Parameters

There are a number of variables: four Holistic Personas that represent real people but have different personalities - participants verified that they representing real people with differences in personalities (Table 3 and [33]); participants with different backgrounds – undergraduate students, postgraduate students, professionals with non-design background (Sect. 4.1); known individual preferences for the Holistic Personas - participants have shown their liking for a Holistic Persona (Table 5); undefined problem setting – participants were asked to provide a conceptual design to assist the Holistic Persona who had in addition to weight and memory problem, represented a human (Table 3) with other personality issues. The results (Table 7) indicate that a number of participants have overcome all these variabilities and produced designs of high quality.

6.2 Categorization of Participants

The participants are categorised into quadrants depending on their score in imagination personality factor and spatial ability. The categorisation allows statistical comparison of performance of participants in different categories. The participants who are close to the boundary line could belong to either of the categories. Hence their performance has to be examined closely and adjusted if needed. In this study to maintain integrity of the results no adjustment to the results were made. Our results indicate that there is a positive relationship between spatial ability, imagination and performance in UCD design.

6.3 Literature Support for Design Suitability of the Holistic Persona

Evaluation of the design artefacts for their suitability to the Holistic Persona was based on the literature support for the influence of personality traits on human uses of software applications or products.

Some of the features that some participants used in their design are similar to the following (Table 6): Oliveira et al. [18] finding that extraverts used their mobile phone more often (e.g. participant Id 1029 remark about extraversion personality trait and mobile phone usage) and extraverts and conscientious people were more satisfied with the level of service they received from their mobile phone service provider; Butt and Phillips [19] finding that extraverts not only receive more calls but spend more time changing the ring tone and wall paper on their mobile phones however the unconscientious, disagreeable and neurotic used SMS in preference to calling; Nov et al. [17] finding that the extraverts tend to be more responsive in a more popular website and emotionally stable people tend to be less influenced by a website's social anchoring; Participant Id 1023's comments are in line with Hamburger and Ben-Artzi [39] and Landers and Lounsbury [40]'s findings that emotionally unstable women seek information online anonymously.

6.4   General Discussion

To score high in the design, the designer had to concentrate on the Holistic Persona, issues she had, overcome their own liking or disliking of the Holistic Persona's personality and provide a solution that is suitable to the Holistic Persona. The rubric for marking is designed to distinguish the designers who would not be distracted by other problems and can provide solution targeted at the Holistic Persona's individual needs. The results indicate that participants, who score above 75 % in the imagination personality factor and spatial ability test, have applied the techniques of UCD in their design work. They can think of design features that suit the Holistic Persona within a short period of time; they are identified as talented aspiring UCD designers. They can 'think on their feet' [41].

This study highlights the importance of the imagination personality trait and spatial ability in performing well in UCD design. Professional software engineers may also have this personality trait and hence our results may be extendable to professionals; which we wish to investigate in future studies. Our study confirms previous research that imagination is important for design work [8, 9, 16, 21, 22] and findings of Ault and John [27] that students with higher spatial ability, perform better in other fields.

The novel techniques presented in this paper facilitates identification of talented aspiring designers early in their studies; they can benefit by receiving advanced training. Likewise the less talented students can be given extra tutoring. For professional establishment, the novel techniques presented in this paper facilitates identification of the personnel talented in design and hence they can be utilised more productively. This study contributes to the understanding of personality traits and abilities required in being a talented designer. Identification of these traits has potential impact on team composition and designer selection.

To the best of our knowledge, this is the first empirical study that reports on a specific link between the performance of conceptual design, spatial ability and the imagination personality of the designers within software engineering and UCD methodologies.

6.5   Threats to Validity of the Study and Measures to Overcome These

Threats to the validity of construct, conclusion, internal and external of the study were identified and measures taken to minimise their effects [42] as described below.

Construct Validity Threats. Construct validity governs generalising the concepts behind the experiment. Since the interaction between personality traits, spatial and design abilities are complex, the research question is exploratory. Anvari and Richards [43] presented results drawn from 23 participants who were undergraduate students (sub-sample of the population presented in this paper) obtained similar results. Anvari and Richards [43] also reported that a small portion of the sample population had pervious training in spatial ability or produced a design that they were familiar with. To mitigate construct validity threats the experiment has to be repeated with samples drawn from a number of different populations.

Conclusion Validity Threats. One of the treats to conclusion validity is low number of participants which affects the statistics used to evaluate the results. There are 33 participants (Table 2) in this study who have completed the design activity, hence the conclusions are indicative only. In order to mitigate 'fishing for the results' threat [42, p. 104], the influence of participant's scores in spatial ability and personality factors on the results were removed by marking the design activity separately and without reference to other results from the study. The design artefacts were remarked again later without reference to original markings using the rubric. The subsequent assessments were in most cases identical with the original ones. Further, the marks for design activity were checked independently by Hien Minh Thi Tran, without knowledge of the participants' performances in spatial ability or their score in personality factors. The independent marking of design artefacts proved the validity of the rubric for inter-assessment. Due to tightness of the rubric, the threat of 'fishing for result' was almost eliminated.

Internal Threats. The internal threats included partial completion of the study, maturation effect, boredom, fatigue, interruption and learning effect. The participants' answers were checked for soundness for each section of the study. Below is an outline of methodologies used to detect data that were not sound.

- Learning effect: to mitigate the learning effect where students learn from the examples given during introduction to UCD, no mention of personalities of personas or users were made. The learning effect from one another is very low as all participants finished this study in one session.
- Boredom or fatigue: the time to answer the personality rating questions was measured but not displayed. A short answer time compared to average answer time would indicate either boredom or fatigue. It was found that one participant's answer time was shorter than expected. His data was excluded as he did not present his design.
- Distraction during the spatial ability test: As the performance in spatial ability test is based on the first ten minutes of the test, any disruption such as slow system response can affect their result. The data for participants who performed well in the test but their performance in the first ten minutes were low were investigated. If the time taken to answer one question is larger than the rest, then the question is ignored. Only one participant was in this situation.
- Lack of incentive to design well: As no rewards were offered for the design work, some participants might not have incentive to perform as well as they could in the design. As the participants who completed the study were motivated to take part hence this was not considered to be a threat.
- Dislike of Holistic Persona: During analysis it was found some participants did not perform well due to the Holistic Persona's personality (e.g. Table 6 participant ID 1031). This threat can affect the results. In this paper no adjustment has been made for such cases.

External Threats. External threats which relate to generalisation of the study are: (1) the results cannot be generalised due to limited sample size; (2) the majority of the sample population in this study are undergraduate students (Sect. 4.1) hence the results would not readily extend to professionals.

We plan to mitigate external threats to generalise the results of this study by conducting horizontal and longitudinal studies. For horizontal studies we plan to repeat the study a number of times using participants from different population pools and include more professionals from various industries. These measures will increase the sample size and provide for mix of population. For vertical studies we plan to observe the students score in their design subjects and their career choices and assess if there is a correlation between their performance in this study and their choices. However, we believe that personality traits are not easily changed and hence our results which rely on personality traits can be extended to professionals.

7   Conclusion and Future Research

In this paper we have presented empirical research in which we investigated four separate research questions and found that: (1) participants think the Holistic Persona resembles a real person and are able to identify the intended personality trait in her; (2) participants indicated that the personality of the Holistic Persona has influenced their conceptual design; (3) participants indicated that they have a preference for a Holistic Persona based on her personality trait (most participants prefer a Holistic Persona who is emotionally stable); (4) participants who are imaginative and have good spatial ability can be seen as talented aspiring designers in use of persona with personality within UCD methodologies, as they were able to think of design features that suit the Holistic Persona within a short period of time. From a practical perspective, we propose that the techniques described for eliciting designs and the use of similar rubrics could be used for the purpose of recruitment of new staff or allocation of staff to software teams. Those identified as lacking in the necessary skills could receive appropriate training or reallocation to more suitable tasks.

This study contributes to the understanding of personality traits and abilities required in being a talented designer. Identification of these traits has potential impact on team composition and designer selection.

In this paper we also presented details of an extensive rubric that we developed to assess the design artefacts. Our rubric provided consistent results for both cases of inter-assessors and intra-assessor.

We plan to investigate other important characteristics for a UCD designer such as interpersonal intelligence, employ sophisticated tools to more accurately measure participants' abstract thinking capabilities and performance.

Acknowledgements. We acknowledge the assistance Hien Minh Thi Tran provided and thank COMP255 Software Engineering Semester 2 2013 students and tutors at Macquarie University.

Appendix I

The following Holistic Persona, Doris, represents an archetypical user of the product or software application which you are designing or recommending to her.

Doris' grand-parents migrated to Tasmania during the early 1940's. Her parents are busy in their professional careers. Doris is studying at the University of Tasmania and is midway through her Bachelor of Arts. Since childhood, she has had interest in music and recently learnt to play guitar.

Doris is an outgoing person and likes to meets people. She likes musical concert and attends all musical events in Hobart. After the concerts, she goes out with her friends to local restaurants. She has a large collection of records and enjoys sharing albums with her friends. Doris is an active member of university clubs. Doris has many friends and enjoys their company. She has been a long member of the 'Assisting Socially Disadvantaged Group', a volunteer group that help refuges and socially disadvantaged people in Tasmania.

Doris is short sighted and has sensitive skin but she often forgets to take her glasses with her or apply sun-screen lotion when she goes out.

Doris is vocal and enjoys debates. She listens to other people's point of view and learns from the experience. Doris' friends feel that Doris is calm, independent and confident. She makes plans for her future and is full of hope. She does not worry if she has to reject requests for help from her friends when she is already committed. She knows her limits. She always meets her commitments with high spirits.

Doris is allergic to peanut but she often forgets to mention this fact while ordering her meals. Doris has read about relationships between height, weight and energy content of various foods.

Doris has realised that she is overweight and wishes to reduce her weight.

References

1. Norman, D.A.: Cognitive engineering. User centered system design, pp. 31–61 (1986)
2. Aoyama, M.: Persona-scenario-goal methodology for user-centered requirements engineering. In: 15th IEEE International Requirements Engineering Conference, RE 2007. IEEE (2007)
3. Goodwin, K.: Designing for the Digital Age. Wiley, Indiana (2009)
4. Anvari, F., Tran, H.M.T.: Persona ontology for user centred design professionals. In: Proceedings of the ICIME 4th International Conference on Information Management and Evaluation. Ho Chi Minh City, Vietnam (2013)
5. Goldberg, L.R.: The structure of phenotypic personality traits. Am. Psychol. **48**(1), 26–34 (1993)
6. Gosling, S.D., Rentfrow, P.J., Swann Jr, W.B.: A very brief measure of the Big-Five personality domains. J. Res. Pers. **37**(6), 504–528 (2003)

7. Svendsen, G.B., Johnsen, J.-A.K., Almås-Sørensen, L., Vitterrø, J.: Personality and technology acceptance: the influence of personality factors on the core constructs of the Technology Acceptance Model. Behav. Inf. Technol. **32**(4), 323–334 (2013)

8. Furnham, A., Bachtiar, V.: Personality and intelligence as predictors of creativity. Pers. Individ. Differ. **45**(7), 613–617 (2008)

9. Poropat, A.E.: A meta-analysis of the five-factor model of personality and academic performance. Psychol. Bull. **135**(2), 322–338 (2009)

10. Mohler, J.L.: Computer Graphics Education: Where and How Do We Develop Spatial Ability? In: Proceedings of Eurographics, Education Papers, pp. 79–86 (2006)

11. Long, F.: Real or imaginary: the effectiveness of using personas in product design. In: Proceedings of the Irish Ergonomics Society Annual Conference (2009)

12. Gardner, H.: Multiple intelligences: the theory in practice. Basic books (1993)

13. Winner, E.: The origins and ends of giftedness. Am. Psychol. **55**(1), 159 (2000)

14. Anvari, F., Tran, H.M.T., Kavakli, M.: Using cognitive load measurement and spatial ability test to identify talented students in three-dimensional computer graphics programming. Int. J. Inf. Educ. Technol. **3**(1), 94–99 (2013)

15. Plucker, J.A., Beghetto, R.A., Dow, G.T.: Why isn't creativity more important to educational psychologists? Potentials, pitfalls, and future directions in creativity research. Educ. Psychol. **39**(2), 83–96 (2004)

16. Field, B.W.: Visualization, intuition, and mathematics metrics as predictors of undergraduate engineering design performance. J. Mech. Des. **129**(7), 735–743 (2007)

17. Nov, O., Arazy, O., Lotts, K., Naberhaus, T.: Motivation-Targeted Personalized UI Design: A Novel Approach to Enhancing Citizen Science Participation, pp. 287–297 (2013)

18. Oliveira, R.D., Cherubini, M., Oliver, N.: Influence of personality on satisfaction with mobile phone services. ACM Trans. Comput.-Hum. Interact. **20**(2), 1–23 (2013)

19. Butt, S., Phillips, J.G.: Personality and self reported mobile phone use. Comput. Hum. Behav. **24**(2), 346–360 (2008)

20. Costa, P., McCrae, R.: Personality Inventory (NEO-PI-R) and NEO Five-Factor Inventory (NEO-FFI) Professional Manual. Psychological Assessment Resources, Odessa (1992)

21. Read, S.J., et al.: The personality-enabled architecture for cognition (PAC). In: Paiva, A.C., Prada, R., Picard, R.W. (eds.) ACII 2007. LNCS, vol. 4738, pp. 735–736. Springer, Heidelberg (2007)

22. Silvia, P.J.: Discernment and creativity: How well can people identify their most creative ideas? Psychology of Aesthetics. Creativity, and the Arts **2**(3), 139 (2008)

23. McCrae, R.R.: Creativity, divergent thinking, and openness to experience. J. Pers. Soc. Psychol. **52**(6), 1258 (1987)

24. Shea, D.L., Lubinski, D., Benbow, C.P.: Importance of assessing spatial ability in intellectually talented young adolescents: a 20-year longitudinal study. J. Educ. Psychol. **93**(3), 604 (2001)

25. Wai, J., Lubinski, D., Benbow, C.P.: Spatial ability for STEM domains: aligning over 50 years of cumulative psychological knowledge solidifies its importance. J. Educ. Psychol. **101**(4), 817–835 (2009)

26. Charyton, C., Jagacinski, R.J., Merrill, J.A., Clifton, W., DeDios, S.: Assessing creativity specific to engineering with the revised creative engineering design assessment. J. Eng. Educ. **100**(4), 778–799 (2011)

27. Ault, H.K., John, S.: Assessing and enhancing visualization skills of engineering students in africa: a comprehensive study. Eng. Des. Graphics J. **74**(2), 12–20 (2010)

28. McMartin, F., McKenna, A., Youssefi, K.: Scenario assignments as assessment tools for undergraduate engineering education. IEEE Trans. Educ. **43**(2), 111–119 (2000)

29. Anderson, L.W., Krathwohl, D.R.: A Taxonomy for Learning, Teaching, and Assessing: A Revision of Bloom's Taxonomy of Educational Objectives, Abridged Edition. Longman, New York (2001)
30. Bailey, R., Szabo, Z.: Assessing engineering design process knowledge. Int. J. Eng. Educ. **22**(3), 508 (2007)
31. Zowghi, D.: Teaching requirements engineering to the Baháí students in Iran who are denied of higher education. In: 2009 Fourth International Workshop on Requirements Engineering Education and Training (REET). IEEE (2009)
32. Brookhart, S.M.: Assessment theory for college classrooms. New Dir. Teach. Learn. **2004** (100), 5–14 (2004)
33. Anvari, F., Richards, D., Hitchens, M., Babar, M.A.: Effectiveness of persona with personality traits on conceptual design. In: 2015 IEEE/ACM 37th IEEE International Conference on Software Engineering (ICSE) (2015)
34. IPIP. International Personality Item Pool. 2013 [cited 2013 2 July]; Available from: http://ipip.ori.org/
35. Field, A., Miles, J., Field, Z.: Discovering Statistics Using R. SAGE Publications Ltd., London (2012)
36. Bodner, G.M., Guay, R.B.: The Purdue visualization of rotations test. Chem. Educ. **2**(4), 1–17 (1997)
37. Brookhart, S.M.: The Art and Science of Classroom Assessment. The Missing Part of Pedagogy. ASHE-ERIC Higher Education Report, vol. 27, Number 1. ERIC (1999)
38. Ehrhart, M.G., Ehrhart, K.H., Roesch, S.C., Chung-Herrera, B.G., Nadler, K., Bradshaw, K.: Testing the latent factor structure and construct validity of the Ten-Item Personality Inventory. Pers. Individ. Differ. **47**(8), 900–905 (2009)
39. Hamburger, Y.A., Ben-Artzi, E.: The relationship between extraversion and neuroticism and the different uses of the Internet. Comput. Hum. Behav. **16**(4), 441–449 (2000)
40. Landers, R.N., Lounsbury, J.W.: An investigation of Big Five and narrow personality traits in relation to Internet usage. Comput. Hum. Behav. **22**(2), 283–293 (2006)
41. Schön, D.A.: The reflective practitioner: how professionals think in action. vol. 5126, Basic books (1983)
42. Wohlin, C., Runeson, P., Höst, M., Ohlsson, M.C., Regnell, B., Wesslén, A.: Experimentation in Software Engineering. Springer, Heidelberg (2012)
43. Anvari, F., Richards, D.: Using Personality Traits and a Spatial Ability Test to Identify alented Aspiring Designers in User-Centred Design Methodologies. In: Proceedings of the ENASE 10th International Conference on Evaluation of Novel Approaches to Software Engineering (2015)

Lorq: A System for Replicated NoSQL Data Based on Consensus Quorum

Tadeusz Pankowski[1]([⊠])

Institute of Control and Information Engineering,
Poznań University of Technology, Poznań, Poland
tadeusz.pankowski@put.poznan.pl

Abstract. In this paper, we discuss a system, called Lorq, for NoSQL data replication. Data replication in the system is based on replication of logs storing update and some control operations. It is guarantied that operations in all logs are eventually applied to their databases in the same order. However, due to possible latency and failures, the time of the application can be different, leading to different levels of consistencies. Applications have possibilities to declare their consistency and latency priorities, from strong consistency to a kind of weak consistencies. In this way, the server level agreement (SLA) is provided. To guarantee strong consistency, a consensus quorum algorithm is used meaning that an update (read) operation is treated successful if a write (read) consensus quorum is reached. Strong consistency ensures that the most up-to-date data is read. To guarantee a weaker consistency, Lorq algorithm utilizes timestamps, which are assigned to both data objects and databases. These timestamps are updated along with update and control operations performed over databases. The algorithm enforce dynamic selection of servers accessed by read operations to ensure required level of consistency and payment depending on consistency level.

1 Introduction

Recently, we observe a rapid development of modern storage systems based on Internet services and cloud computing technologies [24]. Examples of this kind of applications range from social networks [16], Web search [9,10] to e-commerce systems [11]. Data management in such systems is expected to support needs of a broad class of applications concerning different performance, consistency, fault tolerance, and scalability [1]. Development of this new class of systems, referred to as NoSQL systems, differs from conventional relational SQL systems in the following aspects: (a) the data model is usually based on a NoSQL key-value model; (b) data management is focus on intensive simple write/read operations instead of ACID transactions processing; (c) NoSQL system architecture is a multi-server data replication architecture, which is necessary to meet needs concerning the performance, scalability and partition tolerance; (d) a various kinds of consistencies are offered, from the strong consistency to weak consistencies.

© Springer International Publishing Switzerland 2016
L.A. Maciaszek and J. Filipe (Eds.): ENASE 2015, CCIS 599, pp. 62–79, 2016.
DOI: 10.1007/978-3-319-30243-0_4

In replicated systems, the following three features influence the design, deployment and usage of the system: consistency (C), availability (A), and partition tolerance (P). Partition happens when in result of a crash, a part of the network is separated from the rest. According to the CAP theorem [14], all these three features cannot be achieved. Because the partition tolerance is the necessary condition expected by the users, the crucial issue is then the trade-off between consistency and availability/latency.

Applications in such systems are often interested in possibility to declare their consistency and latency priorities [24]. In general, except from strong consistency, a user may expect a weaker kind of consistencies such as: eventual consistency, bounded staleness, read-my-writes, monotonic read, or monotonic read-my-writes. This is similar to declaring isolation levels in conventional SQL databases. In some companies, the price that clients pay for accessing data repositories depends both on the amount of data and on its freshness (consistency). For example, Amazon charges twice as much for strongly consistent reads as for eventually consistent reads in DynamoDB [2]. According to [24], applications *"should request consistency and latency that provides suitable service to their customers and for which they will pay"*. For example, Pileus system [24] allows applications to declare their consistency and latency priorities.

Novelties of this paper are as follows.

1. We propose and discuss a method for replicating NoSQL data. The algorithm is called Lorq (*LOg Replication based on consensus Quorum*). The main features of Lorq are the following: (a) data replication is realized by means of replicating logs storing update operations (treated as a single-operation transactions), and so-called *heartbeat* operation sent by the leader; (b) the processing and replication strategies guarantee that eventually all operations in each replica are executed in the same order and no operation is lost.
2. A special attention is paid to different kinds of consistency, which can be guaranteed by the system. We propose a method based on information stored by client services to guarantee different consistency levels, thereby implementing SLA functionality.

In comparison to Raft [19], we propose a different way for choosing a leader in Lorq. In particular, the procedure is based on timestamps and servers priorities. It simplifies the election procedure significantly. Compared to Pileus [24], that is based on state replication, the replication in Lorq is based on replication of operations. Consequently, the ways to guarantee consistency levels differs significantly from those proposed in Pileus.

The outline of this paper is as follows. The next section reviews problems of NoSQL data replication. In particular, we discuss a key-value model, where timestamps are associated with each data object and with the whole database. The current database timestamp says how up-to-date is the database under consideration. The system architecture and the Lorq algorithm are presented in Sect. 3. We discuss behavior of clients and servers in particular roles. Three roles of servers are: leader, worker and elector. An example illustrates the process of log replication. Some methods for achieving the strong and one of weaker consistencies in Lorq, are discussed in Sect. 4. Finally, Sect. 5 concludes the paper.

2   Replication of NoSQL Data

In modern intensively accessed data stores, a number of goals should be met:

- *Scalability:* The system must be able to take advantage of newly added servers (nodes) for replication and redistribution of data. The aim of adding new hardware is to support large databases with very high request rates and very low latency.
- *Availability:* It is guaranteed that each request eventually receives a response. The case when a response is too late, is often treated as the lack of response at all, and the system can be understood to be unavailable.
- *Partitioning tolerance:* Due to communication failures, the servers in the system can be partitioned into multiple groups that cannot communicate with one another.
- *Consistency:* In conventional databases, a consistent database state is a a a state satisfying all consistency constraints. In replicated databases, consistency means the equality between answers to queries issued against different servers in the system. In the case of *strong consistency* all answers are identical and up-to-date (such as ACID transactions [4]). In the case of a *weak consistency*, some answers can be stale. However, the staleness of answers should be under control, and in the lack of updates, all answers converge to be identical. Then we say about *eventual consistency* [25].

There is a fundamental trade-off between consistency (*Quality of Data*), and latency/ availability and partition tolerance (*Quality of Service*).

To meet the aforementioned needs of practical data-centered and intensively accessed systems, new classes of data repositories are based on NoSQL data models, and database management systems utilizes replication based on quorum consensus algorithms [4,17,19,24].

2.1   NoSQL Data Model

NoSQL data stores were developed as an alternative to well structured relational data models mainly for efficiency reasons. NoSQL data are treated as uniquely identified "containers" of data values. Unique identifiers and indexing on them allow for very fast data access. Additionally, NoSQL data is provided with an automatically updated timestamp, which is used to control the freshness of data. Any modification of data value implies update of the timestamp. However, no complex queries, such as join or secondary key selection, are possible on NoSQL repositories.

NoSQL data stores manage various variants of key-value data models [6] (e.g., PNUTS [9], Dynamo [11], Cassandra [16], BigTable [7], Spanner [10]), Azure Tables [26]).

A NoSQL data object is a key-value pair extended with a timestamp, i.e.,

$$d :: = (x, val, t),$$

where x is a unique identifier, val is a data value, and t is a timestamp. The unique identifier is usually a pair $(PartitionKey, RowKey)$, where $PartitionKey$ identifies the partition data is stored in, and $RowKey$ identifies data in the partition [8]. The value component could be:

- *structureless* – then a data value is a sequence of bytes and an application is responsible for its interpretation, or
- *structured* – data value is a set of pairs of the form $A : v$, where A is an attribute name, and v is a value, possibly nested, i.e.,

$$val :: = \{A_1 : v_1, \ldots, A_n : v_n\}, \ n \geq 0,$$
$$v :: = c \mid val.$$

Further on in this paper, we will assume that values of data objects are structured, and a (NoSQL) database is a pair $DB = (\{\text{set of data objects}\}, t)$, where t is the timestamp of the most recently performed update operation on the database (the most current timestamp of all data in the database). The database timestamp we denote by

$$ts(DB) = t.$$

We distinguish the following operations on NoSQL databases

- update operations: *set, insert, delete, heartbeat,*
- read operation: *read.*

In order to informally define syntax and semantics of operations, we assume that there is a NoSQL database

$$DB = (\{(x, \{A : a\}, t)\}, t_{db}).$$

Operations are specified as follows:

- $DB.set(x', val', t')$ replaces in DB the value and the timestamp of data identified by x'; or nothing changes and an *error* an exception is raised, i.e.,

$$DB.set(x', \{B : b\}, t') = \begin{cases} (\{(x, \{B : b\}, t')\}, t'), & \text{if } x = x', \\ DB, & \text{if } x \neq x'. \end{cases}$$

- $DB.ins(x', val', t')$ either the value of existing data object is changed or the new data object is inserted, i.e.,

$$DB.ins(x', \{B : b\}, t') = \begin{cases} DB_1 = (\{(x, \{A : a, B : b\}, t')\}, t'), \\ \quad \text{if } x = x', \\ DB_2 = (\{(x, \{A : a\}, t), (x', \{B : b\}, t')\}, t'), \\ \quad \text{if } x \neq x'. \end{cases}$$

- $DB.del(x, att, t)$ removes fields with the attribute name att, and $DB.del(x, t)$ removes data object x, i.e., let DB_1 and DB_2 be as above, then

$$DB.del(x, A, t_1) = \begin{cases} (\{(x, \{B : b\}, t_1)\}, t_1), & \text{if } DB = DB_1, \\ (\{(x, \{\}, t_1), (x', \{B : b\}, t')\}, t_1), & \text{if } DB = DB_2. \end{cases}$$

$$DB.del(x, t_1) = \begin{cases} (\{\}, t_1), & \text{if } DB = DB_1, \\ (\{(x', \{B : b\}, t')\}, t_1), & \text{if } DB = DB_2. \end{cases}$$

- $hb(t)$ – *heartbeat* is the operation sent periodically by the leader to prove its activity; updates the database's timestamp, i.e.,

$$DB.hb(t_1) = (\{(x, \{A : a\}, t)\}, t_1).$$

- $read(x)$ – reads the data with identifier x, i.e.

$$DB.read(x) = (x, \{A : a\}, t).$$

2.2   Strategies of Data Replication

Data replication can be realized using:

1. *State propagation:* The leader (a master server) propagates its latest state to workers (slaves, followers), which replace their current states with the propagated data.
2. *Operation propagation:* The leader propagates sequences of operations. It must be guaranteed that these operations will be applied by all workers to their states in the same order.

In both strategies, states of all database replicas will be eventually consistent. However, the freshness of these states is different and depends on the time needed for the propagation. Some serious problems follow from possible crashes of servers or communications between the servers. For instance, it may happen that the leader crashes before propagating the data or operations. In such cases, there must be means to prevent losing this data. From the operational point of view, the replication must take advantages from asynchronous and parallel processing in order to guarantee the required efficiency.

2.3   Consensus Quorum Algorithms

In a quorum-based data replication, it is required that an execution of an operation (i.e., a propagation of an update operation or a read operation) is committed if and only if a sufficiently large number of servers acknowledge a successful termination of this operation [13].

   In a quorum consensus algorithm, it is assumed that: N is a number of servers storing copies of data (replicas), R is an integer called *read quorum*, meaning that at least R copies were successfully read; W is an integer called *write quorum*, meaning that propagations to at least W servers have been successfully terminated. The following relationships hold between N, R and W:

$$W > N/2, \tag{1}$$
$$R + W > N. \tag{2}$$

To commit a read operation, a server must collect the read quorum, and to commit a write operation must collect the write quorum. Condition (1) guarantees that the majority of copies is updated, and (2) that among read copies at least one is up-to-data.

The aim of consensus algorithms is to allow a collection of servers to process users' commands (updates and reads) as long as the number of active servers is not less than $max\{W, R\}$. It means that the system is able to survive failures of some of its servers.

An algorithm based on quorum consensus works properly if a majority of servers is accessible and the most current version of data can be always provided to a client (i.e., it guarantees the strong consistency). Note that for $N = 3, R = 2$, $W = 2$ the system tolerates only one failure, and to tolerate at most two failures, we can assume $N = 5, R = 3, W = 3$. Let p be the probability of a server failure, then the probability that at least n servers will be available is equal to

$$P(N, p, n) = \sum_{k=0}^{n} p^k (1 - p)^{N-k},$$

in particular, $P(5, 0.02, 3) = 0.99992$.

3   Log Replication Based on Consensus Quorum

During last decade, the research on consensus algorithms is dominated by Paxos algorithms [12,18]. Lately, a variant of Paxos, named Raft [19], was presented as a consensus algorithm for managing a replicated log. Lorq is based on ideas underlying Paxos and Raft, and includes such steps as: (1) leader election; (2) log replication, execution and commitment of update operations; (3) realization of read operations on different consistency levels [20,21].

3.1   Architecture

The architecture of Lorq (Fig. 1), like in Raft [19], is organized having in mind: operations, clients, and servers occurring in the system managing data replication.

Operations. We distinguish three *update* operations: *set, insert, delete*, one special control operation *heartbeat* (generated by the leader), and one *read* operation. These operations were discussed in Subsect. 2.1.

Queues. Operations from clients are serialized and put in queues. An operation is represented as an entry of the form:

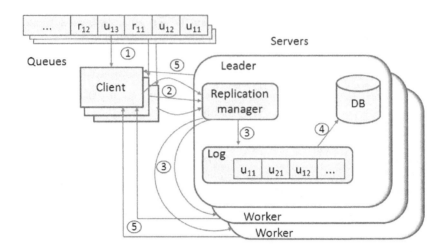

Fig. 1. Architecture of Lorq system. There are update and read operations in queues. Update operations are delivered (1) by clients from queues to one leader (2). A replication module delivers them to leader's log and to logs at all workers (3). Sequences of operations in all logs tend to be identical and are applied in the same order to databases (4). States of all databases also tend to be identical (eventually consistent). A client may read (5) data from any server.

$$entry = (op, arg_1, arg_2),$$

where op is type of the operation, $op \in \{set, ins, del, read\}$; arg_1 and arg_2 are arguments (possibly nulls) of the operation op. Note, that a timestamp will be added later on.

Clients. Each queue is served by one *client*. When client starts, a new session is opened. A client maintains information about timestamps of all committed update and all performed read operations in a session, in tables:

$$c.LastUpdateTimestamo(Key, Timestamp),$$
$$c.LastReadTimestamo(Key, Timestamp),$$

where: c is the client identifier, and the timestamp of data object with key x is returned by COMMITTED(x, t) message (see Figs. 3 and 4), and as result (x, val, t) in response to $read(x)$ operation.

Servers. A server maintains one replica of a database along with the log related to this replica, and runs the software implementing Lorq protocols. One server plays the role of the *leader* and the rest – roles of *workers*. The state of each server is characterized by the server's log and database. The following variables describe the state of a server:

- $lastIdx$ – last log index (the highest position on the log storing an operation),
- $lastCommit$ – the highest log index storing a committed update operation,
- $currentLeader$ – identifier of the current leader, 0 – the leader is not elected,
- $lastActivity$ – the observed latest activity time of the leader.

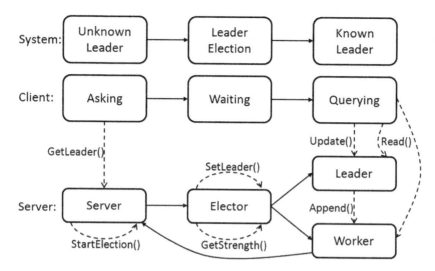

Fig. 2. System states, client and server roles in Lorq. A client can ask about leader, wait for result of election or send queries (update or read). A server can play undefined role (unqualified server), take part in leader election (as elector), or act as leader or worker.

3.2   States and Roles

Lorq system can be in one of the following three states (Fig. 2):

1. UnknownLeader – no leader is established in the system (when the system starts and a short time after a leader failure).
2. LeaderElection – election of a leader is in progress.
3. KnownLeader – a leader is known in the system.

Actors of the system, i.e., clients and servers, can play in those states specific roles.

Client in Asking Role. Initially, and when the system is in UnknownLeader state, a client asynchronously sends the request *GetLeader* to all servers. In response, each available server can return:

- 0 – if a leader can not be elected because the required quorum cannot be achieved (the system is unavailable);
- *currentLeader* – identifier of the leader that is either actually known to the server or has been chosen in reaction to the *GetLeader* request.

Client in Waiting Role. After issuing *GetLeader* request, the client plays the Waiting role. Next, depending on the reply, changes its role to Asking or Querying.

Client in Querying Role. A client reads from a queue the next *entry* (describing an operation), or reads again a waiting one if necessary, and proceeds as follows:

- determines values for c – client identifier, and t – timestamp;
- the *leader.LorqSendEntry*$(c, t, entry)$ operation is sent to the leader and the operation is treated as a *"waiting"* one;
- the *Read*$(c, t, entry)$ operation is handled according to the required consistency type (see Sect. 4).

If the *Update* command replays committed, the corresponding operation is removed out from the queue. If the timeout for responding elapses, the client changes its role to Asking (perhaps the leader failed and the operation will be next reissued to a new leader).

Server in Server Role. A server plays the Server role when the system starts, and when a worker detects that election timeout elapses without receiving any message from the leader (that means the leader failure). A server in Server role starts an election issuing the command *StartElection* to all servers. Next, the systems goes to the LeaderElection state, and all servers change their roles to Elector.

Server in Elector Role. The community of servers attempt to chose a leader among them. The leader should be this server that has the highest value of *lastCommit*, and by equal *lastCommit*, the one with the highest identifier (or satisfying another priority criterion). The election proceeds as follows:

1. A server collects *lastCommit* values from all servers (including itself), and creates a decreasingly ordered list of pairs $(lastCommit, srvId)$.
2. If the list contains answers from majority of servers, then the *srvId* from the first pair is chosen as the leader and its value is substituted to *currentLeader*.
3. The *currentLeader* is announced as the leader. The procedure guarantees that all servers will choose the same leader.

Next, the system goes to the KnownLeader state, the server chosen as the leader changes its role to Leader, and the remainder servers to Worker.

Server in Leader Role. The leader acts as follows (Fig. 3):

1. After receiving an operation $(c, t, entry)$, a leader reads *lastIdx* position from its log. The client identifier (c) and the timestamp (t) from this position are set to variables cL and tL, respectively, denoting *last client (last timestamp) on the leader*. The operation $(c, t, entry)$ is appended to the log by means of the command:

$$myDB.AppendToLeaderLog(cL, tL, c, t, entry).$$

The pair (cL, tL) is used to control the correctness of the append operation. The append (on the leader and any worker) is correct if the previous position on the log contains a client identifier $c = cL$, and a timestamp $t = tL$.

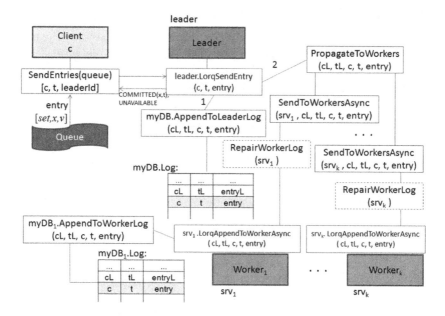

Fig. 3. Sending and propagating of data operations in Lorq system.

2. The operation is propagated asynchronously to all available workers, srv_i:

$$PropagateToWorkers(cL, tL, c, t, entry),$$
$$SendToWorkersAsync(srv_i, cL, tL, c, t, entry).$$

The operation is either appended by the worker to its log, i.e.,

$$myDB_i.AppendToWorkerLog(cL, tL, c, t, entry),$$

or the repairing of the log is carried out first (managed by the leader)

$$RepairWorkerLog(srv_i).$$

The criterion for repairing is whether the last position in the worker's log satisfies $c = cL$ and $t = tL$.

3. If the propagation has completed successfully for majority of servers, the leader initiated the process of applying and committing the replicated operation $PropagateApplyAndCommit(t)$, t identifies the operation, (Fig. 4):

   – first, any worker, srv_i, tries to apply the operation to its database, $myDB_i.ApplyAndCommit(t)$; after the success, the operation is denoted as committed (Y on the log);
   – next, if majority of workers terminates with success, the leader applies the operation in its database, $myDB.ApplyAndCommit(t)$, and denotes it as committed;

- finally, the client is informed about result of the processing: COMMIT-TED – operation was successfully performed and replicated by the majority (equal to the write quorum), or UNAVAILABLE – otherwise.
4. Periodically, defined by the activity timeout, the leader propagates *heartbeat* operation in the same way as update operations. This operation is necessary to:
   - confirm leader's role and prevent starting a new election;
   - for checking log consistency, especially for restarted workers;
   - update database timestamp, t_{db}, in order to control if the database is up-to-date (this is important in answering with required kind of consistency).

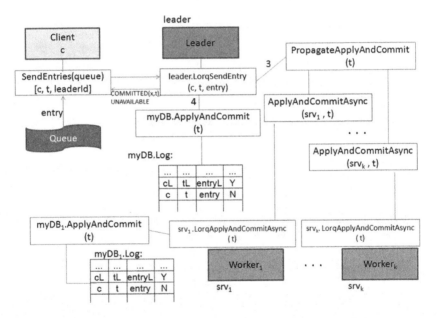

Fig. 4. Applying and committing data operations in Lorq system.

When a new leader starts, then:

- There can be some uncommitted entries in the top of the leader's log, i.e., after the *lastCommit* entry, (*lastCommit* < *lastIdx*). These entries must be propagated to workers in increasing order. If a delivered log entry is already present in worker's log, it is ignored.
- Some *"waiting"* operations in a queue, i.e., denoted as already sent to a leader, could not occur in the leader's log (the reason is that they have been sent to a previous leader and that leader crashed before reaching the write quorum). Then these operations must be again sent by the client from the queue to the newly elected leader.

– After the aforementioned two operations have been done, the client starts delivering the next update operation from the queue.

A server plays the Leader role until it fails. After recovery, it plays a role of a Worker.

Server in Worker Role. Let a worker srv receive a command (see Fig. 3) $SendToWorkersAsync(srv, cL, tL, c, t, entry)$, concerning update or *heartbeat* operation. Then:

1. If log of srv is consistent with the leader's log, i.e., $srv.log[lastIdx]$. $ClientId = cL$ and $srv.log[lastIdx].Timestamp = tL$, the operation is appended to the log, i.e., $myDB_{srv}.AppendToWorkerLog(cL, tL, c, t, entry)$ is performed at position $lastIdx + 1$.
2. If log of srv is inconsistent, i.e., $srv.log[lastIdx].Timestamp < tL$, the worker replays inconsistency and expects that the leader will decide to send all missing items.
3. If log of srv has to more positions, i.e., $srv.log[lastIdx].Timestamp > tL$, all excess positions (with $t > tL$) will be removed and the new operation will be appended at the position as expected (as in the case of consistent log). Note, that excessed positions cannot be committed since the server with the latest committed position is elected to be the leader.

A server plays the Worker role until its failure or failure of the leader – then it returns to the Server role.

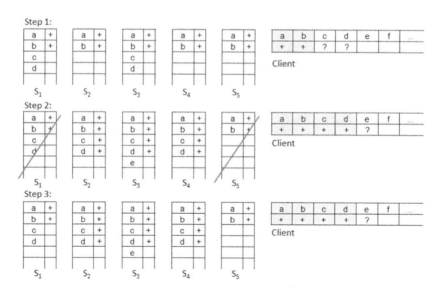

Fig. 5. Illustration to a scenario of managing data replication in Lorq.

3.3   Example

Let us assume that there are five servers in the system ($N = 5$) (Fig. 5), and the write quorum is three ($W = 3$). By "+" we denote committed entries, and by "?" the waiting ones (i.e., a client waits for committing the sent operation). Let us consider three steps in the process of replication presented in Fig. 5.

Step 1. Operations a and b are already committed, bat c and d are waiting, i.e., their execution in the system is not completed. S_1 is the leader that propagated c and d to S_3, and after this failed. We assume that also S_5 failed. There are two uncommitted operations, c and d, in the top of S_3, these operations are also denoted as waiting in the queue.

Step 2. In the next election, S_3 has been elected the leader. The client receives information about the new leader and sends the waiting operations c and d to him. Since c and d are already in the S_3's log, the sending is ignored. S_3 propagates c and d to available workers S_2, and S_4. The write quorum is reached, so they are executed and committed. Next, S_3 receives from a client the operation e, and fails.

Step 3. Now, all servers are active and S_4 is elected the leader. The client receives information about the new leader and sends the waiting operation e to S_4. Next, the leader propagates e as follows:

1. Propagation to S_1: e is appended at fifth position. Since leader's *lastCommit* is 4, thus c and d are executed in the S_1's database and committed.
2. Propagation to S_2: e is successfully appended at fifth position.
3. The leader (S_4) recognizes that the write quorum is already reached. Thus: asynchronously sends to S_1, S_2 and to itself the command to execute and commit e; replies COMMITTED to the client; continue propagations of e to S_3 and S_5.
4. Propagation to S_3: e is already in S_3's log, so the append is ignored. Along with e, the *lastCommit* equal to 5 is sent to S_3. Because of this, e can be executed and committed.
5. Propagation to S_5: there is an inconsistency between logs in S_4 and S_5. We are decreasing *lastIdx* in S_4, $lastIdx := lastIdx - 1$, as long as the coherence between both logs is observed. This happens for $lastIdx = 2$. Now, all entries at positions $3, 4$ and 5 are propagated to S_5. Moreover, operations c, d and e are executed in S_5's database and committed.

In the result, all logs will be eventually identical.

4   Consistency Models for Replicated Data

Some database systems provide strong consistency, while others have chosen a weaker form of consistency in order to obtain better performance and availability. In this section, we discuss how these two paradigms can be achieved in the Lorq data replication system. We will discuss the following consistencies, ordered from weak to strong:

1. Eventual consistency.
2. Bounded staleness.
3. Read-my-writes.
4. Monotonic read.
5. Monotonic read-my-writes.
6. Strong consistency.

1. Eventual Consistency. A reader is guaranteed to see a state of data that existed at some time in the past, but not necessarily the latest state. This is similar to so-called *snapshot isolation* offered by database management systems, or to *consistent prefix* [23]. Eventual consistency is a theoretical guarantee that, *"if no new updates are made to the object, eventually all accesses will return the last updated value"* [25]. In this kind of consistency, reads return the values of data objects that were previously written, though not necessarily latest values.

In Lorq, eventual consistency is realized by reading from any server. It is guaranteed that databases in all servers store past or current states, and that these states were up-to-date sometime in the past. In general, the level of staleness is not known, since the read may be done from a server which is separated from others by communication failure (in a separated partition).

2. Bounded Staleness. A reader is guaranteed that read results are not too out-of-data. We distinguish *version-based staleness* and *time-based staleness* [15]. In time-based staleness, a time bound Δ is specified, and $read(x)$ can be sent to any server whose database has the time-stamp not less than the current time, t_{now}, minus Δ, i.e., to those, where

$$ts(DB) >= t_{now} - \Delta.$$

3. Read-My-Writes. It is guaranteed that effects of all updates performed by the client, are visible to the client's subsequent reads. If a client updates data and then reads this data, then the read will return the result of this update or an update that was done later [23].

In Lorq, the *read-my-writes* consistency is guaranteed by utilizing client's session state recording information about timestamps of updated data. Let

$$lastUpd(x, c) = (\textbf{SELECT } Timestamp \textbf{ FROM } c.LastUpdateTimestamp$$
$$\textbf{WHERE } Key = x).$$

Then operation $read(x)$ can be sent to any server whose database has the time-stamp not less than $lastUpd(x, c)$, i.e., to those, where

$$ts(DB) >= lastUpd(x, c).$$

Note, however, that this consistency does not guarantee monotonicity. It might happen, that two consecutive readings, say in times t_1 and t_2, $t_1 < t_2$, were sent to, respectively, DB_1 and DB_2, where: $ts(DB_1) >= lastUpd(x,c)$, $ts(DB_2) >= lastUpd(x,c)$, but $ts(DB_1) > ts(DB_2)$. Then the data returned by the second read is elder than this returned by the first read. This can be the case when DB_1 and DB_2 are updated by different clients. To avoid such inconsistency, we can require *monotonic read consistency*.

4. Monotonic Read. A reader is guaranteed to see data states that is the same or increasingly up-to-date over time [23]. Assume that a client reads a data object x, $read(x) = (x,v,t)$. Then a client (the same or different) updates x with (x,v',t'), where $t' > t$. If next the user issues another read to this data object, then the result will be: either (x,v,t) or (x,v',t'), but never (x,v'',t''), where $t'' < t$.

In Lorq, the *monotonic read* consistency is guaranteed by utilizing client's session state recording information about timestamps of read data. Let

$$lastRead(x,c) = (\text{SELECT } Timestamp \text{ FROM } c.LastReadTimestamp$$
$$\text{WHERE } Key = x).$$

Then operation $read(x)$ can be sent to any server whose database has the time-stamp not less than $lastRead(x,c)$, i.e., to those, where

$$ts(DB) >= lastRead(x,c).$$

However, monotonic read does not guarantee read-my-writes consistency. It might happen that between two consecutive reads of a data object x, the client updates x. The second read, although it obeys the monotonic read strategy, may not read the new version of x but the old one (the same as by the first read). So, the read-my-write consistency is violated.

5. Monotonic Read-My-Writes. To satisfy both above consistencies, the database, DB, being read should satisfy the condition:

$$ts(DB) >= \max(lastUpd(x,c), lastRead(x,c)).$$

6. Strong Consistency. *Strong consistency* guarantees that a read operation returns the value that was last written for a given data object. In other words, a read observes the effects of all previously completed updates [23,24] performed by any client. The following ways can be taken into account:

1. Some systems, e.g. Pileus [24], recommend sending the *read* operation to the leader. However, this is a good solution only by state propagation strategy. By log propagation, the leader applies an update operation to its database and commits it as the last of all participating servers. So, it can happen that the leader can return out-of-date data object.

2. Analogously to the read-my-writes, we can determine timestamp of the last update operation on the read data object x. However, this time we should consider all clients updating data in the system, i.e.,

$$lastUpd(x) = \max_{c \in Clients} (lastUpd(x, c)).$$

Then $read(x)$ can be sent to any server whose database has the time-stamp not less than $lastUpd(x)$, i.e., to those, where

$$ts(DB) >= lastUpd(x).$$

Drawbacks of this approach are twofolds: first, there may be a large number of clients, so obtaining $lastUpd(x)$ can be costly; second, some clients may be unavailable in the moment of calculation and the method fails.

3. Since Lorq system is based on a consensus quorum algorithm, it is guaranteed that a majority of servers has successfully accomplished execution of all committed update operations in their databases. To guarantee strong consistency, the number of servers we should read from is at least equal to the read quorum (R). Next, from the set of read data objects we chose the object with the latest timestamp. It is guaranteed that among read data there is the latest one.

5   Conclusions and Future Work

We proposed a new algorithm, called Lorq, for managing replicated data based on the consensus quorum approach. Lorq, like another consensus quorum algorithms, is devoted for data-centric applications, where the trade-off between consistency, availability and partition tolerance must be taken into account. A system controlled by Lorq protocol consists of a set of autonomous servers, among them the leader is chosen. Applications have possibilities to declare their consistency and latency priorities, from strong consistency to one kind of weak consistencies. In this way, the server level agreement (SLA) is provided. We briefly discussed different kinds of consistency, and some aspects of correctness of Lorq. The implementation of Lorq makes advantages of the modern software engineering methods and tools oriented to asynchronous and parallel programing [3]. In future work, we plan to extend the Lorq algorithm to take advantages of so-called *replicated data types* [5,22]. We plan also to prepare and conduct some real-system experiments. This research has been supported by Polish Ministry of Science and Higher Education under grant 04/45/DSPB/0149.

References

1. Abadi, D.: Consistency tradeoffs in modern distributed database system design. IEEE Comput. **45**(2), 37–42 (2012)
2. Amazon DynamoDB Pricing: (2014). http://aws.amazon.com/dynamodb/pricing

3. Asynchronous Programming with Async and Await (2014). http://msdn.microsoft.com/en-us/library/hh191443.aspx

4. Bernstein, P.A., Hadzilacos, V., Goodman, N.: Concurrency Control and Recovery in Database Systems. Addison Wesley Publishing Company, Boston (1987)

5. Burckhardt, S., Gotsman, A., Yang, H., Zawirski, M.: Replicated data types: specification, verification, optimality. In: ACM SIGPLAN-SIGACT Symposium on Principles of Programming Languages, POPL 2014, pp. 271–284 (2014)

6. Cattell, R.: Scalable SQL and NoSQL data stores. SIGMOD Rec. **39**(4), 12–27 (2010)

7. Chang, F., Dean, J., Ghemawat, S., Hsieh, W.C., et al.: Bigtable: A distributed storage system for structured data. ACM Trans. Comput. Syst. **26**(2), 1–26 (2008)

8. Chappell, D.: Understanding NoSQL on Microsoft Azure, pp. 1–15. Chappell & Associates, San Francisco (2014)

9. Cooper, B.F., Ramakrishnan, R., Srivastava, U., Silberstein, A., et al.: PNUTS: Yahoo!'s hosted data serving platform. PVLDB **1**(2), 1277–1288 (2008)

10. Corbett, J.C., Dean, J., Epstein, M., et al.: Spanner: Google's globally distributed database. ACM Trans. Comput. Syst. **31**(3), 8 (2013)

11. DeCandia, G., Hastorun, D., Jampani, M., et al.: Dynamo: Amazon's highly available key-value store. SIGOPS Oper. Syst. Rev. **41**(6), 205–220 (2007)

12. Gafni, E., Lamport, L.: Disk paxos. In: Herlihy, M.P. (ed.) DISC 2000. LNCS, vol. 1914, pp. 330–344. Springer, Heidelberg (2000)

13. Gifford, D.K.: Weighted voting for replicated data. In: ACM SIGOpPS 7th Symposium on Operating Systems Principles, SOSP 2079, pp. 150–162 (1979)

14. Gilbert, S., Lynch, N.A.: Perspectives on the CAP Theorem. IEEE Comput. **45**(2), 30–36 (2012)

15. Golab, W., Rahman, M.R., AuYoung, A., Keeton, K., Li, X.S.: Eventually consistent: Not what you were expecting? Commun. ACM **57**(3), 38–44 (2014)

16. Lakshman, A., Malik, P.: Cassandra: A decentralized structured storage system. SIGOPS Oper. Syst. Rev. **44**(2), 35–40 (2010)

17. Lamport, L.: Generalized consensus and paxos. In: Technical Report MSR-TR-2005-33, pp. 1–63. Microsoft Research (2005)

18. Lamport, L.: Fast paxos. Distrib. Comput. **19**(2), 79–103 (2006)

19. Ongaro, D., Ousterhout, J.: In search of an understandable consensus algorithm. In: USENIX Annual Technical Conference, pp. 305–319 (2014)

20. Pankowski, T.: A consensus quorum algorithm for replicated NoSQL data. In: Kozielski, S., Mrozek, D., Kasprowski, P., Malysiak-Mrozek, B., Kostrzewa, D. (eds.) Beyond Databases, Architectures and Structures. CCIS, vol. 521, pp. 116–125. Springer, Heidelberg (2015)

21. Pankowski, T.: Consistency and availability of data in replicated NoSQL databases. In: ENASE 2015 - Proceedings of the 10th International Conference on Evaluation of Novel Approaches to Software Engineering, Barcelona, Spain, 29–30, pp. 102–109. SciTePress (2015), April 2015

22. Shapiro, M., Preguiça, N., Baquero, C., Zawirski, M.: Conflict-free replicated data types. In: Défago, X., Petit, F., Villain, V. (eds.) SSS 2011. LNCS, vol. 6976, pp. 386–400. Springer, Heidelberg (2011)

23. Terry, D.: Replicated data consistency explained through baseball. Commun. ACM **56**(12), 82–89 (2013)

24. Terry, D.B., Prabhakaran, V., Kotla, R., Balakrishnan, M., et al.: Consistency-based service level agreements for cloud storage. In: ACM SIGOPS, SOSP 2013, pp. 309–324 (2013)
25. Vogels, W.: Eventually consistent. Commun. ACM **52**(1), 40–44 (2009)
26. Wood, M.: An Introduction to Windows Azure Table Storage (2013). www.simple-talk.com/cloud/cloud-data/an-introduction-to-windows-azure-table-storage

Heuristic Approaches to Improve Product Quality in Large Scale Integrated Software Products

Sai Anirudh Karre and Y. Raghu Reddy[(✉)]

Software Engineering Research Center,
International Institute of Information Technology, Hyderabad, India
sai.anirudh@research.iiit.ac.in,
raghu.reddy@iiit.ac.in

Abstract. Software quality has always been an important criterion for assessing stability of a product. It is quite challenging for large-scale complex products, especially integrated products, to endure and withstand the competition after a new version release in its market domain. Unlike regular software, integrated software products require detailed exploration on the spread and impact of a defect to improve overall product quality. In this paper, we use heuristic approaches like generalized defect dependency approach, control flow graph based approach, and feature correlation based approach to study the widespread of defects in large software and suggest a metric called defect dependency metric to study the dependency of defects. We implemented the generalized defect dependency approach on an industry dataset and gathered noteworthy results. We provide a comparative a study of the heuristic approaches and comprehended their individual usage with observations. We further discuss the need of adoption of such vision in industries as a standard testing practice to improve quality.

Keywords: Defect dependency · Defect widespread · Heuristic methods · Integrated software product · Software analysis · Software quality · Software metrics · Software reconstruction

1 Research Motivation and Aim

Production cycle of large-scale software products, especially integrated software products should be strategically planned to avoid software failure after product release. An integrated product consists of two more sub-products integrated to achieve some business goals. The sub-products referred as *product pillars* may have themselves been marketed or are marketed as individual products. In integrated software products, minor defects in specific sub-products targeted for a fix in upcoming releases may turn acute in current product version. This is predominant, as not all defects are easy to fix after the product release. Product stake-owners usually bypass minor defects in current release and have them planned during subsequent service packs or maintenance packs due to the complex product design or due to strict release deadlines. During development sprint cycles, software quality teams may spend a lot of time to validate the fix

© Springer International Publishing Switzerland 2016
L.A. Maciaszek and J. Filipe (Eds.): ENASE 2015, CCIS 599, pp. 80–97, 2016.
DOI: 10.1007/978-3-319-30243-0_5

and ensure that the fix does not cascade new defects into the integrated product. The primary objective of quality teams is to identify and avoid as many defects as possible before the product gets released; equally it is costlier to address re-occurred defects and time consuming to fix them post product release. The stability of a large-scale complex product is directly proportional to its quality in design and implementation [1]. Large-scale complex products become victim to both design and implementation issues if it is constructed by merging two or more unstable products. Software acquisition is a common practice in industry. A company acquires its competitor or a company that belongs to new stream to create synergy and to produce integrated solutions to its customer base. It is basic instinct of customers to feel safe using an integrated system which suffices all their business and functional needs using a product with a centralized control than on dis-integrated products that require additional manpower to merge business data together. The individual sub-products commonly referred as pillar products are bound together loosely for various functional and business reasons. For example, different end-users of a banking application may use sub-products like online transaction system, debt management, mortgage management, marketing management, customer service management, reporting system, predictive analysts, etc. in a virtually disintegrated fashion. However, for achieving the business needs, these products are integrated with each other forming a large complex software system. Most of the common defects recorded in banking applications are due to *consistency*. If the user payments in mortgage sub-product are not regularly updated across other sub-products due to a nightly data update job failure, customer service sub-product will be intimating incorrect payment violation notifications to the customers in spite of regular bill payments. In parallel this can create disconnect among reporting teams' as their balance sheets with credit and debit spending never match, creating *reliability* issues to revenue team. In such scenarios, product developers who are independently working as part of mortgage, customer service and reporting sub-products might not be sure of the source of the defect and may not log it as an integrated defect. In above example, severity levels of fixing this defect is high for reporting sub-product when compared with other sub-products. Such defects can cause major breakdown in the deployed product and require stakeholders to identify methods that can check the widespread of a defect and reprioritize the release cycle.

Quality of large-scale software is expected to improve over multiple product versions. The product versions are released in regular intervals and are usually deployed as Software as Service [2, 3]. Such products are developed by large teams that include developers, sustenance engineers, quality engineers, release and build engineers, product managers, product support and maintenance engineers. With such diversity in knowledge and skill, we can find process issues, weak cognition with in teams and un-desired release deadlines contributing towards failure of a complex product deployment. As per Gartner's 2015 Magic Quadrant for Enterprise Integration platforms as a Service Survey [4] most of software industries that develop complex integrated products are still using traditional approaches to develop and maintain quality standards of their existing products as new trends in research are quite tough to adopt. Upon additional interviews with software giants it was found that there is a lot of risk and cost associated on implementing the research as results are unpredictable. This gap can be evaded if there had been an initial study on defect widespread or its dependency on overall product. We define Defect Dependency as a *'scale to identify the widespread of a defect with unknown impact and unknown risk over a module(s) or component(s) or sub-product(s) of a large scale complex software product'*. The research presented in the paper is motivated by the following facts:

1. Achieving software stability in large scale complex products is difficult and not easy.
2. Existing research doesn't have efficient methods to identify widespread of a defect or dependency of a defect over the large integrated complex product.

The specific *research aim* of the work presented in this paper is the following

1. To investigate various approaches like generalized defect dependency approach, control flow based approach, and feature correlation based approach to calculate defect dependency of defect in integrated software products.
2. Perform empirical analysis by implementing these approaches on real time defect datasets and validate the effectiveness of approach across various version releases.

2   Related Work

Previous research shows various methods to improve software quality in large scale complex software products. Ekdahl et al. proposed approaches to improve software integration [5] with low risk and higher quality. Larsson et al. formulated an approach to improve product integration [6] based on software build check-in data. Both these approaches helped large software practitioners to build integrated systems efficiently. Chang et al. suggested a model based object-oriented approach to improve software integration from requirement and reliability perspective [7]. Gotel et al. proposed a standard development approach for Integration software product for achieving high productive products with good quality [8]. Hongyu et al. provided new methodologies to support evolution of software architecture using a dependency model so as to avoid integration issues while merging two different products at architectural level [9]. It solves architectural issues at greater extent as most of the integrated products are incorrectly designed due to lack of artifacts available from both the source products during integration. However, none of the above approaches were proactive enough on forecasting or assessing long term quality issues. Nagappan et al. performed an empirical study on software dependencies and churn metrics to predict failure in software [10]. Although, the study focused on dependency issues, it was limited to a specific piece of software and the impact on large-scale software is unknown. Clarke et al. were the first to propose a model to identify program dependencies for improved quality and maintenance of an industrial software products [11]. Trinitis et al. formulated methodology to integrated software products based on component dependencies for better quality and to avoid functional issues in future version releases [12]. Their work helped quality teams to formulate practical approaches in real-time scenario. New trends and challenges in software integration were discussed and alternate solutions were proposed using an industrial case study by Rognerud et al. [14].

There has been significant published work on defect prediction and forecasting. However, most of these studies are limited to open source software and non-commercial products that do not have the release timelines and market competition as commercial software. Junjie et al. proposed a standard approach to study integration defects using a dependency network of requirements that were drafted based on discussions with client [13]. Unlike all other defect prediction methods, this approach is more compatible to industrial adoption. Lin proposed a similar reusability approach for improving integration using functional requirements as basis of improvising quality and minimizing defects [15]. Shihab performed empirical analysis and found that there are more than 100 research papers published on Software Defect Prediction (SDP) which are mostly into prediction of defects but many do not provide guidance on using the prediction analysis on real time or rarely consider the impact, risk and dependency associated with the predicted or forecasted defects [16]. Practical adoption of SDP in industry to date is limited as a fact that they are too defect-centric and reactive. Most of the organizations need methodologies to identify most defective part of their product and need recommendations to practitioners to prioritize defects so as to avoid breakdown of rest of the product. Chengnian's DRONE defect prediction method using multi-factor analysis [17] is closer to industrial adoption, however, their model is not aimed towards assessing dependency of a defect on overall product.

Our work is focused on the need to understand the defect widespread or defect dependency in large software products. Our previous work [18] focuses on a generic mathematical approach to detect *defect dependency* of a defect using rough set theory [19, 20]. In this paper, we extend our previous work by making the following *unique contributions:*

- We perform a focused heuristic study on implementing our initial approach on a defect dataset of large-scale integrated software product. We implemented our study on a real time Integrated Human Resource Management System (IHRMS) and shared our observations from practical automated evaluation.
- Apart from our initial generalized defect dependency approach, we make use of two other heuristic approaches (control flow based graph and feature correlation based) to identify the defect dependency of a defect in large software and share our insights on implementing these methods in real time.
- We perform a *comparative study* between these approaches and share our comprehension on their usage in industry.

3 Heuristic Approaches

We represent the widespread or dependency of defect by introducing a metric called *Defect Dependency Metric (D^*)*. We use the following heuristic approaches to study dependency of a defect on a large-scale complex integrated software product and calculate the value accordingly:

1. Generalized Dependency Degree based Approach
2. Control Flow Graph based Approach
3. Feature Correlation based Approach

3.1   Generalized Dependency Degree Based Approach

This is a mathematical approach based on Generalized Dependency Degree [19] introduced by Halxuan et al. over Rough sets to calculate dependency of an object or an entity over another in rough sets. His work was extension to rough ret theory which was initially formulated by Pawlak in his work on Rough Set Classification theory [20, 21]. To define rough sets further:

- Consider a rough set over an information system, it can be defined as an approximation space as a pair as $S = (U, A)$ where U is a non-empty finite set called universal set and A is a equivalence relation defined on a U which is a nonempty finite set of attributes i.e., a: $U \rightarrow V_a$ for a ϵ A, where V_a is called the domain of a.
- Here X be a subset of U, then the lower approximation of X by A in S is defined as $\underline{R}X = \{e \in U| [e] \subseteq A\}$, similarly the upper approximation of X by A in S is defined as $\overline{R}X = \{e \in U| [e] \cap A \neq \emptyset\}$ where [e] denotes the equivalence class containing 'e'.

If we redefine above definition in terms of a defect dependency approach, consider a defect dataset (D) of a large scale complex software product (L). Then:

- If P_1, P_2, P_3, P_4 ...... P_N are sub products of L, then consider $D_{P1}, D_{P2}, D_{P3}, D_{P4}$... D_{PN} are defect subsets of respective sub-products of a universal defect dataset D.
- $S = (D, D_e)$ is an approximation space, where D is a non-empty finite defect set and D_e is a equivalence relation defined over all defect subsets D_{Pi} where $\{i \in 1,2,3....n\}$
- To calculate the dependency of a defect subset attributes over another subset, we will evaluate the value for Γ (Generalized dependency degree) which is defined as:

$$D^* = \Gamma(O, H) = \frac{1}{|D|} \sum \frac{|O(x) \cap H(x)|}{|H(x)|} \qquad (1)$$

Here O & H are two equivalent classes generated over an equivalence relation framed from universal set D. Γ provides us the dependency degree of equivalence classes O and H over each other whereas D^* is the notion for defect dependency metric. This is a purely mathematical approach to understand the dependency of a one set over another. Each data point in the dataset is a defect. The lower and upper approximation usually vary between 0 and 10 for large defect dataset, which can be considered as a scale to evaluate the degree of dependency on a real time defect datasets. It has to be noted that the metric value always lies between the lower and upper approximation. The pseudo algorithm to implement defect dependency metric using rough set theory follows:

```
program DEPENDMETRIC(D,P,M,ER,EC)
for i=1 to n do
   read Pᵢ ∈ L //read products from L
for j=1 to m do
   read Mⱼ ∈ Pᵢ //read sub-products/modules from L
begin
for k=1 to z do
   read d_pk //read defects
for l=1 to z
   D = ER(d_pk,R); //Construct equivalence relation on D
for l=1 to z
   D_e = EC(ER(d_pk,R)); // Construct equivalent classes
for l=1 to z
   D*= (EC₁,D); //Calculate Generalized Dependency degree
print D*
end
```

Experiment – Industrial Case Study. The primary author of this paper has been working in integrated product development domain for many years and has contributed to the integration of the integrated product suite in various roles. The primary author is also pursuing graduate studies on a part-time basis. Hence the authors could gain access to all the artifacts and the original data. Due to non-disclosure clauses, the name of the integrated product suite, its product pillars and the organization is being withheld. The product information shown in Table 1 makes use of alternate names to the existing (real) names. However the defect dataset presented in Table 2 shows exactly the same numbers as present in the defect database for the various products and versions of the integrated software product.

About Dataset - Our industry defect dataset contains defects of an Integrated Human Resource Integrated System (IHRIS) product with 5 primary product pillars (as shown in Table 1) that are integrated as a single product suite. Each product pillar has sub-products within which are deployed in an integrated mode. New service pack of the entire integrated product is released in every 2 months. Also a maintenance pack is released twice a month in a calendar year which includes minor fixes for the defects reported between the release timeline. The defect dataset constitutes defects of all the products and sub-products of the integrated suite which are extracted from the defect database of a defect tracking tool called JIRA™. Dataset contains defects raised by QA teams with developers during every sprint cycle along with defects reported by customers post product deployment. The authors worked with quality assurance teams to extract the defects from both sprint cycles and customers together for calculating the metric and evaluated the data as per the requirement stated by product managers.

Study Design - The study was conducted between September 2014 and July 2015 which includes three service packs along with five maintenance packs of the above provided integrated software suite. Product Managers chosen the entire defect dataset i.e., it includes defect counts of all the sub-product(s) together so as to generate equivalence classes for all the sub-products and products. Defect Dependency metric will be applied over these equivalence classes and the metric value is calculated for all the defects. The value of metric is the indicator for improvement study.

QA teams progressively compared and presented the results to product management team so that they can prioritize the defects and take an executive decision on implementing a plan for a new feature over a stable product(s) or sub-product(s) in upcoming service packs. This section describes the steps involved on calculating the metric using the industry dataset:

- Each defect in this dataset is a data point. All defects related sub-products are considered as sub-sets of universal defect set (D) which include 16 sub-products (M) spread across 5 product pillars (P). For example, if Web Services Manager is a pillar product, it contains Export Mgmt., Integration Mgmt. & Web Service Admin mode as its sub-products projected as sub-sets.
- Each set contains open defects of its sub-product and they are entitled to be calculated together. Here D the universal defect set contains defects of all sub-products i.e. D = {p_1 U p_2 U p_3 U…………….. U p_{16}} where p_i is a sub-product.

Equivalence relation and Equivalence classes are constructed using all the p_i sets, later they are applied to calculate $\Gamma(p_1, p_2,..., p_{16})$ to generate overall defect dependency metric D^*

Assumptions – While we initially considered the entire defect dataset, it was not completely pruned. It contained duplicate defects, chained defects, un-formatted defect reports which are not yet triaged and currently in unassigned or open state.

Table 1. Product information.

S. No	Product	Sub-product
1	Learning Management System (*LMS*)	Admin Mgmt. (L_1)
		Learner Mode (L_2)
		Manager Mode (L_3)
2	Human Resource System (*HRS*)	Hire Mgmt. (H_1)
		Compensation Mgmt. (H_2)
		Succession Mgmt. (H_3)
		Performance Mgmt. (H_4)
3	Business Intelligence System (*BIS*)	BI Dashboards (B_1)
		Data Downloader (B_2)
		Data Uploader (B_3)
4	Work Force Manager (*WFM*)	Attendance Mgmt. (F_1)
		Payroll Mgmt. (F_2)
		Reimbursement Mgmt. (F_3)
5	Web Services Manager (*WSM*)	Export Mgmt. (W_1)
		Integration Mgmt. (W_2)
		WSM Admin Mode (W_3)

Implementation Setup - The implementation was programmatically developed using .NET 4.0 and SQL. Equivalent relation and its classes were generated using a custom packages created using Microsoft Integration Services. Below is the implementation flow:

- Data Extract Package (**E**) is developed to extract and load defect dataset from JIRA^{TM} database (**J**) into a Testing Database (**T**). Metric Package (**M**) is responsible to generate equivalent relation and its equivalent classes. Reporting Tool (**R**) is used to display the metric results.
- This setup was implemented on Intel Xenon E5-2660 @ 2.20 GHz (8 cluster processors) with 64 bit Windows Server 2008 R2 SP1 Enterprise as operating system along with 16 GB of RAM (Fig. 1).

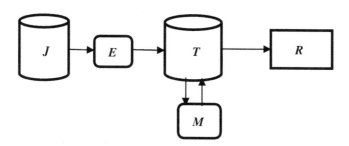

Fig. 1. Implementation flow.

Results. The metric was implemented over open defects logged across 3 service packs {*V1, V2, V3*} and 8 maintenance packs {*V1.1, V1.2, V1.3, V2.1, V2.2, V3.1, V3.2, V3.3*} releases. *V1* was the base version where we first started implementing this metric and *V3.3* was the last. Figure 2 graph contain initial overall metric value for the entire product suite was high i.e., *6.78* in *V1* version and it was significantly improved to *1.08* until version *V3.3*. Figure 3 graph provides the insight of metric value by product. Table 2 provides metric details for all the open defects as part of sub-products across its product pillars. O_L, O_H, O_B, O_F, O_W being the overall metric for respective product. QA team has been evaluating the metric by end of every sprint release separately to study the defect dependency and have been comparing the metric values for prioritizing the defective module so that it can be fixed with defined criticality.

From version *V1* to version *V3* we found a significant rise in metric value on every standard service pack release i.e. *V2* and *V3*. We studied the cause of this increase and found that rise in metric is due to dependency among the new features introduced in the respective pillar products. However, as the maintenance pack(s) were released with subsequent fixes, we found downtrend in metric results within a version i.e. between *V1* to *V1.3* etc. At the end of every version, we were able to isolate the defect dependency to a greater extent at module level in entire integrated software product. We identified a great fall in defects having higher widespread stabilizing the overall product.

Table 2. Drilldown metric data of sub-products (M) w.r.t their product-pillars (P).

P	M	V1	V1.1	V1.2	V1.3	V2	V2.1	V2.2	V3	V3.1	V3.2	V3.3
LM	O_L	1.84	1.49	1.24	0.99	1.26	1.15	0.53	0.8	0.41	0.28	0.14
	L_1	0.19	0.18	0.14	0.17	0.14	0.11	0.07	0.09	0.03	0.03	0.03
	L_2	0.37	0.33	0.26	0.21	0.21	0.16	0.05	0.14	0.11	0.07	0.02
	L_3	1.28	0.98	0.84	0.61	0.91	0.88	0.41	0.57	0.27	0.18	0.09
HRS	O_H	2.47	2.1	1.88	1.71	1.97	1.78	1.13	2.54	1.65	1.28	0.56
	H_1	0.45	0.39	0.33	0.29	0.51	0.45	0.31	0.44	0.31	0.17	0.08
	H_2	0.39	0.31	0.32	0.29	0.39	0.32	0.29	0.28	0.19	0.12	0.07
	H_3	0.22	0.21	0.16	0.15	0.18	0.13	0.12	0.14	0.11	0.05	0.02
	H_4	1.41	1.19	1.07	0.98	0.89	0.88	0.41	1.68	1.04	0.94	0.39
BI	O_B	1.02	0.93	0.81	0.62	1.08	0.96	0.72	0.98	0.72	0.42	0.19
	B_1	0.27	0.21	0.18	0.13	0.31	0.28	0.22	0.34	0.21	0.11	0.07
	B_2	0.32	0.31	0.27	0.17	0.45	0.41	0.29	0.52	0.44	0.29	0.12
	B_3	0.43	0.41	0.36	0.32	0.32	0.27	0.21	0.12	0.07	0.02	0
WFM	O_F	1.15	0.96	0.89	0.73	1.05	0.85	0.71	1.2	0.73	0.38	0.19
	F_1	0.31	0.25	0.19	0.12	0.44	0.37	0.31	0.58	0.31	0.21	0.09
	F_2	0.24	0.21	0.2	0.11	0.21	0.17	0.14	0.24	0.15	0.06	0.02
	F_3	0.6	0.5	0.5	0.5	0.4	0.31	0.26	0.38	0.27	0.11	0.08
WSM	O_W	0.3	0.26	0.22	0.22	0.24	0.1	0.07	0.17	0.06	0.04	0
	W_1	0.16	0.15	0.13	0.13	0.12	0.07	0.04	0.09	0.04	0.04	0
	W_2	0.05	0.05	0.05	0.05	0.09	0.03	0.03	0.07	0.02	0	0
	W_3	0.09	0.06	0.04	0.04	0.03	0	0	0.01	0	0	0
Overall		6.78	5.74	5.04	4.27	5.6	4.84	3.16	5.69	3.57	24	1.08

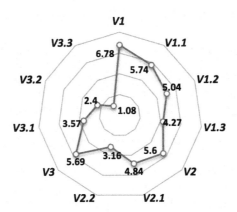

Fig. 2. Trend graph of overall metric of entire product suite across versions.

Observations and Remarks. Below observations were captured after implementation concluded as part of retrospection session conducted between Product Managers and QA teams for trend analysis.

- There has been significant improvement on stability of the product. We found exponential decrease in environment and performance related defects across releases.
- By end of *V3.3* version release, standard evaluation results found that there was about 71 % decrease in overall defects reported by customers post product release and 52 % decrease in internal defects raised by QA teams during sprint cycles when compared with older versions.

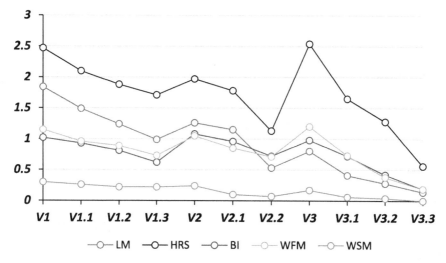

Fig. 3. Trend graph of overall metric per sub-product across versions.

Most of the functional defects which were dependent were proactively identified and were resolved in timely fashion. This decreased the risk of software failure during product deployments. Proactive defects constitute 12 % among overall defects recorded across versions before deployment.

- During this implementation, we found few architectural flaws in two of the sub-product(s) which required total makeover in terms of integration. This wouldn't have been possible if the metric was never implemented. We consider this to be significant contribution of our approach on real time scenario.
- It was also identified that it is too costlier to re-design the sub-modules when the product is actively used by most of the customers. Hence, the faultier sub-products are being disintegrated and are being planned to be merged as components in one of the existing product for better product stability.

3.2   Control Flow Graph Based Approach

Control Flow Graph approach is a generic approach which uses Control Flow graphs as base artifact. This method helps us to study the defect dependency on a defect level across the entire large integrated software product. Below are the steps involved in the approach:

- Consider a defect d recorded in a large software complex product (L)
- Generate a Control flow graph of defect flow across the entire product suite
- Track and identify all possible artifacts like sub-products (p), modules (m), classes (c), blocks(b), loops (l), methods (n) etc., which can be depicted from for the control flow graph using control flow specification language (CFSL) [24] as per respective large scale complex product design
- Let ($\sum p + \sum m + \sum c + \sum b + \sum l + \sum n$) be minimum approximation of entities effected during defect flow and $\sum L$ be the maximum approximation of all the entities calculated using the available control flow graph
- $\sum L - (\sum p + \sum m + \sum c + \sum b + \sum l + \sum n)$ is considered as range of the defect. When the range is divided by $\sum L$ then it is considered as the spread per artifact for the entire large product L.
- When the above resultant value is subtracted with 1, we get the spread for overall large product L. This is considered to be the weightage of defect range D^* mathematically represented as below:

$$D^* = 1 - \frac{\sum L - (\sum p + \sum m + \sum c + \sum b + \sum l + \sum n)}{\sum L} \quad (2)$$

- The scale of D^* here is between 0 and 1. Control flow graphs can be automatically generated using standard software testing tools for large software like RedHat JBPM[1], Soot[2] and Dr. Garbage[3] etc., using control flow specification language to generate pseudo code graphs, block graphs etc.

Assumptions – Control flow specification language is represented in XML format. One has to externally read the XML file and compute the count the desired artifacts. As part of this approach, we assume that it is possible to capture and generate the control flow of a defect over a product.

Example - We illustrate the approach using a bug report as an example from product defined in Table 1.

Table 3. Example defect report in IHRIS Integrated Software Product.

Defect#101	Incorrect tax calculation in QTD payroll
Product	Payroll Mgmt. (WFM)
Cause	Corruption in Employee Rating in Performance Mgmt. caused incorrect flow into WFM module. Compensation was incorrect calculated causing issue.
Fix	Added Exception in Tax calculation for QTD Employee payroll w.r.t data validation from Performance and Compensation modules.

- Figure 4 is the control flow graph of Defect#101 and the modules linked with defect are Performance Mgmt., WFM Module, Compensation and the products are HRS

---

[1] http://www.jbpm.org/.

[2] http://sable.github.io/soot/.

[3] http://www.drgarbage.com.

(Human Resource System) and WFM (Workforce Mgmt.). Control flow contains blocks in bold and italic, along with other main modules. The figure also highlights product and its sub-product to show how overlapped they are in terms of integration (Table 3).

- ΣL is *76784* which was computed for the complete IHRIS product and $(\Sigma p + \Sigma m + \Sigma c + \Sigma b + \Sigma l + \Sigma n)$ value for the Defect#101 is computed to be *7861*.
- By using Eq. (2), D^* value for the defect#101 is *0.1023*.

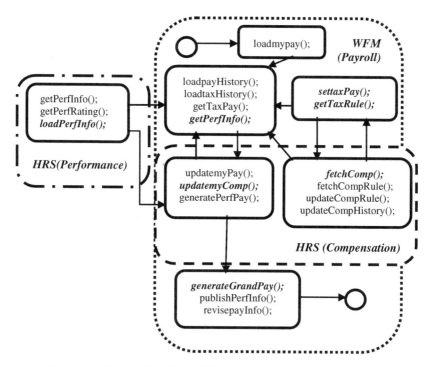

Fig. 4. Control flow graph of defect#101, methods in **block**-*italic* are defective.

Using this approach, D^* value can be computed for all the defects reported in a specific version and defects with high D^* value can be prioritized accordingly. If the D^* value is similar for two or more defects, product managers can take a call to prioritize defects as per business and functional need. This approach has to be re-applied for all the defects individually to estimate the defect dependency of an individual defect over an entire large integrated product. This approach also helps QA teams to easily evaluate the dependency test cases which are difficult to test and fix in real time especially for large and complex software products.

3.3   Feature Correlation Based Approach

Large scale software development is hard. Many software projects fail due to lack of knowledge on dependency of a product feature over another which is an undeniable truth about the software industry. The primary idea of this approach is to understand the correlation of the features from overall defects recorded per feature and estimate the defect dependency among the features in a large integrated software product. We adopt standard statistical [25] methods to evaluate the dependency over software features using defects as criteria for assessing the metric. Below are the steps involved in the approach:

- We will have to pre-process and prune our defect dataset to perform a co-variance study on product features. Firstly, list down the features available in the product.
- Capture defects counts for against each feature across versions or sprint releases or product release so as to construct the desired test dataset
- Now calculate the co-variance (cv) (as per Eq. (3)) between features for the available defect counts and generate a Co-variance matrix (CM). Using Co-variance matrix, we should be able to understand the relation between the features which help us to deduce dependency among each other. Below equation is to calculate co-variance between two features x and y which belongs to same product:
- *Note*: N = n−1 if the co-variance is calculated for a small sample. Else, we need to use the entire population size for large datasets.

$$cv = \frac{\sum (xi - \bar{x})(yi - \bar{y})}{N} \tag{3}$$

- The positive co-variance value indicates increasing linear relationship between the features, whereas the negative co-variance value indicates decreasing relationship.
- Later calculate standard deviation (sd) of each feature i.e. $\{x, y\}$ and calculate Pearson Correlation co-efficient (r) to understand the strength of relation, which can be defined as below:

$$r = \frac{cv(x, y)}{sd(x) * sd(y)} \tag{4}$$

- If $|r| \geq 2/\sqrt{N}$ then the relationship is statistically exists between specified features, else there is no relationship between the specified features. This is a *causation* validation (c) method to understand the dependence of features among defect dataset. Causation validation can be considered as our defect dependency metric (D^*).
- We illustrate below example to demonstrate the method. Table 4 contains the defect counts of features $\{F1, F2, F3, F4\}$ which are captures across 4 different sprint cycles. Using below example, we will be identifying the relationship between the features using defect counts as evaluation criteria.
- Table 5 contains the basic statistics which are required to construct the Pearson Correlation co-efficient, co-variance, correlation and co-variance matrix to identify the relationship among the features.

Table 4. Sample feature-sprint cycle defect count set.

Feature / Cycle	F1	F2	F3	F4
Sprint Cycle 1	21	34	9	6
Sprint Cycle 2	19	31	4	11
Sprint Cycle 3	16	29	8	12
Sprint Cycle 4	17	19	2	9

- Table 6 is the co-variance matrix which contains positive and negative values for few feature combinations. If we validate heuristically, *F2* and *F3* are highly related as the value the covariance is high and the rest are highlighted in bold-italic.

Table 5. Statistics of sample defect data.

Feature	Size	Mean	Std. deviation	Variance
F1	4	17.5	12.76	163
F2	4	28.25	6.5	42.25
F3	4	5.75	3.304	10.91
F4	4	9.5	2.64	7

- Similary, *F1* and *F3* are least related as their covariance value is too low.
- There is no definite scale for co-variance as it depends on the size of population of dataset used to construct the covariance matrix.

Table 6. Co-variance Matrix of features from sample defect data.

CM	F1	F2	F3	F4
F1	163	*0.334*	*0.091*	−0.400
F2	*0.334*	42.25	*2.338*	−0.553
F3	*0.091*	*2.338*	10.91	−0.744
F4	−0.400	−0.553	−0.744	7

- Table 7 provides causation validation on features across defect dataset. If the value is +ve, there exists a dependence relationship between the features. Else the depedence relation don't exist. For our sample defect dataset, *F1–F3* and *F2–F3* are strongly dependent to each other.

Table 7. Causation validation of feature relationship.

D*	F1	F2	F3	F4
F1	-	−ve	*+ve*	−ve
F2	−ve	-	*+ve*	−ve
F3	*+ve*	*+ve*	-	−ve
F4	−ve	−ve	−ve	-

- Using this methods, project managers and quality teams will be able to understand the actual dependent features within defect dataset. This approach is statistical in nature and can be statistically validated for improved results on larger defect datasets.
- The above steps are to be repeated for every desired interval i.e. every sprint cycle or test cycle or release cycle to learn the pattern defect dependency over features and formulate the stability of the product.

4   Comparison and Scope of Implementing Approaches

In this section, we compare and comprehend above proposed approach to understand their ease of usage and study the likelihood of adoption in real-time (Table 8).

Table 8.   Detailed comparision of proposed approaches.

Approach / Category	Generalized Dependency Degree based Approach	Control Flow Graph based Approach	Feature Correlation based Approach
Defect Dataset	apt for large	any size	any size
Scope	prioritize most widespread defects	improve control flow among sub-products	improve features and address functional issues
Implementation	programmatically achieved	partially programmatically achieved	programmatically achieved
Verification	empirical	formal	statistical
Validation	n-fold cross-validation	informal inspection	statistical
Advantages	easy to evaluate across sub-products	easy to evaluate at defect level	easy to evaluate at feature level
Challenges	difficult to study at a single defect level	difficult to study if it is not possible to generate control flow	difficult in case of unavailability of functional specifications
Automation	non-generic	partially generic	generic

In contrast, not all above approaches might help software practitioners on addressing software quality issues in large software. In reality, it is critical to construct a control flow graph for a large software due to its complexity. Such software products should be first refactored and later be inspected to understand defect dependency. Also, not all software products have recorded software specification documents. Especially in case of legacy systems, there can be few details available which might only suffice basic understanding of the product. However lack of design documents might not help us implement feature based correlation approach. Software practitioners might have to address functional requirements of their complex product before implementing above proposed method.

5 Future Work

In recent years, there is moderate growth of transfer of research on new technologies from academia to industry [22]. There were many lessons learnt from industrial case studies over a decade [23]. As part of our current work we presented new methods to compute defect dependency and was successfully able to implement them in real world defect dataset. Initially it has become difficult for us to convince our quality teams to adopt and automate the approach as the metric was not substantially showing any improvement. In due course of implementation across various release versions we were able to realize the significance of the defect dependency. As a future work, we will be assessing the metric more comprehensively by getting feedback from developers and quality teams on how significant this method helps them to prioritize the defect as part of regular work. We will be implementing the feature correlation approach on open-source defect datasets and also explore new approaches which can help evaluate the defect dependency at all levels of software production cycle instead restricting to specific artifact.

6 Summary

In this paper we present our work on need of defect dependency metric and its successful practical implementation on real-time industry dataset. Apart from our initial study we have also proposed few new approaches to calculate and verify defect widespread or defect dependency over a large scale complex software product. Software quality in large scale software products has been challenging, especially during integration or dis-integration of legacy products in industry. This has been our driving force to study approaches to defect dependency. We are assertive to note that the proposed approaches are generic, simple and heuristic in nature with less complexity and can be easily adopted in industry without any technical challenges. We strongly recommend software practitioners to implement any of these approaches and record the defect dependency metric as a standard and use it as a measure for assessing the quality of large integrated software products.

Acknowledgements. The Authors Would like to Acknowledge Product Managers and Solutions Architects from Sumtotal Inc. and Factset Research Systems Inc. for Sharing Their Valuable Assistance, Suggestions and Feedback on Implementing Our Research into Reality.

References

1. Yoshida, M., Iwane, N.: Towards the software life cycle cost for integrated software product line systems. In: International Conference on Industrial Informatics, pp. 910–916. IEEE Press, Singapore (2006)
2. Dong, J., Wang, J., Sun, D., Lu, H.: The research of software product line engineering process and its integrated development environment model. In: International Symposium on Computer Science and Computational Technology, pp. 66–71. IEEE Press, Shanghai (2008)

3. Saaksjarvi, M.: Software application platforms: from product architecture to integrated application strategy. In: 26th Annual International Proceedings of Computer Software and Application Conference, pp. 435–443. IEEE Press, Oxford (2002)

4. Pazzini, M., Natis, Y.V., Malinverno, P., Iijima, K., Thompson, J., Thoo, E., Guttridge, K.: Magic Quadrant for Enterprise Integration Platform as a Service, Worldwide, Report: G00270939, Gartner Press (2015)

5. Ekdahl, F., Crnkovic, I.: How to improve software integration. Inf. Softw. Technol. J. (2005)

6. Larsson, S., Crnkovic, I.: Product integration improvement based on analysis of build statistics. In: European Software Engineering Conference, pp. 505–508. IEEE Press, Dubrovnik (2007)

7. Chang, C.-H., Chu, W.C., Lu, C.-W.: Improving software integration from requirement process with a model-based object-oriented approach. In: International Conference on Secure System Integration and Reliability Improvement, pp. 175–176. IEEE Press, Yokohama (2008)

8. Gotel, O., Kulkarni, V., Scharff, C., Neak, L.: Integration starts on day one in global software development projects. In: IEEE International Conference on Global Software Engineering, pp. 244–248, Bangalore (2008)

9. Pei, H., Crnkovic, I.: Using dependency model to support software architecture evolution. In: 23rd IEEE/ACM International Conference Automated Software Engineering-Workshops, pp. 82–91, L'Aquila (2008)

10. Ball, T., Nagappan, N.: Using software dependencies and churn metrics to predict field failures - an empirical case study. In: Proceedings of International Symposium on Empirical Engineering and Measurement, pp. 364–373. IEEE Press, Madrid (2007)

11. Clarke, L.A., Podgurski, A.: A formal model of program dependences and its implications for software testing debugging and maintenance. Proc. IEEE Trans. Softw. Eng. **16**(9), 965–979 (1990)

12. Trinitis. C., Walter, M.: How to integrate inter-component dependencies into combinatorial availability models. In: Proceedings of Annual Reliability and Maintainability Symposium (RAMS) Proceedings. Modeling and Simulation Techniques, pp. 226–231 (2004)

13. Wang, J., Li, J., Wang, Q.: Can requirements dependency network be used as early indicator of software integration bugs? In: Proceedings of 21st IEEE International Requirements Engineering Conference, pp. 185–194, Rio De Janeiro (2013)

14. Rognerud, H.J., Hannay, J.E.: Challenges in enterprise software integration: an industrial study using repertory grids. In: Proceedings of International Symposium on Empirical Software Engineering and Measurement, pp. 11–22, Lake Buena Vista (2009)

15. Lin, J.-M.: Cross-platform software reuse by functional integration approach. In: Proceedings of 21st International Conference on Computer Software and Application Conference, pp. 402–408, Washington (1997)

16. Shihab, E.: Practical software quality prediction. In: Proceedings of International Conference on Software Maintenance and Evolution, pp. 639–644, Victoria (2014)

17. Tian, Y., Lo, D., Sun, C.: DRONE: predicting priority of reported bugs by multi-factor analysis. In: Proceedings of International Conference on Software Maintaince (ICSM), pp. 200–209, Netherlands (2013)

18. Karre, S.A., Reddy, Y.R.: A defect dependency approach to improve software quality in integrated software products. In: Proceedings of International Conference on Evaluation of Novel Approaches to Software Engineering, pp. 110–117, Barcelona (2015)

19. Yang, H., King, I., Lyu, M.R.: Generalized dependency degree between attributes. Proc. J. Am. Soc. Inf. Sci. Technol. **58**(14), 2280–2294 (2007)

20. Pawlak, Z.: Rough classification. Int. J. Hum. Comput. Stud. **51**(15), 369–383 (1999)

21. Gediga, G., Düntsch, I.: Rough approximation quality revisited. Proc. J. Artif. Intell. **132**(2), 219–234 (2001)
22. Laird, L., Yang, Y.: Transferring software engineering research into industry - the Stevens way. In: Proceedings of IEEE/ACM 2nd International Workshop on Software Engineering Research and Industrial Practice (SER&IP), pp. 46–49 (2015)
23. Wohlin, C.: Empirical software engineering research with industry: top 10 challenges. In: Proceedings of 1st International Workshop on Conducting Empirical Studies in Industry (CESI), pp. 43–46, (2013)
24. Smelik, R., Rensink, A., Kasternberg, H.: Specification and construction of control flow semantics. In: IEEE Symposium on Visual Languages and Human-Centric Computing. IEEE Press, pp. 65–72 (2006)
25. Anderson, T.W.: An Introduction to Multivariate Statistical Analysis, 3rd Edition. Wiley India Pvt Ltd, India (2009). ISBN-10:8126524480, ISBN-13:978-8126524488

Towards a CBSE Framework for Enhancing Software Reuse: Matching Component Properties Using Semi-formal Specifications and Ontologies

Andreas S. Andreou[1] and Efi Papatheocharous[2(✉)]

[1] Department of Computer Engineering and Informatics,
Cyprus University of Technology, Limassol, Cyprus
andreas.andreou@cut.ac.cy
[2] Swedish Institute of Computer Science, SICS Swedish ICT, Kista, Sweden
efi.papatheocharous@sics.se

Abstract. A novel Component-based Software Engineering (CBSE) framework is proposed in this work that focuses on enhancing the reuse process by offering support for locating appropriate components. The architecture of the framework comprises of five interrelated layers, namely Description, Location, Analysis, Recommendation and Build. The scope of this work is to describe in detail the first and third layers, and provide the means to evaluate the suitability of candidate software components for reuse. The overall aim is to facilitate components' profiling and offer efficient matching of system and software requirements to increase the reusability potential of components. A specifications profile is created for each component using a semi-formal natural language that describes certain properties. A dedicated parser recognizes parts of the profile and translates them into instance values of a dedicated CBSE ontology that encodes these properties. Matching is then performed at the level of ontology instances between the available components and the components required by the developer. The framework recommends components based on a suitability ratio that calculates their distances from the desired properties.

Keywords: Software engineering · Components · Reuse · Semi-formal specifications · Ontology

1 Introduction

Component-based software engineering (CBSE) has emerged during the last two decades as a recognizable approach within the software development process that relies on extensive reuse of existing components and has attracted considerable research attention [1]. The most significant advantages of reusing existing software components parts instead of developing systems from scratch, either small-grained units (functions, classes) or large-grained fully-fledged systems (Components Off The Shelf, COTS), are typically the acceleration of the development process, the increased dependability of the reused software and the reduction of the associated process risks. However, these

© Springer International Publishing Switzerland 2016
L.A. Maciaszek and J. Filipe (Eds.): ENASE 2015, CCIS 599, pp. 98–121, 2016.
DOI: 10.1007/978-3-319-30243-0_6

benefits have been explicitly reported in only 33 % of the studies according to the systematic literature study [1]. Hence, software development with and for reuse still suffers from certain weaknesses that hinder their full exploitation potential. In our opinion, one of the most challenging weaknesses is the lack of efficient mechanisms to assess the suitability of candidate components for reuse. This is exactly the problem dealt within this work.

According to Szyperski's definition in (2002), *"A software component is a unit of composition with contractually specified interfaces and explicit context dependencies only. A software component can be deployed independently and is subject to composition by third-parties"* [2]. This is particularly relevant with the way systems are developed today, as a lot of investment is put in using or buying ready-made components, through large-grained software reuse. The resulting systems are more qualitative and their time-to-market is significantly reduced, while at the same time, cost savings can be realized.

In the domain of CBSE two primary types of roles are distinguished: the software developer that develops the component from scratch and the reuser-developer or consumer, that is, the developer that makes use and integrates the ready-made components to develop a new software system. There are several alliances and agreements that need to be formed between software creators, vendors and owners. Completing a software product on time, within budget and with the required quality depends heavily on these relations, as well as on the methods and/or techniques utilized to support the development process. Mili et al. [3] define software reuse as "the process whereby an organization defines a set of systematic operating procedures to specify, produce, classify, retrieve and adapt software artefacts for the purpose of using them in its development activities."

Nowadays, although the software components industry is steadily growing, and many emerging concepts such as Software as a Service (SaaS), Open Source Software (OSS) components and Components Off The Shelf (COTS) become more and more common in the way software is developed, there is still lack of efficient support to components' management, storing and retrieval. Although there are multiple brokers that try to serve reusers or consumers, and related communities are formed (for example the large Open Source community), still nowadays the need for more appropriate tools is emphasized. Tool support is in a way unavoidable for CBSE to succeed [1]. Even though many efforts are recognized to exist today, Barn and Brown [4] talk about the development of new generation tools of appropriate methods and tools that will encourage reuse and wider CBSE practice.

In a recent systematic mapping study of the CBSE area it was identified that the majority of the literature studies address primarily new solutions' functionality, while interaction (e.g., between components, component compositions, reusability property) and quality concerns are the second and third most common research topics respectively [1]. In addition, among the list of research gaps reported, two of them significantly motivate the present work: Gap 4 and Gap 5 (as mentioned in the study above). The first indicated that CBSE concepts are still not fully integrated in industry or into the overall development and maintenance processes. In addition, the latter, also indicated that further research is needed to investigate how functionality, methodology and management must be further developed for CBSE to work in the first place, how CBSE can work efficiently and how components may be assessed. These research gaps pin-pointed by Vale et al. [1] indicate that there is still great need for methodological approaches to improve and automate the processes of modelling, searching, retrieving and analyzing candidate components for integration.

To this end, the present work proposes a new CBSE reusability framework as an extension of the work in [5]. The architecture of the framework (as originally presented in [5]) comprises of five interrelated layers, namely Description, Location, Analysis, Recommendation and Build. The first layer of the framework is the key component to the process as it is responsible to profile component specifications using an expressive and easily understood (by component developers and reusers) semi-formal natural language structure. The purpose is to make it possible to capture properties useful for components' matching in an intuitive manner. This profile is then transformed into a more formalized ontological representation and a simple, yet efficient way, to use this representation for automatically matching components based on the suitability level of candidate components that is calculated by comparing ontology tree instances. The matching process is carried out in the third layer and the recommended solutions (components) are provided to the fourth layer of the framework that yields detailed recommendations, as to which of the candidate components may be best integrated and why.

In this work we focus and extend the implementations of the first and third layers. The framework focuses on the identification of components and their assessment in terms of required features (functional or non-functional properties). It demonstrates their suitability for integration according to a prescribed (or desired) requirements profile. The main novel aspects of this, is that the CBSE reusability framework approach consists of: (i) profiling of the components using the Extended Backus-Naur Form, which describes the desired properties of the required components, and (ii) an automatic search and retrieval mechanism for finding appropriate components for reuse. The latter utilizes the profiling scheme and without human intervention it delivers the most suitable components in three sequential steps: parsing the ontology profiles of the requested and available components, executing the matching algorithm and recommending the best matches. To the best of our knowledge existing approaches in the relevant literature do not offer such properties of filling-in the gap of automation and management of components' CBSE and reuse processes, neither have proper support for managing non-functional properties. The latter is also mentioned as Gap 6 in study [1].

The most significant differences between this work and that of [5] may be summarized to the following:

(a) The profile used to describe the components is modified and enhanced so that both horizontal and vertical expansion is feasible. Horizontal expansion refers to adding new values for a fixed (pre-defined) property, while vertical means the ability to add new properties. In the latter case the parsing mechanism is modified accordingly to be able to recognize the extension.

(b) The matching process is extended and includes the option of assigning weights to certain properties. This addition makes it possible to increase the properties' significance and this is primarily used in the comparison between available candidates. Therefore, the overall suitability of components can be adjusted based on what reusers consider more important when looking for appropriate component-solutions.

(c) The recommendation layer is also slightly enhanced with information that reveals possible incompatibilities between the successful candidates and what the reuser tries to find. Such incompatibilities are mostly focused on differences between programming platforms used to develop the candidates, or operating systems supported, and would potentially result in increase of the time and effort required by the reuser to integrate the component with the rest of the system. This case only applies if the properties that present incompatibility have been declared as desired and not as constraints.

(d) The experimental process was significantly extended and now includes a second, larger stage of experiments with increased levels of complexity and size as regards the targeted software application that is to be developed through reuse activities, thus touching also upon issues of scalability and efficiency.

The rest of the chapter is organized as follows: Sect. 2 provides a brief literature review on the subject. The proposed approach CBSE reusability framework for pro-filing and matching components is described in Sect. 3. The section starts with an overview of the reusability framework, continues with a presentation of the semi-formal description of components specifications and ends with the presentation of the details of the matching process, including the a dedicated CBSE ontology and the matching algorithm. Section 4 describes the experimental process which is divided into two stages and reports some interesting findings on the assessment of the proposed approach framework. Finally, Sect. 5 concludes the chapter and suggests further research steps.

2 Literature Overview

The literature overview of this section focuses on relevant publications on matching required properties and components. The relevant component search and retrieval literature is rich with studies about COTS, while Quality of Service (QoS) is one of the most frequently used mechanisms for component matching. In addition, ontologies have offered promising common ground to the CBSE process, either for describing metrics or properties for assessing components, or for supporting in some way their matching process. A brief outline of some of those studies follows.

Zaremski and Wing [6] were among the first, to the best of our knowledge, to use formal specifications to describe the behavior of software components and to determine whether two components match. Chung and Cooper [7] presented an approach that supports iterative matching, ranking and selection of COTS represented as sets of functional and non-functional requirements. The work of Iribarne et al. [8] presented an extension of approaches dealing with component search and service matching in which components offer several interfaces. More specifically, they addressed service gaps and overlaps extending the traditional compatibility and substitutability operators to deal with components that support multiple interfaces. Yessad and Boufaida [9] proposed a Quality of Service (QoS) ontology for describing software components and used this ontology to semantically select relevant components based on the QoS specified by the developer. Pahl [10] presented an approach for component matching by encoding transitional reasoning about safety and liveness properties into description logic and a Web standards compliant ontology framework. Yan et al. [11] attempted to address the lack of semantic description ability in component searching and retrieval by introducing a conceptual ontology and a domain ontology. The authors represented a component ontology library by a conceptual and a component graph. During the retrieval process, the retrieval pattern graph was matched with the component graph using a component retrieval algorithm based on graph patterns. Kluge et al. [12] suggested an approach for matching functional business requirements to standard application software packages via ontologies. Seedorf and Schader [13] introduced an enterprise software component ontology to establish a common understanding of enterprise software components, i.e., their types and relationships to entities in the business domain. Alnusair and Zhao [14] proposed a semantic-based approach for retrieving relevant components from a reuse repository utilizing an ontology model comprising of three axes, source-code, component, and domain-specific ontology. Their experiments suggested that only pure semantic search that exploits domain knowledge tends to improve precision.

Although it is evident from the above studies that matching of component specifications through the use of ontologies is not a new concept, their results also show that it is a promising and worth pursuing research subject. Their results exhibit several improvements but also emphasize the need for expansions. What is more important to highlight, is the fact that current studies do not cover adequately practical aspects of component reusability. This is because they: (i) express component services in abstract ontology forms and/or provide matching algorithm descriptions sometimes with and other times without the use of ontology information, or (ii) do not provide concrete, yet simple, descriptors of the component properties, which may be reused by tools or methods that could further aid the reuse process. This chapter aspires to address this need by introducing an integrated CBSE reusability framework for components' reuse, which offers a layered approach that guides the reuse process. The details of the framework are presented next.

3   CBSE Reusability Framework

3.1   Overview

The proposed CBSE reusability framework is depicted in Fig. 1 and consists of five layers (sub-systems). Each layer supports a part of the CBSE development process as follows: (i) The Description layer is responsible for creating the component profiles, which includes the properties for the components offered or required. A developer (either component developer or reuser) defines the functional and non-functional requirements that are provided by or required from existing components depending on the role the developer has within the process. The former essentially provides the functional behavior and properties of the available components in terms of functionality, performance, availability, reliability, robustness etc., and the latter provides the required properties. (ii) The Location layer offers the means to search, locate and retrieve the components of interest that match the profile. (iii) The Analysis layer provides the tools to evaluate the level of suitability of the candidate components and yield matching results that will guide the selection of components for reuse. (iv) The Recommendation layer uses the information received from the profiling activities and produces suggestions to reusers as to which of the candidate components may be best integrated and why, through a cost-benefit analysis. (vi) The Build layer essentially comprises a set of integration and customization tools for combining components and building larger systems.

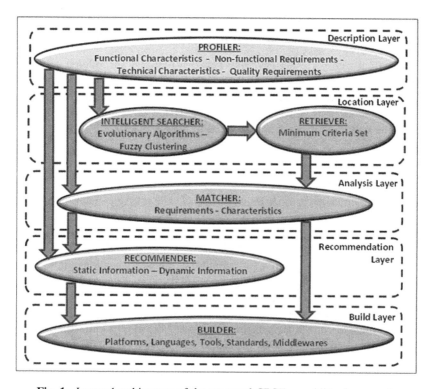

Fig. 1. Layered architecture of the proposed CBSE reusability framework.

One of the challenges that the present work addresses is the issue of narrowing down the component requirements for searching and locating appropriate components, considering a minimal set of criteria and associating the various candidates with a ratio value of suitability. The latter can enable reaching to a plan (or recommendation) on how to progress with a project, and how to integrate components into one fully-functioning system. Therefore, in this work, we focus to describe only on the details of the activities carried out in the Description and the Analysis layers. We focus to describe the process for conducting automatic matching between required and offered properties of components based on a structured semi-formal natural language and using ontologies. The proposed matching process consists of the following three steps:

Step 1. The required functional and non-functional properties of the component(s) are first described in a specifications profile using a semi-formal natural language. Functional properties specify a function that a system or system component must be able to perform [15]. Non-functional properties are software requirements that describe not what the software must do but how the software must do it [15]. The standards (ISO/IEC) were used as inspiration on what kind of properties one might use to describe specifications. Details on the profile descriptions are given in Subsect. 3.2.

Step 2. In this step, the profile specified is automatically parsed and certain textual parts are recognized. These are then translated into instance values of a dedicated CBSE ontology (details of the CBSE ontology are described in Subsect. 3.3.1). This ontology is built so as to highlight various development issues from the perspective of components reusability.

Step 3. The final step performs matching between required and offered components' properties, the latter being stored also as instances of the CBSE ontology. This matching takes place automatically at the level of ontology items and a suitability ratio is calculated that suggests which components to consider next for possible integration. Details on the matching process are provided in Subsect. 3.3.2.

3.2   Level 1: Description Layer

Nowadays, the metrics and properties met in Service Level Agreements (SLA) tend to become standard in the software industry, especially for applications executing on distributed systems and the Cloud. The same concepts may easily be applied in our case where we target at providing a profiling scheme able to capture the properties of components for the purpose of reusing them in building larger applications. In this context, there are various approaches to SLA metrics, like those suggested by Czajkowski et al. [16], Emeakaroha et al. [17], Mili et al. [19] and Paschke and Schnappinger-Gerull [18]. These studies make some useful categorization either in the context of performance metrics from both the hardware perspective (e.g., availability, failure frequency, processor time, etc.) and the software perspective (e.g., service times, response times, solution times, etc.), or from the point of view of the type of property described (e.g., time and scalar metrics). These categorizations have been carefully studied and certain concepts have been adopted and adapted in this work so as to reflect better the concepts of components description that are deemed necessary to support efficient reuse. The latter is realized by supporting effectively the process of finding the appropriate components for each case.

The first layer of the proposed CBSE reusability framework supports a specific type of component profiling, which uses information revolving around three axes: functional, non-functional and reusability properties. The selection of these axes was made targeting at describing a component from the perspective of the core functional aspects offered, the quality features and other constraints with direct effect on the functional properties, as well as a third viewpoint focusing on reusability issues. One may argue that the latter two types of properties may overlap. This is actually true as there is a thin line separating certain properties, while others may have the same meaning (e.g., use of standards). Nevertheless, we decided to differentiate between the two so as to emphasize on reuse issues and offer a way to handle information that may not involve general quality properties but at the same time is of particular importance to a component consumer, like for example those reported in the ISO-9126 standard. This becomes clearer in the description of the types of properties used to profile components that follows:

(i) <u>Functional Properties.</u> One or more functional aspects included in the component are described. More specifically, the services offered by the component are outlined, accompanied with the structure of the published interface (i.e., provides/requires, detailing what services must be made available for the component to execute and what services are offered by the component during execution). Component contracts are also reported with the related Pre-conditions, Post-conditions, Invariants and Exception handling descriptions (i.e., cases where pre/post-conditions or invariants might be violated per method).

(ii) <u>Non-functional Properties.</u> Non-functional constraints, such as quality properties are reported. Performance indicators, resources requirements (e.g., memory and CPU) and other quality features (i.e., quality attributes based on the ISO 9126 standard, like availability (MTBF) and reliability) are described.

(iii) <u>Reusability Properties.</u> The aspect of reusability of the component is described. It involves general information about the component related to its context, legacy and ways of current use, its flexibility and other factors that are considered useful to reusers. Properties here can include the application domain the component is developed for, the programming languages used, the operating system(s) that is able to execute on, the type of openness/extensibility (i.e., black, glass, grey, white), its price, developer information (i.e., details about the company or individual that created the component), a list of protocols and standards the component supports (e.g., JMS/Websphere, DDS/NDDS 4.0, CORBA/ACE TAO, POSIX, SNMP and .NET), as well as information about accompanying documentation (like design, administration and user manuals, and test cases). Some of the above properties even though important for the component' utilization, they are made optional in the implementation and thus it depends on the component developers to provide the corresponding information.

The component properties descriptions are written in the Extended Backus-Naur Form (EBNF). Expressing the component descriptions in the EBNF notations allows us to formally prove key properties, such as well-formedness and closure, and hence help validate the semantics. The proposed grammar has been developed with the Another Tool for Language Recognition (ANTLR) parser generator (http://www.antlr.org/). ANTLR is a parser and translator generator tool that allows language grammars' definition in an EBNF-like syntax.

Table 1 presents the EBNF description of a component. As previously mentioned, this description is used as a template from both the component developer and the reuser. The developer's motivation to provide this information in the best possible way is to increase the chances and frequency of successful reuses and the reuser needs to specify this information so as to be able to search and find the best possible alternatives for integration. One may observe that component properties descriptions will have to present some differences in the information provided from the two types of users.

Table 1. Profile of a component in EBNF form.

DIGIT ⇐ 0 | 1 | 2 | 3 | 4 | 5 | 6 | 7 | 8 | 9 ;   INTEGER ⇐ DIGIT {DIGIT};

CHAR ⇐ A | B | C | ... |W | a | b | c | ... | W | ! | @ | # | ... ;   STRING ⇐ CHAR {CHAR} ;

Variable_type ⇐ CHAR | INTEGER | ... ;   Variable_name ⇐ STRING

Primary_Type ⇐ ' Input ' | ' Output ' | ' Security ' | ' Multimedia ' | ' Networking ' | ' GUI ' | ... ;

Secondary_Type ⇐ ' Authentication ' | ' Data processing ' | ' Video ' | ' Audio ' | ' File access ' | ' Printing ' | ... ;

Details_Description ⇐ CHAR { CHAR } ;

Min_Max_Type ⇐ 'Minimize ' | 'Maximize' |

Required_Type ⇐ ' CONSTRAINT ' | ' DESIRED ' |

Service ⇐ ' S ' INTEGER Primary_Type, Secondary_Type { Details_Description } Required_Type ;

Service_List ⇐ Service { Service }

Operator ⇐ ' exists ' | ' implies ' | ' equals ' | ' greater than ' | ' less than ' | ...

Condition ⇐ Variable_Name Operator { Value } { Variable }

Precondition ⇐ Condition { Condition }; (* IF THESE ARE PROVIDED BY DEVELOPER/VENDOR *)

Postcondition ⇐ Condition { Condition }; (* IF THESE ARE PROVIDED BY DEVELOPER/VENDOR *)

Invariants ⇐ Condition { Condition }; (* IF THESE ARE PROVIDED BY DEVELOPER/ DEVELOPER/VENDOR *)

Exceptions ⇐ Condition { Details_Description } { Exceptions }; (* IF THESE ARE PROVIDED BY DEVELOPER/VENDOR *)

Method ⇐ ' M ' INTEGER { Variable Variable_Type } { Precondition } { Postcondition } { Invariant } { Exception } ; (* IF THESE ARE PROVIDED BY COMPONENT DEVELOPER/VENDOR *)

(* ==== INTERFACING ====== *)

Service_analysis ⇐ ' Service ' INTEGER ' : ' ' Method ' INTEGER ' : ' STRING Method { Method } ;

(* ==== NON-FUNCTIONAL PROPERTIES ======= *)

Performance_indicators ⇐ [' Response time ' (INTEGER) Min_Max_Type Required_Type | ' Concurrent users ' (INTEGER) Min_Max_Type Required_Type | ' Records accessed ' (INTEGER) Min_Max_Type Required_Type | ...] { Performance_indicators } ;

Resource_requirements ⇐ [' memory utilization ' (INTEGER) Min_Max_Type Required_Type | ' CPU reqs ' (INTEGER) Min_Max_Type Required_Type | ...] { Resource_requirements } ;

Quality_features ⇐ [' Availability ' (INTEGER) Min_Max_Type Required_Type | ' Reliability ' (INTEGER) Min_Max_Type Required_Type | ...] { Quality_features }

...

(* ==== END OF NON-FUNCTIONAL PROPERTIES; NEW ITEMS MAY BE ADDED HERE ======= *)

(Continued)

```
(* ==== REUSABILITY PROPERTIES ======= *)
Application_domain ⇐ ' Medical ' Required_Type | ' Financial ' Required_Type | '
       Business ' Required_Type | ... {Application_domain} ;
Programming_language ⇐ ' C '  Required_Type | ' C++ ' Required_Type | ' Java '
       Required_Type | ' VB ' Required_Type | ... ; { Programming_language}
Operating_systems ⇐ ' Windows ' Required_Type | ' Linux ' Required_Type | ' Unix '
       Required_Type | ' IOS ' Required_Type | ' Android' Required_Type | ...   {
       Operating_systems } ;
Openness ⇐ ' black ' Required_Type | ' glass ' Required_Type | ' grey ' Required_Type | '
       white ' Required_Type;
Price ⇐ INTEGER ;
Development_info ⇐ STRING; Developer ⇐ STRING; Version ⇐ STRING; (* IF THESE
       ARE PROVIDED BY DEVELOPER/VENDOR *)
Protocols_Standards ⇐ [ '  JMS/Websphere ' Required_Type | ' DDS/NDDS '
                Required_Type | ' CORBA/ACE TAO ' Required_Type | ' POSIX '
                Required_Type | ' SNMP ' Required_Type |... { Protocols_Standards
                }];
Documentation ⇐ [ ' Manuals ' Required_Type | ' Test cases ' Required_Type | ... ] ; (* IF
       THESE ARE PROVIDED BY DEVELOPER/VENDOR *)
...

(* ==== END OF REUSABILITY PROPERTIES; NEW ITEMS MAY BE ADDED HERE
====== *)


SPECIFICATIONS PROFILE :
     'Specifications Profile ' STRING ;  'Descriptive title ' STRING ;
     'Functional Properties :' Service_List ;
     'Interfacing :' Service_analysis { Service_analysis };
     'Non-functional Properties :' Performance_indicators ;   Resource_requirements;
Quality_features ; ...
     'Reusability   Properties   :'   Application_domain;      Programming_language;
                     Operating_systems;        Openness;        Price;
                     Protocols_Standards;  Documentation ; ...
```

These differences are denoted in the comment lines (text in green which starts and ends with the symbol '*') and refer mostly to information about contracts, developer details and documentation, which are not among the key information that reusers would need to define when searching for components, and they rather constitute peripheral component information from the reusability property descriptions. A key point here is the ease of extensibility of the profile presented in 1. We distinguish two types of expansion, horizontal and vertical. The horizontal expansion is realized by adding new values at the end of certain properties where applicable. This is indicated by the ellipsis (i.e., the punctuation mark consisting of three dots) after the last property value, for example after 'GUI' for Primary Type. The vertical expansion is similarly depicted in two specific parts of Table 1, namely the non-functional and the reusability properties, and it may be achieved by adding any new properties expressing them in the proper EBNF format and by modifying the parsing module so that it transforms the new property elements to the correct instances of the revised ontology scheme. This feature is not yet automatically supported; it is supported conceptually and it is left as part of our future work on the supporting software tool.

While reading the profile from top to bottom, the reuser finds the definitions used for the component items in the template. The reuser starts by filling-in this information, giving a name and selecting a list of (one or more) services the component is required to offer. Each service is defined by a primary functionality type, a secondary informative type and thirdly, an optional description. Primary types include general functionality offered, like I/O, security and networking, while the secondary type explicitly expresses the kind of function it executes, like authentication, video streaming, audio processing etc. For example, a service could be [*Security*, *Login Authentication*]. If a service is sought for, then the reuser assigns a *Requirement* value, either *Constraint*, which means it is absolutely necessary and a candidate component is rejected if it does not offer it, or *Desired*, which simply adds points to the suitability value of a candidate component. Interfacing information comes next where each service is decomposed into the various methods that implement its logic; a method is analyzed to its constituent parts of *Pre-conditions*, *Post-conditions*, *Invariants* and *Exceptions* (if any). This piece of information can be provided by the component developer. Non-functional requirements or properties are defined next by the reuser and developer (creator) respectively, the former denoting what the search is for (and can be either defined as mandatory or desired), and the latter denoting what the component has to offer. Finally, both the reuser and the developer fill-in general information useful for reusability purposes (application domain, programming language, OS etc.) with the reuser again denoting the level to which a certain feature is required (defined as mandatory or optional). It should also be mentioned that certain features in the sought profile may be assigned to specific values along with a characterization as to whether this feature should be minimized (i.e., the value denotes an upper acceptable threshold) or maximized (i.e., the value denotes a lower acceptable threshold) in the suitable components offered. For example, if response time should be confined under 15 s, then next to that performance indicator the values (15, *minimize*) should be entered.

3.3 Level 3: Analysis Layer

3.3.1 Dedicated CBSE Ontology

A dedicated CBSE ontology is developed to reflect development issues based on the reusability of components. The ontology essentially addresses the same property axes and adheres to the same semantic rules of the component profile so that an automatic transformation of the latter to instances of the ontology is feasible. Figure 2 depicts the largest part of the ontology; some details have been intentionally left out to make the graphical representation more readable. A component is fully described by instances of the ontology items and can therefore be used as the basis for the matching process that is described next. This process works at the level of the ontology tree rather than the

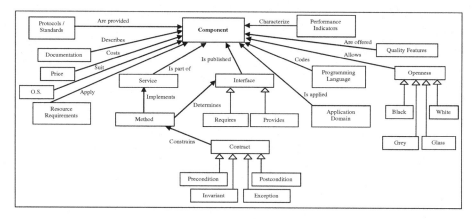

Fig. 2. The CBSE ontology based on three axes: (i) Functionality, (ii) Non-functional, and (iii) Reusability properties.

textual descriptions of the profile as comparison between required and available components is easier and more profound, both computationally and graphically (visually).

3.3.2 Matching Process

The matching process defined in this work was inspired by considering the strengths and weaknesses of similar approaches identified in the relevant literature. Some researchers focus on components retrieval issues and propose different methods for description processing, like simple string (e.g., Mili et al. [6]), signature matching (e.g., Zaremsky and Wing [21]) and behavioural matching (e.g., Zaremsky and Wing, [7]). The proposed approach may be considered as a hybrid method comprising string and behavioral matching but in a different manner than the aforementioned studies.

More specifically, the cornerstone of the matching process is a dedicated parser which identifies parts of the profile (functional and non-functional behavior, interfaces, performance indicators, etc.) and translates them into the CBSE ontology. The parser first checks whether the profile is properly described in the context and semantics of the structure presented in Table 1 using the ANTLR framework. Once successful, the parser proceeds with recognizing the parts of the profile and building the ontology tree of instances following the algorithm presented in Fig. 3. The parser essentially builds ontology tree instances which describe the requested and the available components. The next step is the matching of properties between ontology items. The tree instance of the required component is projected on top of all other candidates assessing the level of requirements' fulfilment in multiple stages. The first stage requires that all constraints are satisfied. In this case, the list of services sought must be at least a subset of the services offered. The second stage, executed once all constraints are satisfied, calculates the level of suitability of each candidate component. A demonstration example for this stage is given in the first part of the experimental section.

A requested component P_r defines in its profile a set of constraints K that must be satisfied including number and type of services, performance and quality factors, resource requirements, protocols/standards and documentation. The matching between the discrete items in the profile of P_r and those of a candidate component P_c is determined through the following rules:

Rule (A): P_c is a *suitable* candidate for P_r if and only if every item $k \in K$ is satisfied by the corresponding item in P_c. We denote this by $P_c \equiv candP_r$.

Rule (B): P_c is an exact match of P_r if and only if every item l defined in P_r is offered by P_c. We denote this by $P_c \equiv P_r$.

Clearly rule (B) subsumes rule (A). The level of suitability is calculated for each suitable candidate as the ratio of matched profile items required (i.e. that are actually

```
Let Method(i)=set of methods implementing Service i
Trace 'Specification Profile' store STRING Name
Create Node Name
Start Parsing
   Trace 'Service List'
   Read N Services
   Trace 'Interfacing'
   For i=1 to N
   { Create Instance of Service i under node Name
      For each method j ∈ Method(i) do
         { Create Method j as node attached to Service i
           Determine Arguments A of Method j
           Create A as part of Interface node
           Determine Contracts for A and j's logic
           Create Preconditions, Post conditions, Invari-
ants, Exceptions
                 for j
         }
   }
   Trace 'Non-functional Properties'
   Read NOT_NULL non-functional properties
   For all NOT_NULL non-functional properties do
   Create Instances Performance indicators, Resource re-
quirements,
        Quality features
   Trace 'Reusability Properties'
   Read NOT_NULL reusability properties
   For all NOT_NULL reusability properties do
      Create Instances Application domain, Programming
language,
           Operating systems, Openness, Price, Protocols
and Standards,
           Documentation
End Parsing
```

Fig. 3. Algorithmic approach for the parsing process and ontology transformation.

offered by the candidate component) to the total items outlined in P_r. More specifically, a dissimilarity value is calculated which indicates, in case of multiple suitable candidates, which one is closer to what has been requested.

We distinguish two types of properties, one of binary type (offered 'yes'/'no') and one of numerical type (e.g., price, response time). Matching properties of the former type presumes that all constraints are by default satisfied and its level is calculated simply by following the equations described hereafter.

The binary dissimilarity is calculated as:

$$R_{bin} = \frac{1}{M} \sum_{i=1}^{M} \delta_{i,c,r} \qquad (1)$$

where

$$\delta_{i,c,r} = \begin{cases} 0, & \text{if property } i \text{ required in } P_r \text{ is offered by } P_c \\ 1, & \text{if property } i \text{ required in } P_r \text{ is not offered by } P_c \end{cases} \qquad (2)$$

and M the number of binary properties defined in Pr.

The numerical type is associated with minimum and maximum acceptable values. Therefore, matching of numerical properties is essentially another assessment of dissimilarity, which is performed by measuring how far from the optimal value (either maximum or minimum) lies the offered property value. We distinguish two cases:

(i) The property is mandatory (constraint). The candidates in this case satisfy the lower or upper bound of the defined feature value. Therefore, the distance between the values of the required and offered components is calculated by:

$$dC_{i,MAX} = \frac{max_{v_i} - v_i}{max_{v_i} - min_{v_i}} \qquad (3)$$

for feature value maximization, and

$$dC_{i,MIN} = \frac{v_i - min_{v_i}}{max_{v_i} - min_{v_i}} \qquad (4)$$

for minimization, while the total numerical dissimilarity for the constraints is calculated as:

$$R_{num,const} = \frac{1}{T} \sum_{i=1}^{T} dC_{i,\{MAX,MIN\}} \qquad (5)$$

(ii) The property is, not mandatory, but desired. In this case some of the values of the candidates satisfy the bounds defined in the desired components and some do not. Therefore, the distance between the desired property values v_d and the values offered by the candidate components v_i is calculated by:

$$dD_{i,MAX} = 1 + \frac{v_d - v_i}{max_{v_i, v_d}} \tag{6}$$

$$dD_{i,MIN} = 1 - \frac{v_d - v_i}{max_{v_i, v_d}} \tag{7}$$

for feature value maximization and minimization respectively. The total numerical dissimilarity for the desired features is then calculated as:

$$R_{num,des} = \frac{1}{M} \sum_{i=1}^{M} dD_{i,\{MAX,MIN\}}. \tag{8}$$

In the above equations, max_{v_i, v_d} is the maximum value of the property between all candidates and the desired component, while T and M are the numbers of numerical properties that are mandatory and desired respectively.

The total value for the numerical properties is:

$$R_{num} = \frac{R_{num,const} + R_{num,des}}{2} \tag{9}$$

The total dissimilarity value for a suitable candidate component is then calculated as:

$$R_{tot} = \frac{R_{bin} + R_{num}}{2} \tag{10}$$

It is clear from the above that the closer the dissimilarity value to zero the better the suitability level of a component. The recommendation task ranks suitable components in ascending order of dissimilarity and suggests the top n candidates.

4   Experimental Evaluation

A series of experiments was designed and executed so that the usefulness, applicability, effectiveness and efficiency of the proposed CBSE reusability framework are assessed. Specifically, two sequential experimental stages were followed. The first stage comprised of searching and retrieving various components based on a set of properties, while the second involved investigating targeted reusability development activities and assessed in addition scalability. The second stage of experiments is considered a significant extension of the first, as it was considerably longer, in-depth and comprises of actual developments activities to implement a simple application with reuse and through the use of the proposed CBSE framework. Both experimental stages were used as feedback (based on the evaluation obtained) for the overall improvement of the proposed framework.

The experimental stages were carried out in total by 25 subjects, 20 of which were graduate (master level) students at the Cyprus University of Technology and the remaining 5 were software practitioners. The students hold an undergraduate degree in Computer Science and/or Engineering that included courses in Software Engineering (SE) and at the time of the experimentation they followed an advanced SE course with emphasis on CBSE and reusability. The practitioners consisted of software developers working in the industry, 3 of which extensively making use of component reuse for the last 5 years and 2 of which are responsible for producing components for internal reuse in their company for the last 3 years.

4.1   Experimental Stage A'

In the first experimental stage (A'), all subjects underwent a short period of training (approximately 2 h) on the proposed CBSE reuse framework focusing mostly on the profiling scheme and the semi-formal structures of the natural language used. The target was to provide a first evaluation of the usefulness, applicability, effectiveness and efficiency of the framework.

The experiments conducted thus aimed at addressing the following four main questions regarding the proposed framework: (**Q1**) *How easy and straightforward is it for locating appropriate components?* The question mainly focuses on the ease of use, level of understandability and effective utilization of functional, non-functional and reusability properties to seek and locate candidate components sought for. (**Q2**) *How "complete" is the process for locating appropriate components?* Answering this question will essentially define whether there is enough information supported from the framework or if there exist key information that a reuser would like to search for and is yet not supported. The word complete appears in quotes as completeness is not a property that may easily be quantified. Nevertheless, for the purposes of this evaluation, we assume that completeness denotes the level to which the proposed process supports the profiling (and therefore the processing) of all possible sources of information describing component properties. (**Q3**) *How accurate are the results (i.e., the recommended components)?* This question refers to the quality of the results in terms of correctness and specifies the end-user's (the reuser in our case) satisfaction level. (**Q4**) *What is the efficiency of the process in terms of time/effort required by reusers to locate and retrieve the components they need?* This question refers to the quality of the results in terms of efficiency and effort required to spend and again relates to the reuser satisfaction levels.

A total of 100 synthetic components were randomly generated with the help of the practitioners who inspected the elements produced and suggested corrections so as to correspond to realistic cases and resembling real-world components. The components created were divided into 7 major categories: Login (10), Calendar (10), Address Book (10), Calculator (10), Task/Notes Manager (10), Clock (10) and GUI Widgets (Wallworks (15), Window Style (15), Background/Fonts Style (10)). The multiple instances of the synthetic components for each category differed on attributes such as programming language, OS, openness, protocols/standards and documentation, as well as on the performance indicators.

The EBNF profile of each component was then created, followed by its transformation into an ontology instance of the component tree. Each subject was then asked to perform 10 different searches using a simple form (see Fig. 4) where basically they inputted the desired functionality (primary, secondary), the values for certain performance indicators and their level of requirement (mandatory or desired). This information was also transformed in EBNF and then the ontology tree instance of the search item (component) was also created. Each search tree instance was then automatically matched against the available component instances in the repository. As this process is essentially an item-to-item matching of the tree instances, the classic metrics of precision and recall are not applicable here since the components retrieved were only those that satisfied all constraints for functionality and the rest of the features. Therefore, the candidate components returned were only the suitable ones which then competed on the basis of satisfying the rest of the properties sought for, calculating the level of suitability, as defined in Eq. (10).

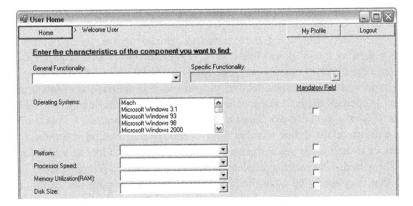

Fig. 4. Excerpt of the component search form.

Table 2 shows details of the experimental process while one of the reusers was searching for a Task Manager component. Components' functionality and features appear in the first column, preferences for the required component in the right most column and the five (retrieved) candidates in the columns in between. The lower part of this table lists the figures for the dissimilarity calculation described in Eqs. (1)–(10). The figures clearly suggest that Component #2 is the candidate that best satisfies the search preferences, followed by Components #1, #4 and #5, that have similar characteristics to each other.

This process was executed 10 times by each subject for each component category and the results were gathered and assessed qualitatively under the four main questions (Q1–Q4), described in the beginning of the present section, related to ease of use, completeness, accuracy and efficiency of the process and the results obtained. At the end, the participants in the experimental study were asked to rate the approach on a five-point Likert scale ranging from 1-Very Low to 5-Very High to obtain the focal point of each question.

The findings of the experimental results (Stage A') suggested the following with respect to the questions:

Table 2. Candidates' evaluation when seeking for a Task Manager component (C denotes constraint and D desired).

Task Manager	1	2	3	4	5	SEARCH FOR
Service Primary	input	input	input	input	input	Input (C)
Service Secondary	Data processing	Data processing	Data processing	Data processing	Data processing	Data processing (C)
Response Time (sec) (min)	10	12	*8*	*8*	9	12 (C)
Concurrent Users (max)	50	*100*	40	80	*100*	20 (C)
Memory utilization (KB) (min)	2	3	4	*1*	2	4 (C)
Total task supported (max)	200	1800	700	1900	*2000*	1500 (D)
Download history time (sec) (min)	6	8	22	*4*	20	18 (D)
Reliability (max)	90	*95*	92	93	90	90 (C)
Availability (max)	95	98	97	*99*	96	95 (C)
Application domain	ANY	ANY	ANY	ANY	ANY	ANY (C)
Programming language	C/C++	C/C++	Java	C/C++	.NET	C/C++ (D)
Operating systems	Windows	Windows	Windows Android	Windows Linux	Windows	Windows (C)
Openness	white	white	black	grey	white	White (D)
Documentation	Manual, Test Cases, Code, Comments, Design doc	Code, Comments, Design doc	Manual, Test Cases	Manual, Test Cases	Manual, Test Cases, Code, Comments	Code (D), Comments (D), Design doc (D)
Evaluation						
R_{bin}	0	0	0,714286	0,571429	0,285714	
R_{num}	0,8244589	0,47316	0,811688	0,270996	0,59632	
R_{tot}	**0,4122294**	**0,23658**	**0,762987**	**0,421212**	**0,441017**	

(Q1) *How Easy and Straightforward is it for Locating Appropriate Components?* All subjects agreed that the method was quite easy to follow once trained, with a median rating of 4 (High). The training was mentioned that it was not too difficult to go through and in terms of effort required it was acceptable. It is even easier to carry out the search with the use of the dedicated supporting tool, as some of the subjects stated; after their first few searches they felt quite comfortable with the approach and faced no problems in using it.

(Q2) *How "Complete" is the Process for Locating Appropriate Components?* Completeness was the feature that brought to light some questioning. Initial values by students rated this aspect with 4 (High), while practitioners gave the value of 2 (Low). Some follow-up questions in the interviews we conducted the difference was obvious where it originated from. Practitioners, as they are more experienced with the variability of components in the real-world, emphasized that the approach should be more flexible and allow for more metrics and properties to take part in the profiling of a component. After a round of discussions, through which the open nature of the profile scheme for a component was explained and exemplified, and emphasis was given on how new properties may be inserted to satisfy further needs, practitioners were asked to rate again the question. They recognized that extensibility was just a matter of profile design and thus the current one could be extended. The approach is able to cover any possible features or properties a reuser may seek, as long as the structured form followed for describing components encompasses these items. Therefore, practitioners agreed that the approach offers great flexibility in this respect and rated again completeness giving a median value of 4 (High).

(Q3)   *How Accurate are the Results (i.e., the Recommended Components)?* The components retrieved by the proposed approach were found suitable and among the top alternatives for all cases. It was also observed that the components returned as best candidates did not always possess the optimal numerical values in the corresponding properties sought, that is, the best values for the specific features (i.e., lowest time performance); they rather exhibited a good balance between numerical properties and also presented good ratings for the binary properties. This is clear in Table 2 where the optimal numerical values offered by the suitable components are marked in boldface and italic; it is evident that Component #4 holds the majority of optimal numerical values, yet it is not among the top 2.

(Q4)   *What is the Efficiency of the Process in Terms of Time/Effort Required by Reusers to Locate and Retrieve the Components They Need?* The total time and effort spent to locate the appropriate components was quite limited, rated as 2 (Low) being confined to the actions required to describe the properties of the components sought. Automation of the whole process for returning appropriate components back to the reuser was acknowledged to have a decisive positive effect on the total time that had to be devoted, as stated from the practitioners.

The results from the first experimental stage, and especially Q3, gave birth, to a possible modification/extension of the approach. This modification included an additional implementation and application of a priority or weighting scheme for the framework properties. With this scheme the reuser will be able to define the properties considered as more significant than the rest and therefore, change the assessment of candidate components to take this significance into account too, along with the rest aforementioned similarity factors. This modification is explained further in Experimental Stage B' (Subsect. 4.2).

4.2   Experimental Stage B'

With similar experimental design, the second experimental stage was conducted. During the second experimental stage (B'), the proposed CBSE reusability framework was used by the reusers with the target to implement a small-scale software application and assess in addition scalability.

The same group of subjects, were asked to make use of the proposed framework and locate appropriate components that can be reused. They were given the following instructions. Develop a software Web application that supports the following:

- Multiple users
- User authentication mechanisms
- Management of client records (insert, update, delete)
- Management of product records (insert, update, delete)

- Order placement for purchasing products (search and browse products, place in or remove from shopping cart products)
- Card payment processing
- Logistics support (issue invoices, audit trails).

The target of the second experimental stage was twofold: First, to expand the use of the framework to a larger and functionally demanding experimental setup. The setup is more realistic, includes complex development tasks and comes across to integration issues for CBSE (resulting from reusing of existing components, such as the issue of synthesis and compatibility of individual parts). Second, to assess scalability and efficiency of the approach when scaling up complexity, handling at the same time challenges raised from the previous experimental stage.

As such, to meet the first target the approach was slightly extended at the Recommendation level so as to include a software module that performs checks to detect profound issues affecting compatibility, like the programming language or the operating system, and suggest a different ranking of the appropriate components based on the expected extra costs (time/effort) arising from such issues. This kind of recommendations was provided only in cases where the possible incompatibilities were associated with properties that were not declared as constraints.

To meet the second target, the framework was extended with the addition of a new element that provides a mechanism that allows a reuser to define varying degrees of significance among the desired properties. A weighting scheme was therefore applied during the process of describing the properties of the component sought using a Likert scale of 3 values indicating 1-low, 2-medium and 3-high level of significance.

A pool of 350 synthetic components was created and made available through a server. Each functional characteristic was satisfied by at least 5 generated components with varying properties (e.g., resource requirements, performance indicators, programming language, etc.). The reuser was handed a randomly generated list of properties (constraints and desired ones) to guide the selection of components that were appropriate for each case and was left free to interact with the system to set their priorities as regards the significance of the component features and then locate the most suitable ones for the functional tasks described above. As with the previous stage, each reuser was given access to the server using a simple GUI for searching and retrieving components based on the concepts of the proposed approach, with search properties being defined using primarily pull down menus, drop-down lists and check-boxes (Fig. 4). Then, these property definitions were automatically transformed to their EBNF counterparts and corresponding ontology notions with no extra effort or visibility on behalf of the reuser.

The experimental stage B' spanned approximately one week's time, by the end of which the experiences obtained were shared among all participants in a closed session and the framework was rated once again. The results of the experiment were assessed in a similar way to the previous one:

(Q1) *How Easy and Straightforward is it for Locating Appropriate Components?* Subjects answered that even with performing a wider-scope task the approach is still quite easy and straightforward. They rated it with a median rating of 4 (High). A threat to the validation of this result is however the fact that subjects were not the first time to have worked with the tool. The large size of the application that required the search of multiple components and the increasing complexity of the development task, minimizes the effect of this threat.

(Q2)   *How "Complete" is the Process for Locating Appropriate Components?* The extension of the framework to accommodate new values for fixed (pre-defined) properties as well as new types of properties was received positively by the experiment participants. They gave a median rating of 4 (High). A comment received during the discussions was that even if the second experimental process the subjects undertook is more realistic to the real working conditions in terms of complexity, the type of developments they might face in the future would definitely contribute to the level of richness of the properties, and thus enhance further the overall completeness levels.

(Q3)   *How Accurate are the Results (i.e., the Recommended Components)?* The accuracy of the returned components was rated with a median rating 2 (Low). This was due to the random nature of the generated components, as well as of the list of properties each participant was supplied with, i.e., there were cases where the properties sought were not perfectly aligned between them. For example, the use of a component for displaying the list of products had quite short response time than that of the component inserting a product in the shopping cart. Therefore, participants discussed for a more realistic generation of component properties within the framework. Nevertheless, everybody agreed that this "anomaly" did not violate the outcome of the experimental process as at this stage what was important was to assess the applicability of the approach to more complicated situations. Thus the scalability issue of the framework even if not evaluated explicitly, was considered promising. In addition, the accuracy potential of the results was slightly improved with the weighting scheme applied in this experimental stage. The weighting scheme enabled reusers to narrow down the list of matches, especially in cases where the candidate components were similar or very close to each other with respect to the properties set. In addition, the recommendation module worked fairly well in the majority of the cases, although some participants pointed out that its use was not always helpful. There were cases where the incompatibility of the programming platforms in which the components were built hindered their composition (or at least recommended them not to be integrated), but their combination was by far better than that of other, that appeared as more compatible ones. This observation, combined with the fact that if a wrapper could easily be developed to handle the incompatibility issues, led to the conclusion that the recommendation module should be further enhanced with more sophisticated ways of suggesting the use or not of specific types of components. Nevertheless, this was already a known "weakness" of the recommendation engine, as its purpose was just to demonstrate how its use may offer enhanced support to the selection of similar components, something which was acknowledged by all participants.

(Q4)   *What is the efficiency of the process in terms of time/effort required by reusers to locate and retrieve the components they need?*

Overall, the efficiency was found again high (median value was 4), despite the fact that the search process was multifaceted compared to experimental stage A'. Indeed the results confirmed that the size of the application under development did not add significantly to the complexity of the way the approach was used, but rather affected the time for locating all component instances for each case as expected.

5 Conclusions

This work addressed a specific topic in the area of component based software engineering and more specifically the issue of automatic search and retrieval of software components by matching specifications. A new CBSE reusability framework was proposed which comprises different layers for describing, analyzing, locating and assessing the appropriateness of available components.

The work focused on the activities of the matching process between required and offered properties. This process initially produces a special form of natural-language-based profile written in EBNF, the latter being highly descriptive, while it allows formally proving key properties and validating the semantics. The profile describes three different categories of components' properties, that is, functional, non-functional and general reusability properties. A specially designed module parses the profile, recognizes certain sections and elements, and then translates them into instances of a special form of component-based ontology developed to support the component specification matching activities. Using this profile developers/vendors of components offer details of what they have to offer to potential reusers who use the profile to describe what they look for using the same EBNF notation. The profiles are transformed into ontology trees, something that enables faster comparison between characteristics as this commences at the level of ontology instances. The matching process assesses if hard constraints are violated (i.e., absolutely necessary properties required are not offered by candidates) and if not, it calculates a dissimilarity metric that dictates the level of appropriateness of components for possible integration.

A two stage experimental process was followed, the first focusing on demonstrating and evaluating the applicability of the proposed approach, while the second further investigated efficiency and scalability issues through a more complicated reuse context. The experiments provided strong evidences that the proposed approach is accurate, complete and efficient, and therefore it may be regarded as suitable for adoption in the everyday practice of software reuse.

The framework introduced in this work may be conceived as a promising new idea with ample room for extensions and enhancements. Our future work will include several research steps, some of which are outlined here: First of all, a more thorough experimentation will be carried out to validate the applicability and efficacy of the proposed framework. To this end, a series of experiments will be conducted utilizing open source components. Second, the retrieval parts will be enhanced by optimization techniques (e.g., evolutionary algorithms) for automating the process of locating candidate components. Finally, the dedicated software tool that supports the whole framework will be extended with capabilities for EBNF editing and ANTLR parsing during the construction of component profiles, as well as graphical representation and visual inspection/comparison of ontology tree instances.

Acknowledgement. The work is partially supported by a research grant for the ORION project (reference number 20140218) from The Knowledge Foundation in Sweden.

References

1. Vale, T., Crnkovic, I., de Almeida, E.S., da Mota Silveira Neto, P.A., Cerqueira Cavalcanti, Y., de Lemos Meira, S.R.: Twenty-eight years of component-based software engineering. J. Syst. Softw., **111**, 128–148 (2016). ISSN 0164-1212. http://dx.doi.org/10.1016/j.jss.2015.09.019
2. Szyperski, C.: Component Software: beyond object-oriented programming, 2nd ed., Addison Wesley, Essex, England (2002)
3. Mili, H., Mili, A., Yacoub, S., Addy, E.: Reuse based software engineering: techniques, organization, and measurement. Wiley-Blackwell, New Jersey (2002)
4. Barn, B., Brown, A.W.: Methods and tools for component based development. In: Proceedings of IEEE Technology of Object-Oriented Languages (TOOLS 1998) (1998)
5. Andreou, A.S., Papatheocharous, P.: Automatic matching of software component requirements using semi-formal specifications and a CBSE ontology. In: Proceedings of the 10th International Conference on Evaluation of Novel Approaches to Software (Barcelona, Spain, April 29–30) (2015)
6. Mili, H., Radai, R., Weigang, W., Strickland, K., Boldyreff, C., Olsen, L., Witt, J., Heger, J., Scherr, W., Elzer, P.: Practitioner and SoftClass: a comparative study of two software reuse research projects. J. Syst. Softw. **25**(2), 147–170 (1994)
7. Zaremski, A.M., Wing, J.M.: Specifications matching of software components. ACM T Softw. Eng. Meth. **6**(4), 333–369 (1997)
8. Chung, L., Cooper, K.: Matching, ranking, and selecting components: a COTS-aware requirements engineering and software architecting approach. In: Proceedings of the International Workshop on Models and Processes for the Evaluation of COTS Components at 26th International Conference on Software Engineering, (Edinburgh, Scotland, UK, May 23–28, 2004). ICSE, pp. 41–44 (2004)
9. Iribarne, L., Troya, J.M., Vallecillo, A.: Selecting software components with multiple interfaces. In: Proceedings of the 28th Euromicro Conference (Dortmund, Germany, September 4–6, 2002). EUROMICRO 2002, pp. 26–32. IEEE Computer Society Press (2002)
10. Yessad, L., Boufaida, Z.: A QoS ontology-based component selection. Int. J. Soft Comput. (IJSC) **2**(3), 16–30 (2011). doi:10.5121/ijsc.2011.2302
11. Pahl, C.: An ontology for software component matching. Int. J. Softw. Tools Technol. Trans. **9**(2), 169–178 (2007)
12. Yan, W., Rousselot, F., Zanni-Merk, C.: Component retrieval based on ontology and graph patterns matching. J. Inf. Comput. Sci. **7**(4), 893–900 (2010)
13. Kluge, R., Hering, T., Belter, R., Franczyk, B.: An approach for matching functional business requirements to standard application software packages via ontology. In: Proceedings of the 32nd Annual IEEE International Computer Software and Applications Conference (Turku, Finland, July 28 - August 1, 2008). COMPSAC 2008, 1017–1022 (2008). doi:10.1109/COMPSAC.2008.147

14. Seedorf, S., Schader, M.: Towards an enterprise software component ontology. In: Proceedings of the 17th Americas Conference on Information Systems (Detroit, Michigan, August 4–7, 2011) AMCIS (2011)
15. Alnusair, A., Zhao, T.: Component search and reuse: An ontology-based approach. In: Proceedings of the IEEE International Conference on Information Reuse and Integration (Las Vegas, USA, August 4–6, 2010). IRI2010, pp. 258–261 (2010)
16. ISO/IEC/IEEE 24765:2010, 2010, Systems and software engineering - Vocabulary, ISO/IEC/IEEE 24765:2010
17. Czajkowski, K., Foster, I., Kesselman, C., Sander, V., Tuecke, S.: SNAP: A protocol for negotiating service level agreements and coordinating resource management in distributed systems. Job scheduling strategies for parallel processing, pp. 153–183. Springer, Berlin Heidelberg (2002)
18. Emeakaroha, V.C., Brandic, I., Maurer, M., Dustdar, S.: Low level metrics to high level SLAs-LoM2HiS framework: Bridging the gap between monitored metrics and SLA parameters in cloud environments. In: Proceedings of the International Conference on High Performance Computing and Simulation (HPCS), pp. 48–54. IEEE (2010)
19. Mili, H., Ah-Ki, E., Godin, R., Mcheick, H.: An experiment in software component retrieval. Inf. Softw. Technol. **45**(10), 633–649 (2003)
20. Paschke, A., Schnappinger-Gerull, E.: A categorization scheme for SLA metrics. Serv. Oriented Electron. Commer. **80**, 25–40 (2006)
21. Zaremski, A.M., Wing, J.M.: Signature matching: A key to reuse. ACM **18**(5), 182–190 (1993)

Helping Program Comprehension of Large Software Systems by Identifying Their Most Important Classes

Ioana Şora[1($\boxtimes$)]

Department of Computer and Software Engineering,
University Politehnica of Timisoara, Timisoara, Romania
ioana.sora@cs.upt.ro

Abstract. An essential prerequisite before engaging in any maintenance activities of complex software systems is the good comprehension of the existing code. Program comprehension is supported by documentation, which can be either developer documentation or documentation obtained by reverse engineering. In both cases, but especially in the case of reverse engineered documentation, this means a large amount of detailed documents that have to be carefully studied. Processing such large and detailed information can be made easier if there is an executive summary - a short document pointing to the most important elements of the system.

In our work we propose a tool to automatically extract such a summary, by identifying the most important classes of the system. Our approach consists of modeling the static dependencies of the system as a graph and applying a graph ranking algorithm. How we build the dependency graph is the key for the success of the approach. We empirically determine how different dependency types should be taken into account in building the system graph. The proposed approach has been validated by experiments on a set of open source real systems.

Keywords: Reverse engineering · Program comprehension · Key classes · Recommender tool

1 Introduction

Program comprehension [1] is an important software engineering activity, which is necessary to facilitate reuse, maintenance, reengineering or extension of existing software systems.

In the case of large software systems, program comprehension has to deal with the huge amount of code that implements it. When starting with the study of an unknown system, software engineers are overwhelmed by the amount of information, which makes it difficult to filter out the important elements from a lot of details.

Documentation can help with program comprehension. Assuming that the documentation is up-to-date, there are still additional requirements related to the

© Springer International Publishing Switzerland 2016
L.A. Maciaszek and J. Filipe (Eds.): ENASE 2015, CCIS 599, pp. 122–140, 2016.
DOI: 10.1007/978-3-319-30243-0_7

contents of the documentation such that it is effective for facilitating the early stages of work: very useful are documents such as architectural overviews, or describing what is called the core of the system. Detailed and scattered implementation documentation is of little use, as are large class diagrams that are reverse engineered from the code. This has been confirmed by the experiments described in [2], where most subjects did not appreciate reverse engineered diagrams to be helpful due to the information overload in these class diagrams.

In our work we help program comprehension of object oriented software systems by identifying their most important classes [3], [4]. This gives a set of good starting pointers for studying the system. We consider that the importance of a class is given by the amount and types of interactions it has with other classes. Thus, a natural approach of identifying the most important classes is based on ranking them with a graph-ranking algorithm.

In this work we adapt PageRank [5] to use it for the purpose of ranking classes of software systems according to their importance for the design of the system. The key here for obtaining a ranking which is indeed effective for the goal of program comprehension is to use an adequate graph model of the system.

Section 2 describes our approach of modeling the structure of software systems by static dependencies and the way we use this for identifying the most important classes of the system. We define two parameters of the graph model, given by the weights of dependency types and dependency directions. Section 3 presents experimental results. We do first an empirical fine-tuning of the parameters of the graph model, then apply our approach to a set of relevant open-source projects. In Sect. 4 we will discuss our results and draw the conclusions of our experiments, while also comparing with related work. Section 5 draws the conclusions of this paper.

2   Ranking Classes According to Their Importance

2.1   Building the Right Model

We model the software system as a graph having as nodes classes or interfaces. If an edge exists from node A to node B, this means, in PageRanks terminology, that node A recommends node B as important. Applying the right strategy for determining where and how to place the recommendation edges is the crucial element for the effectiveness of the ranking approach.

In our model, the recommendations derive from the program dependencies identified by static analysis with help of the model extractors of the ART tool suite [6]. If A depends on B, this means both that A gives a recommendation to B but also that B gives a recommendation to A. We call the edge from A to B a *forward recommendation*, while the edge from B to A is a *back recommendation*.

The forward recommendation, resulting directly from a dependency, is obvious: a class which is used by many other classes has good chances to be an important one, representing a fundamental data or business model. But also the reverse is true: a class which is using a lot of other important classes may be an important one, such as a class containing a lot of control of the application or an important front-end class. If only the directed dependency would be considered as a recommendation, then library classes would rank very high while the classes containing the control would remain unacknowledged. Thus the reason for having back recommendations.

Recommendations may also have weights. A class is not necessarily recommending all its dependency classes with an equal number of votes. It will give more recommendation votes to those classes that offer it more services. Thus recommendation weights are derived from the type and amount of dependencies.

Static dependencies in object oriented languages are produced by various situations. There are different classifications of the mechanisms that constitute dependencies [7]. In accordance with these, we distinguish between following categories of dependencies between two classes or interfaces A and B:

- inheritance: A extends B
- realization: A implements B
- field: A has at least one member of type B
- member access: A member of B is accessed from code belonging to A
- method call: A calls a method of B. We can further distinguish if it is a static method call or a method call on a class instance. Every distinct method of B which is called is counted as a new dependency.
- parameter: A method of A has at least one parameter of type B
- return type: A method of A has the return type B
- local variable: A local variable of type B is declared in code belonging to A
- instantiation: An instance of B is code belonging to A
- cast: A type-cast to B occurs in code belonging to A

Two classes A and B can be at the same time in several dependency relationships: for example, A can have members of type B, but in the same time it can have a method with parameters of type B and overall it can call several different methods of B.

The strength of the recommendation is proportional with the strength of the dependency which takes into account both the number of dependency relationships and the types of dependency relationships between the two classes.

The strength of a dependency can be estimated using an approach based on an ordering of dependency types according to their relative importance. Establishing the relative importance of static dependency types is a subject of empirical estimation and different authors use different frameworks for this [7]. In this work, we continue to use the ordering of dependency types used previously in the context of architectural reconstruction by clustering in [8]. In summary, we take as reference for the weakest type of dependencies the local variables dependency type and assign it weight 1. On the next level of importance, level 2, we put the dependency strength given by one distinct method that is called. Usually several distinct methods of a class are called, thus these weights will sum up to a significant value. Also on level 2 are dependencies generated from creating instances. Dependencies due to parameters, return values or having a member dependency is assigned weight 3 while inheritance and realization have weights 4. We will empirically validate this assumption of dependency weights in the context of class ranking in Sect. 3.

The weight of the forward recommendation from A to B is given by the dependency strength of the cumulated dependencies from A to B. The weight of the back recommendation from B to A is a fraction F of the weight of the forward recommendation from A to B. We identified that, while a class is important if it is both used by other classes and it is also using other classes, the second argument should have a smaller weight in the global reasoning, only a fraction F of the dependency strength. We illustrate this idea with the simple example presented in Subsect. 2.2 and we also empirically investigate values for this fraction in Sect. 3.

2.2   A Simple Example

We illustrate the idea of our approach using as an example a simplified program structure with four classes A, B, C, D. Class A is the front-end component of the application, B is the main business component, C a helper, and D some utility or library class.

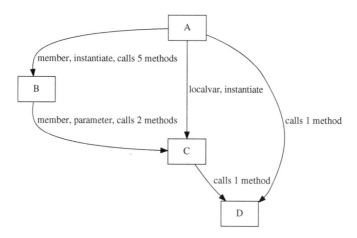

Fig. 1. Example: graph of program dependencies.

Figure 1 depicts the dependencies between the 4 classes. Class A has a member of type B, it instantiates objects of type B and calls five different methods of class B. Also, class A has a local variable of type C and instantiates an object of type C. Class B has a member of type C, has member functions with parameters of type C, and calls 2 different methods of C. Both classes A and C call one static method of class D.

We use this simple example to explain the importance of using a weighted dependency graph, taking into account the dependency strengths induced by different dependency types, and also of using back-recommendations.

In a first try, we consider the dependency graph directed and unweighted. If PageRank is applied on the directed graph of Fig. 1, without back-recommendations, we obtain the following ranking: D(0.41), C(0.29), B(0.16),

A(0.12). This ranking places the deepest classes on a top level, bringing the utility class D on the top position. The utility class D can be considered a library class with high reuse potential, however D is not the most important class of the system and not so important for program comprehension. This shows that simply applying PageRank on the directed graph defined by the dependencies is not a valid method of identifying the classes that are important for program comprehension.

In a second try, back-recommendations are included and the unweighted graph from Fig. 1 will be completed with a reverse edge for every original edge. Applying PageRank on this new graph results in a new ranking: A(0.29) C(0.29) B(0.21) D(0.21). This order brings on top two classes of medium importance (A and C), while ranking the key class B as low as the utility class D.

In a third try, we introduce weights reflecting the type and amount of dependencies, using the empirical values defined in the previous section. Following weights result: AB=15, AC=3, AD=3, BC=11, CD=2. Back-recommendations are given a fraction F of the weight of the forward recommendation. We experiment with different values for F. If F=0 (no back-recommendations) the ranking results D(0.38), C(0.3), B(0.19), A(0.11), which is wrong since it brings the utility class on top. If F=1, the ranking is B(0.36), A(0.29), C(0.24), D(0.08). If F=1/2, the ranking is B(0.34), C(0.29), A(0.24), D(0.11). These last two rankings reflect very well the situation of B being the most important class, while D plays only a small role as an utility class. A and C are of medium importance. Since this example is generic and small, we cannot argue whether A should be ranked above C or not.

More experiments on real-life systems are described in Sect. 3 and they will show that PageRank can be used as an effective means to identify key classes for program comprehension if it is applied to a correct model of recommendations. We argue that this model has to take into account both the strength of the dependencies and also include back-recommendations, with a fraction $0 < F < 1$ bringing the best results.

3   Experimental Results

3.1   Experimental Setup

In order to validate the proposed ranking tool, we apply it on a set of relevant open source systems. We run our tool that implements the ranking approach described in Sect. 2, using weighted recommendations, according to the type and amount of dependencies as well as back-recommendations.

In all the experiments, we limit the examination of the tool produced ranking to the top 30 ranked classes, independent from the size of the system. We consider that a percentage limit of 15 % or even 10 % of the system size would result in candidate sets which are too big for the purpose of the tool, that of facilitating an easy start in program comprehension.

Thus we have to experimentally prove that the top 30 ranked classes are indeed the most important classes of the analyzed systems.

Unfortunately, the identification of the most important classes of a system may be, up to a certain degree, subjective to different opinions of different experts. The reference solution will be the reduced set resulting from the intersection of different expert opinions. In order to validate the tool, we could do an experiment asking different software experts to judge the top rankings produced by the tool. This scenario requires a big effort and, in the end, the objectivity of our experts may be questionable.

We chose to rely for the validation of the tool output on the comparison with reference solutions extracted from developers documentation. The kind of developer documentation that is useful for our validation is usually found in documents described as "architectural overview", "core of the system", "introduction for developers", etc. It may consist either in pruned diagrams or even free text descriptions. Of course, developers documentations may be outdated or not accurate. In order to reduce these risks, we preferred as case studies systems that provide both developers documentation and documentation from other sources, mainly systems included in the *Qualitas Corpus* - a curated collection of software systems intended to be used for empirical studies on code artifacts. These systems have been also analyzed in other works and their structure has been discussed by several sources, thus we can define as reference solution an intersection of different expert opinions. In this way we establish unbiased reference solutions to compare the solutions produced by our tool.

In the next Subsect. 3.2 we present the detailed analysis and discussion of one system. We use this system to perform the empirical validation of the value of fraction F representing the back-recommendations and to show the importance of choosing the weights that quantify dependency strengths.

Some more systems are then analyzed and presented in Subsect. 3.3.

In Chapter 4 we will discuss our results and draw the conclusions of our experiments, while also comparing with related work.

3.2 Detailed Analysis of the First Case Study

In this subsection we present the detailed analysis and discussion of a system, Apache Ant. Apache Ant[1] is a Java library and command-line tool to compile, build, test and run Java applications. We analyze release 1.6.1, feeding as input ant.jar containing the core part of ant. It contains 524 classes. A developer tutorial[2] indicates the following key classes to understand the design of the Ant core: `Project`, `Target`, `UnknownElement`, `RuntimeConfigurable`, `Task`, as depicted in Fig. 2. Besides these main classes, `IntrospectionHelper`, `ProjectHelper2` and `ProjectHelperImpl` are mentioned in the documentation as important.

---

[1] http://ant.apache.org/.

[2] http://codefeed.com/tutorial/ant_config.html.

The `Project` class is instantiated whenever Ant starts and, with the help of helper classes, the `Project` instance parses the `build.xml` file. The `Target` class represents the targets specified in the `build.xml` file. Once parsing finishes, the build model consists of a project, containing multiple targets. A target is a container of tasks, represented by specializations of the `Task` class.

Each task in Ant has a reference to its `RuntimeConfigurable` instance. Prior to the task being executed, it would need to be configured from its `RuntimeConfigurable` instance.

The class `UnknownElement` was introduced to allow the model to support storing information about tasks whose classes were not known at parse-time. `UnknownElement` extends `Task`, allowing it to be stored in the Ant object model.

We consider the following set of 8 classes as the reference solution: `Project`, `Target`, `UnknownElement`, `RuntimeConfigurable`, `Task`, `IntrospectionHelper`, `ProjectHelper2` and `ProjectHelperImpl`. Ant has been also analyzed for the detection of key classes in [9], and the same set of classes has been used as a reference solution.

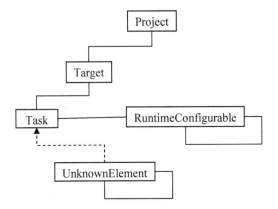

Fig. 2. Core classes of Ant described in the developers tutorial.

We perform an empirical fine-tuning of our recommender tool in order to get its ranking results as close as possible to the reference solution.

We use the detailed analysis of this case study to answer following questions, for the fine-tuning of the recommender tool:

Q1. Which is the role of dependency directions? More specifically, are back-recommendations needed? If yes, then which is the relative contribution of back-recommendations compared to that of forward recommendations?

In our experiments, we will consider the following possibilities for dependency directions:

– F=0: no back recommendation, only forward recommendation determined by the dependency relationship.
– F=1: back-recommendations have the same weight as forward recommendations.
– F=1/2, F=1/4: back-recommendations have a smaller weight than forward recommendations

Q2. Which types of dependencies are relevant for the goal of this recommender tool? We will investigate whether all dependency types are equally important or if there are some dependency types that can be ignored without affecting the quality of the result or even improving it.

For dependency types and weights, we consider the following profiles:

- *AllDep*: dependencies of all types are considered and summed up, with equal contributions
- *CallsOnly*: only method calls are considered, ignoring all other types of dependencies. The number of distinct methods called is taken into account in the global dependency strength.
- *InterfOnly*: only dependency relationships induced by elements visible from the interface are counted (inheritance, implementation, method parameters), ignoring all details such as local variables, member accesses and method calls.
- *AllWeighted*: all dependency types, but weighted such that interface elements have a higher weight than method calls while local variables use brings the smallest weights. This weighting schema is the one mentioned in Subsect. 2.1.

Table 1. Experimental results summary for Ant.

		F=0	F=1	F=1/2	F=1/4
AllDep	Top 10	0.38	0.38	0.25	0.38
	Top 15	0.63	0.63	0.63	0.63
	Top 20	0.63	0.88	1.00	0.88
	Top 30	0.75	1.00	1.00	1.00
	Top 50	0.75	1.00	1.00	1.00
AllWeight	Top 10	0.38	0.38	0.25	0.38
	Top 15	0.50	0.63	0.63	0.75
	Top 20	0.63	0.88	1.00	0.88
	Top 30	0.75	1.00	1.00	1.00
	Top 50	0.75	1.00	1.00	1.00
CallsOnly	Top 10	0.38	0.38	0.25	0.25
	Top 15	0.44	0.38	0.50	0.50
	Top 20	0.75	0.63	0.88	0.88
	Top 30	0.75	0.89	0.89	1.00
	Top 50	0.75	1.00	1.00	1.00
InterfOnly	Top 10	0.50	0.25	0.25	0.38
	Top 15	0.63	0.25	0.38	0.38
	Top 20	0.75	0.38	0.38	0.50
	Top 30	0.75	0.63	0.63	0.75
	Top 50	0.75	0.75	0.75	0.88

In our experiments we will generate and study all the possible combinations resulting from values for dependency weights and the fraction F of back-recommendations. We want to find out which combination favors the retrieval of most of the classes of the reference set. The summary of these experiments is depicted in Table 1. The values in the table represent the percentage of the classes of the reference set that are retrieved in the top N(where N=10, 15, 20, 30 and 50) ranked classes.

A first conclusion that can be drawn from Table 1 is that all dependency types have to be considered, because ignoring certain dependency types (as in the profiles *CallsOnly* and *InterfOnly*) has a negative impact. While both the *AllDeps* and *AllWeighted* profiles allow for combinations leading to the retrieval of all the classes of the reference solution in the top 20 ranked classes, this is not possible in any combination with the *CallsOnly* and *InterfOnly* profiles.

A second conclusion that can be observed by analyzing the columns of Table 1 is that the worst results are obtained when no back-recommendations are used (F=0). Using back-recommendations (F=1) improves the results, but the improvement is bigger when $F < 1$ (with F=1/2 and F=1/4).

Figure 3 presents the top 30 ranked classes when analyzing Ant with our tool configured with the *AllWeighted* profile.

	F=0	F=1	F=1/2	F=1/4
1	*Project*	*Project*	*Project*	*Project*
2	FileUtils	*Task*	*Task*	*Task*
3	Location	Path	BuildException	BuildException
4	BuildException	BuildException	Path	Path
5	*Task*	FileUtils	FileUtils	FileUtils
6	FilterSet	Commandline	Commandline	Parameter
7	*Target*	AbstractFileSet	Parameter	Commandline
8	ChainReaderHelper	Execute	AbstractFileSet	Reference
9	ProjectComponent	Parameter	Execute	*Target*
10	BuildEvent	*ProjectHelper2*	Reference	AbstractFileSet
11	*RuntimeConfigurable*	Java	*Target*	Execute
12	Path	Zip	*UnknownElement*	*UnknownElement*
13	Reference	*UnknownElement*	DirectoryScanner	*RuntimeConfigurable*
14	FilterSetCollection	DirectoryScanner	ComponentHelper	ComponentHelper
15	ComponentHelper	*ProjectHelperImpl*	*ProjectHelper2*	*IntrospectionHelper*
16	PropertyHelper	*Target*	*IntrospectionHelper*	ProjectComponent
17	DataType	DefaultCompilerAdapter	*ProjectHelperImpl*	DirectoryScanner
18	*UnknownElement*	Reference	*RuntimeConfigurable*	*ProjectHelperImpl*
19	Parameter	ComponentHelper	ProjectComponent	Location
20	Os	Javadoc	Zip	BuildEvent
21	BuildListener	*IntrospectionHelper*	TokenFilter	*ProjectHelper2*
22	Condition	TokenFilter	ModifiedSelector	TarEntry
23	*IntrospectionHelper*	Ant	Javadoc	ModifiedSelector
24	LineTokenizer	Javac	Javac	Condition
25	JavaEnvUtils	CommandlineJava	DefaultCompilerAdapter	EnumeratedAttribute
26	Watchdog	MatchingTask	Ant	ZipShort
27	Commandline	Rmic	EnumeratedAttribute	Resource
28	InputRequest	FilterChain	BuildEvent	MailMessage
29	TimeoutObserver	ModifiedSelector	Java	TokenFilter
30	AbstractFileSet	ExecTask	Rmic	FileSelector
Found:	*6/8*	*7/8*	*8/8*	*8/8*

Fig. 3. Top fragment of the ranking of Ant classes using the *AllWeighted* profile.

We can see that with F=0, only 6 out of the 8 classes of the reference set are found. Introducing back-recommendations brings an improvement: with F=1, 7 out of 8 classes are found, while with F=1/2 and F=1/4, all the 8 classes are found in the top 30 ranking. The detailed analysis of Ant validates our assumption, described with help of the simple example in Sect. 2.2, that back-recommendations are needed but they should be assigned weaker strengths than their forward recommendation counterparts. Taking F=1/2 and F=1/4, all classes of the reference set are found in the top 30 ranking for the analyzed system. Using the value F=1/4 enables to get the last hit on position 21 compared to F=1/2 where the last hit is found earlier, at position 18. In future work, more experiments could be done to fine-tune the value of the back-recommendation fraction F. In this work, the following experiments use the value F=1/2.

By examining the classes that occupy top positions in all rankings, we notice the constant presence of certain classes that were not included in the reference solution, so we manually analyzed them in order to decide if their high ranking can be considered dangerous false positives or if they should be rightfully included in the set of key classes. Among these classes, Path, Parameter, Reference, Commandline, and BuildEception represent some fundamental data structures that are very much used and this is the reason that they are ranked on top positions. The classes ComponentHelper, AbstractFileset, DirectoryScanner have a controlling function which makes them interesting to be studied. It is interesting to notice that these 3 classes are also found in top positions in the ranking obtained in [9]. The top ranked classes obtained for Ant in [10] and [11] have also similarities with our ranking.

3.3   More Experimental Results

We completed a series of experiments on an additional set of systems. In the experiments described in this section we use the value F=1/2 for the back-recommendations, as it resulted from the set of experiments described in the previous subsection.

The analyzed systems are: JHotDraw, JEdit, ArgoUML, Wro4j and JMeter.

Analysis of JHotDraw.   JHotDraw[3] is a highly customizable graphic framework for structured drawing editors. Its source code and binaries are freely available.

We analyze here JHotDraw, release 6.0b.1. We take advantage of the capabilities of our ART model extractor tools [6] that can handle compiled code, and directly feed it as input the jhotdraw.jar file from the binary distribution, which proves to contain 398 implementation classes. The architecture of the system is documented by its developers, the documentation provides a short description of the core architectural classes and interfaces, enumerating the most important artifacts in the opinion of the system developers. The case study of JHotDraw has been analyzed also in [12], in order to produce

---

[3] http://www.jhotdraw.org/.

a more precise class diagram, in terms of relationships, than the one provided by the authors of JHotDraw. We noticed a couple of classes considered important and added to the diagram: DrawingEditor, textttStandardDrawingView, CompositeFigure. Thus we conclude that the set of important artifacts (classes and interfaces) for an executive summary of JHotDraw is formed by these pointed out by the developers, completed with the three classes added in the study of [12]: Figure, Drawing, DrawingView, DrawApplication, Tool, Handle, DrawingEditor, StandardDrawingView, CompositeFigure. This set of 9 classes is further considered the reference summary of the whole system comprising 398 classes.

The top 30 classes in the ranking produced by our tool are: Figure, DrawingView, FigureEnumeration, DrawingEditor, Undoable, StorableInput, StorableOutput, CollectionsFactory, Drawing, DrawApplication, Standard DrawingView, ConnectionFigure, CommandTool, AbstractCommand, Composite Figure, DrawApplet, AbstractTool, Connector, HTMLTextAreaFigure, Text Figure, ConnectionTool, HandleEnumeration, PolyLineFigure, Handle, RelativeLocator, Locator, FigureChangeListener, DesktopEventService, DecoratorFigure.

We can see that all the nine classes which are in the reference are ranked in the top 30. This means that our tool finds all the classes of the reference solution, ranking them in the top 7.5 % classes of the 398 examined. Eight classes from the reference set are actually ranked in the top 20, while five of them are in the top 10. The first places of the ranking are also taken by the most important classes.

Analysis of JEdit. JEdit[4] is a cross platform programmer's text editor written in Java. We analyze the code of release 5.1.0, with 1266 classes.

Developer documentation is available[5] and it gives the following introductory overview of jEdit implementation: The main class of jEdit is jEdit, which is the starting point for accessing various components and changing preferences. Each window in jEdit is an instance of the View class. Each text area you see in a View is an instance of JEditTextArea, each of which is contained in its own EditPane. Files are represented by the Buffer class. The Log class is used to print out debugging messages to the activity log. Plugin developers have to extend EBPlugin.

In summary, the developers documentation point out the following classes of interest: jEdit, View, EditPane, Buffer, JEditTextArea, Log, EBMessage. We take this set of 7 classes as the reference solution.

The top 30 classes in the ranking produced by our tool are: jEdit, View, JEdit-Buffer, Buffer, TextArea, Log, Interpreter, NameSpace, SimpleNode, GUIUtilities, EditPane, TokenMarker, CallStack, ParserRuleSet, Misc-Utilities, VFS, VFSBrowser PluginJAR, JEditTextArea, TextAreaPainter, VFSFile, Selection, Mode, Primitive, DisplayManager, Gutter, SearchAnd-Replace, EditBus, EBMessage, Parser.

---

[4] http://jedit.org/.

[5] http://community.jedit.org/cgi-bin/TWiki/view/Main/JEditSourceCodeIntro.

We can see that all the seven classes which are in the reference are ranked in the top 30. This means that our tool finds all the classes of the reference solution, ranking them in the top 2.5 % classes of the 1266 examined. Out of these, six classes from the reference set are ranked in the top 20. Actually, the only class which did not make it into the top 20, class `EBMessage`, is not so much a core class but it is mentioned in the summary as important for plugin developers, being important only in this context. Four of the classes in the reference set are found in the top 10. The first places of the ranking are also taken by the most important classes.

Analysis of ArgoUML. ArgoUML[6] is a well-known open source UML modeling tool. In this work we analyze its release 0.9.5, having detailed architectural descriptions in Jason Robbins's dissertation[7] which created the fundamental layer for ArgoUML. The analyzed jar contains a total of 852 classes.

The set of key classes as identified from the architectural description is composed by the following 12 classes: `Designer`, `Critic`, `CrUML`, `ToDoItem`, `ToDoList`, `History`, `ControlMech`, `ProjectBrowser`, `Project`, `Wizard`, `Configuration`, `Argo`.

Our analysis resulted in the following top 30 ranked classes: `Project Browser`, `Designer`, `ToDoItem`, `ColumnDescriptor`, `CrUML`, `Project`, `UMLUser InterfaceContainer`, `TreeModelPrereqs`, `Critic`, `UMLAction`, `MMUtil`, `FigNodeModelElement`, `NavPerspective`, `Notation`, `Wizard`, `UMLModelElement ListModel`, `PropPanel`, `Configuration`, `TableModelComposite`, `ToDoList`, `Argo`, `PropPanelModelElement`, `ParserDisplay`, `CodePiece`, `FigEdge ModelElement`, `UMLChecklist`, `ModuleLoader`, `SelectionWButtons`, `Argo EventPump`, `NotationName`.

We notice that 6 out of the 12 classes in the reference solution are ranked in the top 10, while 9 classes are found in the top 20 and 10 classes are found in the top 30.

Analysis of Wro4j. Wro4j[8] is an open source web resource optimizer for Java. We have used release 1.6.3, containing 337 classes.

The classes that are mentioned in the design overview[9] as important for understanding the design of the system, and which are further considered as the reference solution in our experiment, are the following 12 classes: `WroModel`, `WroModelFactory`, `Group`, `Resource`, `WroManager`, `WroManagerfactory`, `ResourcePreProcessor`, `ResourcePost-Processor`, `uriLocator`, `uriLocatorFactory`, `WroFilter`, `resourceType`.

The first 30 classes as ranked by our tool are, in order: `WroManager`, `Resource`, `WroConfiguration`, `BaseWroManagerFactory`, `ResourcePre-Processor`, `WroTestUtils`, `WroUtil`, `WroModelFactory`, `Injector- Builder`,

[6] http://argouml.tigris.org.
[7] http://argouml.tigris.org/docs/robbins_dissertation.
[8] https://code.google.com/p/wro4j/.
[9] https://code.google.com/p/wro4j/wiki/DesignOverview.

ResourceType, Context, HashStrategy, Resource- PostProcessor, WroModel, WroFilter, WroRuntimeException, ProcessorDecorator, UriLocatorFactory, WroManagerFactory, CacheStrategy, PreProcessorExecutor, ReadOnlyContext, LifecycleCallbackRegistry, Injector, LifecycleCall back, WildcardExpanderModelTransformer, ResourceWatcher, Default-WroModelFactoryDecorator, Group, UriLocator.

We observe that 5 out of the 12 classes in the reference solution are found in the top 10 ranked, while 10 classes are found in the top 20 and all 12 classes are found in the top 30.

Analysis of JMeter. Jakarta JMeter[10] is a Java application for testing of Web Applications. We analyze version 2.0.1, its core found in ApacheJMeter_core.jar which contains 280 classes. Design documentation[11] and other works that analyzed this system [13] mentions following classes: AbstractAction, JMeterEngine, JMeterTreeModel, JMeterThread, JMeterGUIComponent, Sampler, SampleResult, TestCompiler, TestElement, TestListener, TestPlan, TestPlanGUI, ThreadGroup.

The first 30 classes as ranked by our tool are, in order: JMeterUtils, JMeterProperty, GuiPackage, SampleResult, JMeterTreeNode, JMeter- Thread, SaveService, AbstractTestElement, JMeterTreeModel, MainFrame, JMeterContext, PropertyIterator, JMeter, Sampler, CompoundVariable, ThreadGroup, JMeterTreeListener, Test- Compiler, MenuFactory, Thread GroupGui, AbstractJMeterGuiComponent, Arguments, CollectionProperty, SampleEvent, Value- Replacer, JMeterGUIComponent, StandardJMeter Engine, Result- Collector, GenericController.

We observe that 3 out of the 13 classes in the reference solution are found in the top 10 ranked, while 7 classes are found in the top 20 and 8 classes are found in the top 30.

4   Discussion and Comparison with Related Work

4.1   Summary of Experimental Results

In Table 2 we summarize the results obtained in our experiments. For each one of the five analyzed systems, we represent in this table the raw data describing it: its size, the size of the reference solution, the number of classes found if the cut threshold is placed after the first 10, 15, 20 or respectively the first 30 ranked classes. The execution time includes both the analysis of dependencies and building the model of the system and the applying of the ranking.

We compute the recall and precision for our approach, defined as in [13]:

The *recall*, showing the technique's retrieval power, is computed as the percentage of key classes retrieved by the technique versus the total number of key classes present in the reference set.

---

[10] http://jmeter.apache.org/.
[11] http://wiki.apache.org/jmeter/.

Table 2. Experimental results summary.

	JHotDraw	Ant	jEdit	ArgoUML	Wro4j	JMeter	Avg.Precis	Avg.Recall
System size	398	524	1266	852	337	280		
Execution time	1 min	2 min	3 min	2.5 min	1 min	1 min		
Reference set	9	8	7	12	12	13		
Hits in Top 10	5	2	4	6	5	3	42 %	42 %
Hits in Top 15	7	5	5	6	8	5	40 %	61 %
Hits in Top 20	8	8	6	9	10	7	40 %	81 %
Hits in Top 30	9	8	7	10	12	8	30 %	90 %

The *precision*, showing the technique's retrieval quality, is computed as the percentage of key classes retrieved versus the total size of the result set.

The last columns of Table 2 present the average values of recall and precision computed from our experimental data concerning the six analyzed systems.

We consider this a good result, since the measured recall guarantees the user a good start for program comprehension, having assured two thirds of the relevant classes by examining a very small number of classes (only 10-15 classes), independently on the size of the whole system. Also, in case of 4 systems out of the six analyzed, all the relevant classes have been found in the top 30.

The precision values in our experiments are disadvantaged by the very small size of the reference solution, which is in average 10 classes. However, we did not add further classes to these reference sets, in order to keep them fair by avoiding subjectivity. Also, while in most systems it would be difficult to rank with precision all classes, this reduced top set is that which is unanimously agreed as the most important. On the other hand, a user which uses our tool to analyze a new system does not know the exact size of this top set. He or she will use the tool with the expectation to find the top 10 or top 20 classes. If we examine the top fragments of the rankings produced by the tool, we notice there several classes that are certainly not irrelevant, although they were not included in the reference top set.

In our opinion, program comprehension is effectively supported by the tool in the following scenario: the tool identifies a small number of classes as key classes. These classes give the starting points for the examination of the system by a software engineer doing maintenance or evolution activities. For practical effectiveness, most often is not worth to move the cut threshold below the top 20 ranked classes, due to the increased effort of manual investigation. The very short and general executive summary of the system is quickly and easy retrieved in this top set. After getting this executive summary, the user can continue the analysis tasks either by parsing the documentation, beginning from the discovered key classes, or he/she may apply other techniques such as feature localization [14] to track more localized areas of interest.

4.2   Comparison with Related Work

There are several approaches trying to identify the most important software artifacts (classes, packages, functions) from a software system. They present differences in following aspects:

- the primary information that is extracted and analyzed: the majority uses static analysis [15], [16] but there are also approaches based on dynamic analysis [9], [11].
- the criteria used to define the importance of a class: the majority derives the importance of a class from the ways it interacts with other classes, given by design metrics (such as coupling), network metrics of the topology of the interactions between the classes, or a combination of these. Other approaches use the number of changes recorded by the versioning system [17] as an indicator of the importance of a class. There were also attempts to use textual information such as class names [18] as hints for the importance of a class.
- the techniques for identifying the key classes are mostly based on network analysis [16], including here also webmining techniques [13], and more recently machine learning [15], [19]. Also interactive tools for pruning of reverse engineered class diagrams are developed [20].

Comparing the results obtained by all these different approaches is difficult, because they are using different software systems as case studies and not all publications describe the raw data of their experiments such as the rankings that they obtained. Where such data was available we compared the results with our results for the same systems.

Coderank [21] was one of the first works to introduce the concept of calculating PageRank values for a graph resulting from static dependencies between the software artifacts such as classes of a project. However, there is little experimental validation that supports the claims about their ability to help program comprehension by identifying relevant components of real software systems.

An important work in detecting key classes of software systems belong to Zaidman et al. [13], [22], [9]. They uses a graph-ranking algorithm, HITS, in order to detect key classes of a software system. They combine this webmining technique with dynamic and static analysis, and perform experiments on two systems. With dynamic analysis they attain an average recall of 92 % and precision 46 %. However, a major drawback of this approach is that dynamic analysis relies very much on the user finding good execution scenarios. It also presents scalability issues and has a high execution time (1h45). Zaidman also combined this webmining technique with static analysis but concluded that the static analysis was not able to achieve a reasonable precision and recall. Here their best reported results were an average recall of 50 % and precision 8 %, while the execution time is still high (over 1 hour).

In our work we have proven that static analysis can be used to successfully and efficiently identify key classes, our results near the values obtained by [13] with dynamic analysis, while the execution time in our case is just a couple of minutes. We think that a major enabling factor for our positive result here is our recommendation model, which takes into account all possible types of static dependencies with appropriate weights, while Zaidman uses coupling metrics that take into account only method calls. We also appreciate in the work of [13] the extensive description of their result sets in case of Ant and JMeter, which allowed us to compare with our result sets for these two systems. We retrieved a couple of classes from outside the reference set that appear both in their and our top ranking result set, leading to a future reconsideration of the reference sets.

Kamran et al. [11] develop their own version of a dynamic coupling metric. Their results, obtained on analysing the Ant system, compete with those obtained in [13] but significantly reduce the execution time. It is interesting to note that the some classes present in the top ranking of Ant, while not included in the reference set, are the same in our approach and in [11].

Steidl et al. [16] start from static analysis to retrieve important classes of a system. Their approach calculates a centrality index for the nodes of the dependency graph obtained by static analysis. They performed an empirical study to find the best combination of centrality measurement of dependency graph. They used as baseline for validation of results opinions of several software developers. They found out that centrality indices work best on an undirected dependency graph including information about inheritance, parameter and return dependencies. Using the Markov centrality leads to the best results, with a precision between 60 % and 80 % in the top 10 recommendation set. Their experiments were performed on a set of 4 systems. However, they do not compute the recall of their method, nor do they mention the members or the sizes of the reference sets. From the data presented, one could conclude that the baseline sets for each system were larger, being reunions of different expert opinion instead of intersection of such, resulting in more that 10 classes in the baseline. Theses larger baseline solutions may have favored the count of hits in the top 10, as opposed to the smaller reference solutions used in our experiments. We appreciate that the retrieval power of this technique is similar with ours.

Meyer et al. [10] propose an automated way to identify the important classes of a software system based on K-core decomposition. They show that the classes in the highest K-cores are the ones that are the most important, but in order to reduce the number of classes k-core values should be used in conjunction with other network metrics as centralities. They discuss their results on 3 systems, two of the systems being Ant and JHotDraw and obtaining rankings that have many similarities with the ones obtained in our work. Pan et al. [23] use K-core decomposition to find the most important packages of a software system.

Perin et al. [24] use PageRank on the graph of static dependencies. They report experiments on several systems, including Ant, Jmeter and Jedit. However, the set of top ranked classes is very different from the sets of top ranked classes reported for these systems in our work, and is different as well from those reported in [9], [11], [10].

Osman et al. worked on condensing class diagrams by including only the important classes. They used a very different approach, based on machine learning [15]. They use design metrics extracted from available forward design diagrams to learn and then to validate the quality of prediction algorithms. Nine small to medium size open source case studies are analyzed, taking as baseline available forward design diagrams which contain from 11 to 57 classes, representing between 4 % and 47 % of the project size. In a follow-up, Osman et al. [18] built a classifier that is based on the names of classes in addition to design metrics, but the results show that combining text metrics with design metrics leads to modest improvements over using design metrics only.

Thung et al. [19] uses machine learning combining design metrics and network metrics in the learning process. Introducing network metrics besides the design metrics improves the results of [15] by almost 10 %. However, in [19] network metrics and design metrics are computed as distinct and independent attributes and used in the learning process. In our approach, the network metric (PageRank) is adapted to be computed on the weighted graph resulting after the design metrics (measuring dependency strengths and coupling) are applied, and thus we believe that the concept of recommendation is better adapted to its particular purpose.

The work of Hammad [17] starts from another point of view regarding the importance of classes: they consider that the classes that were important to the design of the system are these often impacted by design changes. They measure the design importance of a class as the number of commits that impact the class, and this is also measured for the sets of classes that collaborate.

5   Conclusions

In this work, we develop a method and tool for automatically identifying the most important classes of a software system, in order to facilitate the start of program comprehension activities.

Our approach is based on static analysis, used to build a graph model of the system, and the PageRang graph ranking algorithm.

In order to obtain a ranking that is relevant for our goal, the graph model of the system has to be carefully built for this purpose. We define two parameters of the graph model: the weights of dependency types and the dependency directions, which we call forward recommendations and back recommendations. We have experimentally determined that all types of static dependencies between classes have to be taken into account, weighted according to the relative importance given by the dependency type and number of occurrences. Also, experiments have shown that back-recommendations are necessary, but should be assigned only a fraction $0 < F < 1$ of the weight of their corresponding forward recommendations.

We have validated our approach by analyzing six open source systems and comparing the top ranked classes with these described as important in developers documentation. The results have shown our technique's retrieval power, which is able to find an average of 90 % of the classes of the reference sets indicated in the developers documentation as ranked in the top 30 by our tool.

References

1. von Mayrhauser, A., Vans, A.: Program comprehension during software maintenance and evolution. Computer **28**(8), 44–55 (1995)
2. Fernández-Sáez, A.M., Chaudron, M.R.V., Genero, M., Ramos, I.: Are forward designed or reverse-engineered UML diagrams more helpful for code maintenance?: A controlled experiment. In: Proceedings of the 17th International Conference on Evaluation and Assessment in Software Engineering. EASE 2013, 60–71. ACM, New York (2013)
3. Sora, I.: Finding the right needles in hay - helping program comprehension of large software systems. In: ENASE 2015 - Proceedings of the 10th International Conference on Evaluation of Novel Approaches to Software Engineering, Barcelona, Spain, 29–30, pp. 129–140 (2015), April 2015
4. Sora, I.: A PageRank based recommender system for identifying key classes in software systems. In: 10th IEEE Jubilee International Symposium on Applied Computational Intelligence and Informatics, SACI 2015, Timisoara, Romania, May 21–23, 2015, pp. 495–500 (2015)
5. Page, L., Brin, S., Motwani, R., Winograd, T.: The PageRank citation ranking: Bringing order to the web. Technical Report 1999–66, Stanford InfoLab Previous number = SIDL-WP-1999-0120, November 1999
6. Şora, I.: Unified modeling of static relationships between program elements. In: Maciaszek, L.A., Filipe, J. (eds.) ENASE 2012. CCIS, vol. 410, pp. 95–109. Springer, Heidelberg (2013)
7. Briand, L., Daly, J., Wust, J.: A unified framework for coupling measurement in object-oriented systems. IEEE Trans. Softw. Eng. **25**(1), 91–121 (1999)
8. Sora, I., Glodean, G., Gligor, M.: Software architecture reconstruction: An approach based on combining graph clustering and partitioning. In: 2010 International Joint Conference on Computational Cybernetics and Technical Informatics (ICCC-CONTI), pp. 259–264, May 2010
9. Zaidman, A., Calders, T., Demeyer, S., Paredaens, J.: Applying webmining techniques to execution traces to support the program comprehension process. In: Ninth European Conference on Software Maintenance and Reengineering, 2005. CSMR 2005, pp. 134–142, March 2005
10. Meyer, P., Siy, H., Bhomwick, S.: Identifying important classes of large software systems through k-core decomposition. Advances in Complex Systems 17(07n08) 1550004 (2014)
11. Kamran, M., Azam, F., Khanum, A.: Discovering core architecture classes to assist initial program comprehension. In: Lu, W., Cai, G., Liu, W., Xing, W. (eds.) Discovering Core Architecture Classes to Assist Initial Program Comprehension. LNCS, vol. 221, pp. 3–10. Springer, Heidelberg (2013)
12. Guéhéneuc, Y.G.: A reverse engineering tool for precise class diagrams. In: Proceedings of the 2004 Conference of the Centre for Advanced Studies on Collaborative Research. CASCON 2004, IBM Press 28–41 (2004)
13. Zaidman, A., Demeyer, S.: Automatic identification of key classes in a software system using webmining techniques. J. Softw. Maintenance Evol.: Res. Pract. **20**(6), 387–417 (2008)
14. Dit, B., Revelle, M., Gethers, M., Poshyvanyk, D.: Feature location in source code: a taxonomy and survey. J. Softw.: Evol. Process **25**(1), 53–95 (2013)

15. Osman, M.H., Chaudron, M.R.V., Putten, P.v.d.: An analysis of machine learning algorithms for condensing reverse engineered class diagrams. In: Proceedings of the 2013 IEEE International Conference on Software Maintenance. ICSM 2013, Computer Society 140–149. IEEE, Washington, DC (2013)

16. Steidl, D., Hummel, B., Juergens, E.: Using network analysis for recommendation of central software classes. In: 2012 19th Working Conference on Reverse Engineering (WCRE), pp. 93–102, October 2012

17. Hammad, M., Collard, M., Maletic, J.: Measuring class importance in the context of design evolution. In: 2010 IEEE 18th International Conference on Program Comprehension (ICPC), pp. 148–151, June 2010

18. Osman, M., Chaudron, M., Van Der Putten, P., Ho-Quang, T.: Condensing reverse engineered class diagrams through class name based abstraction. In: 2014 Fourth World Congress on Information and Communication Technologies (WICT), pp. 158–163, December 2014

19. Thung, F., Lo, D., Osman, M.H., Chaudron, M.R.V.: Condensing class diagrams by analyzing design and network metrics using optimistic classification. In: Proceedings of the 22Nd International Conference on Program Comprehension. ICpPC 2014, pp. 110–121. ACM, New York (2014)

20. Osman, M., Chaudron, M., Van Der Putten, P.: Interactive scalable abstraction of reverse engineered uml class diagrams. In: 2014 21st Asia-Pacific Software Engineering Conference (APSEC), vol. 1. 159–166, December 2014

21. Neate, B., Irwin, W., Churcher, N.: Coderank: a new family of software metrics. In: Software Engineering Conference, 2006. Australian 10 pp.-378, April 2006

22. Zaidman, A., Du Bois, B., Demeyer, S.: How webmining and coupling metrics improve early program comprehension. In: 14th IEEE International Conference on Program Comprehension, 2006. ICpPC 2006, pp. 74–78 (2006)

23. Pan, W., Hu, B., Jiang, B., Xie, B.: Identifying important packages of object-oriented software using weighted k-core decomposition. J. Intell. Syst. **23**(4), 461–476 (2014)

24. Perin, F., Renggli, L., Ressia, J.: Ranking software artifacts. In: 4th Workshop on FAMIX and Moose in Reengineering (FAMOOSr 2010). 120 (2010)

A Case Study for a Bidirectional Transformation Between Heterogeneous Metamodels in QVT Relations

Bernhard Westfechtel[✉]

Applied Computer Science I, University of Bayreuth, Universitaetstrasse 30,
95440 Bayreuth, Germany
bernhard.westfechtel@uni-bayreuth.de

Abstract. Model transformations constitute a key technology for model-driven software engineering. In additional to unidirectional transformations, bidirectional transformations may be required e.g. for round-trip engineering or bidirectional data conversion. Bidirectional transformations may be difficult to perform if the metamodels of source and target models differ significantly from each other, as it is the case for object-relational mappings. In this paper, we present a bidirectional transformation between Ecore models and relational schemata written in QVT Relations. The case study demonstrates that it is possible to encode a bidirectional transformation between heterogeneous metamodels in a single relational specification. Simultaneously, the case study also shows some inherent limitations of what can be achieved by bidirectional transformations.

1 Introduction

In *model-driven software engineering* [1], software development is driven by the construction of high-level models which are transformed over multiple stages into executable code. For MDSE, key enabling technologies are required for defining modeling languages as well as defining and executing model transformations.

In object-oriented modeling, the abstract syntax of a modeling language is defined by a *metamodel*. To this end, the Object Management Group (OMG) provides the *Meta Object Facility* standard (*MOF* [2]), whose subset EMOF (Essential MOF) has been implemented in the Eclipse Modeling Framework (*EMF*) [3].

For *model transformations*, the OMG issued the *QVT* standard (*Queries, Views, and Transformations*), which defines a family of model transformation languages at different levels of abstraction [4]. The most high-level language is *QVT Relations* (*QVT-R*), which supports the declarative specification of transformations between MOF-based models. QVT-R addresses a wide spectrum of model transformation scenarios, including enforcing and checking, unidirectional and bidirectional, batch and incremental, and n:1 transformations.

© Springer International Publishing Switzerland 2016
L.A. Maciaszek and J. Filipe (Eds.): ENASE 2015, CCIS 599, pp. 141–161, 2016.
DOI: 10.1007/978-3-319-30243-0_8

This paper focuses on a particularly interesting feature of QVT-R: the declarative specification of *bidirectional transformations*. Rather than writing two unidirectional transformations separately, a transformation developer may provide a single relational specification which may be executed in both directions. This approach saves specification effort and ensures the consistency of forward and backward transformations.

Bidirectional transformations are required e.g. for *round-trip engineering*. Furthermore, integration of heterogeneous tools calls for *data converters* which ideally perform lossless transformations in all directions.

However, lossless transformations in all directions require that transformations are *mutually invertible*: From the target model produced by the forward transformation, the backward transformation should reconstruct the original source model; vice versa for the opposite direction. This requires bidirectional transformations which are *bijective*. In the case of *heterogeneous metamodels*, bijectivity is not achievable.

This paper presents a bidirectional transformation for *object-relational mappings*. The transformation demonstrates an important advantage of QVT-R: A fairly complex bidirectional transformation may be encoded as a single relational specification. In languages supporting only unidirectional transformations such as e.g. ATL [5], the transformation developer would have to provide two separate transformation definitions — one for each direction.

On the other hand, the case study also demonstrates inherent limitations of bidirectional transformations in the presence of heterogeneous metamodels. Due to information loss, it is not possible to reconstruct a class model completely by running a forward transformation followed by a backward transformation. Thus, the presented bidirectional transformation is not bijective. Furthermore, the backward transformation essentially can process only relational schemata which were generated by the forward transformation.

2   Model Transformations

A *model* is an abstraction of a system allowing predictions or inferences to be made [6]. A model is expressed in a *modeling language*. A *metamodel* defines the abstract syntax of a modeling language, usually with the help of class diagrams and additional constraints (written e.g. in OCL). A model obeying the rules defined in a metamodel is called an *instance* of that metamodel.

A *model transformation* operates on a set of models, each of which may be either read, created, or updated. A *single-source-single-target transformation* takes a single *source model* as input and produces a single *target model* as output. A transformation is called *exogenous* (*endogenous*) if the source and target metamodels are different (the same). The case study presented in this paper deals with an exogenous single-source-single-target transformation.

A transformation may be modeled as a *function* from a source model to a target model. A transformation is *total* if it may be applied to any instance of the source metamodel, *deterministic* if it returns a unique target model for a given source model, *injective* if it returns different target models for different source models, *surjective* if it can generate any instance of the target metamodel, and *bijective* if it is both injective and surjective.

As defined so far, a transformation is *unidirectional*: It can generate an instance of the target metamodel from an instance of the source metamodel, but not vice versa. A *bidirectional transformation* is a pair of opposite unidirectional transformations (called *forward* and *backward transformation*).

In the context of round-trip engineering and bidirectional data converters, it is highly desirable that both forward and backward transformation are *total* and *mutually inverse*. Totality ensures that the transformations may be applied to all instances of the respective metamodels. Mutual inversion ensures consistent behavior: Applying the backward transformation after the forward transformation returns the original model; likewise for the opposite direction.

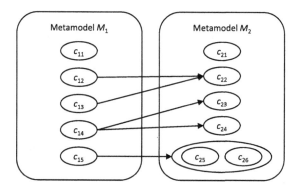

Fig. 1. Mappings between heterogeneous metamodels.

However, in practical applications these requirements may at best be approximated. If the forward and the backward transformation are both total and mutually inverse, there is a bijective (1:1) mapping between source models and target models. Such a mapping does not exist in the case of *heterogeneous metamodels*. This is illustrated in Fig. 1, where c_{ij} denote concepts defined in metamodels (in terms of classes, attributes, or references): c_{11} cannot be mapped at all, c_{12} and c_{13} are mapped to the same concept c_{22}, c_{14} may be mapped non-deterministically to c_{23} or c_{24}, and c_{15} has to be simulated by the set of concepts $\{c_{25}, c_{26}\}$.

3   QVT Relations (QVT-R)

QVT-R is a declarative language for specifying both uni- and bidirectional model transformations as well as consistency checks. This section gives a brief overview of QVT-R; see [4] for a comprehensive description and [7] for a tutorial.

In QVT-R, a *transformation* may be defined on $n \geq 2$ models; here, we assume $n = 2$. The models involved in a transformation are typed by *metamodels*. A metamodel defines the elements from which models may be composed, and constraints on their composition. In this way, it defines a set of models conforming to the metamodel. In the following, models and metamodels are denoted by lowercase and uppercase letters. The expression $m \in M$ states that m conforms to the metamodel M.

A transformation is specified in terms of rules, each of which defines a *relation* between source and target patterns. A relation consists of *domains*, each of which defines a pattern in one model. A domain has a unique root object and is marked by a *domain qualifier* (checkonly or enforce) which controls how the domain may be used in a transformation (see below). Furthermore, a relation may have a when *clause* which serves as a precondition for applying the relation. A relation may also comprise a where *clause* which essentially acts as a postcondition. Finally, *variables* may be declared in a relation which are used in domains, the when and the where clause.

A transformation is executed in the direction of a specific model. In *checking mode*, the transformation is executed on a pair of already existing models $m_1 \in M_1$ and $m_2 \in M_2$. If m_2 is selected as target model, it is checked whether for each relation and each instance of a source pattern in m_1 satisfying the when clause, a corresponding target pattern instance exists in m_2 such that the where clause is satisfied, as well. Domain qualifiers are immaterial in checking mode.

In *enforcing mode*, the target model is updated such that it is consistent with the source model. Thus, QVT-R provides for *incremental transformations*. A *batch transformation* is treated as a special case (m_2 is empty). To establish consistency, it is checked for each relation and each source pattern instance whether a corresponding instance of the target pattern already exists. If there is no such instance, it is created if the target pattern is qualified by enforce; otherwise, an inconsistency is reported. Furthermore, the check is performed also in the opposite direction. If there is no matching source pattern instance, the target pattern instance is deleted if its domain is qualified by enforce; otherwise, an inconsistency is reported.

Ideally, a transformation may be executed in both modes in either direction. Thus, a *bidirectional transformation* may be defined by a single specification. In this case (to be considered in this paper), all domains should be qualified by enforce. For a *unidirectional transformation*, source and target domains should be qualified by checkonly and enforce, respectively. Transformations which are run only in checking mode should mark all domains by checkonly.

4   Problem

An *object-relational mapping* constitutes a wide-spread use case for model transformations. The QVT standard includes a small example of a unidirectional mapping of simple UML-like models to relational schemas (see Appendix A.3.1 of the standard). In contrast, we developed a more sophisticated bidirectional transformation between Ecore models (class models in EMF) and relational schemas which covers large parts of the Ecore metamodel.

4.1   Metamodels

An excerpt from the *Ecore metamodel* is shown in Fig. 2. An Ecore model consists of a tree of *packages*. A package owns a set of *classifiers* which are partitioned into *classes* and *data types*. Classes are organized into a *multiple inheritance hierarchy*. Each class owns a set of *structured features* which are classified into *attributes* and *references*. A feature has a multiplicity, defined by a *lower bound* and an *upper bound*. A feature may be designated as changeable, volatile, transient, or derived. Multi-valued features consist of collections which may be *ordered* and *unique*. Attributes and references are typed by data types and classes, respectively. A data type may be an externally defined Java type, or an *enumeration type* defined in the model. A reference may be designated as a *containment reference*, implying exclusiveness, existential dependency, and absence of cycles. Furthermore, unidirectional references may be grouped into pairs, making up *bidirectional references*.

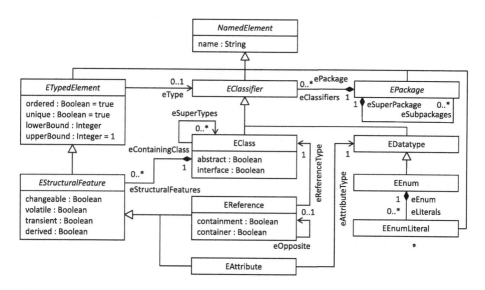

Fig. 2. Ecore metamodel (excerpt).

Figure 3 displays our metamodel for schemas of relational databases. A *schema* consists of a set of *tables*, each of which has a set of named *columns*. In a column, a single value is stored, which is typed by one of a set of predefined

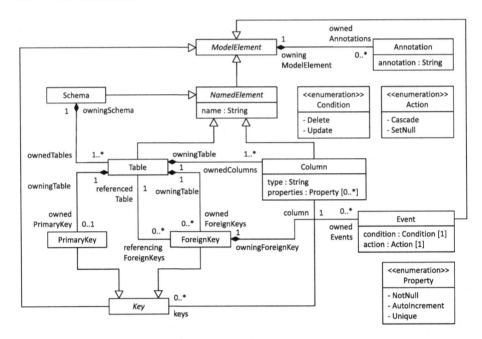

Fig. 3. Schema metamodel.

SQL data types. A *key* refers to a column which identifies a tuple in a relation in a unique way. A *primary key* serves to uniquely identify tuples of its owning relation. A *foreign key* references another relation, which must have a matching primary key. Please note that we make the simplifying assumption that each relation has at most one primary key which is composed of one column.

Properties and events are used to control the dynamic behavior of updates. Each column may be decorated with a number of *properties*: NotNull excludes null values, AutoIncrement defines a counter, and Unique excludes duplicates. Furthermore, *events* may be defined on foreign keys as pairs of conditions and actions. The *conditions* Delete and Update refer to the deletion and update of the referenced target tuple, respectively. The *action* Cascade defines cascading deletions, while SetNull sets the reference to null when the respective event is fired.

4.2   Transformation Approach

In Ecore models and relational schemas, data are modeled in significantly different ways. Heterogeneity impedes the development of a bidirectional transformation. Below, we first present an approach to transform an Ecore model into a relational schema. Next, we address the opposite direction. Finally, we discuss the options to synthesize a bidirectional transformation.

Forward Transformation. For the sake of simplicity, we assume a few non-essential restrictions regarding Ecore models: The whole Ecore model is defined in a single package; only single inheritance is allowed; attributes must have data types which can be mapped to SQL types, multi-valued features are assumed to be unordered; with respect to multiplicities, only single- and multi-valued features are distinguished (ranges [0..1] and [0..*], respectively).

The transformation to be described below may be applied to all Ecore models satisfying these restrictions. However, the transformation ignores operations as well as volatile, transient, and derived features. Unlike the simple transformation from UML-like models to relational models in the QVT standard [4], where an object is represented by a single tuple, objects are spread over multiple tuples which are tied together by unique object identifiers. In the presence of multi-valued features, a representation by a single tuple is not possible; furthermore, the inheritance hierarchy is not flattened to provide for a modular transformation. More specifically, the transformation works as follows:

1. Each package is mapped to a schema. In the schema, an object table is created which manages unique identifiers (integers).
2. Each class is mapped to a table with a primary key.
3. Inheritance is mapped as follows: A root class maintains a foreign key into the object table. A subclass maintains a foreign key into the superclass table.
4. A single-valued attribute is mapped to a column.
5. A containment reference is mapped to a column and a foreign key in the opposite table (i.e., the table for the child class).

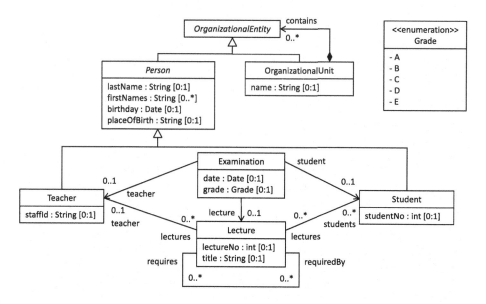

Fig. 4. Sample Ecore model of a campus management system.

6. A single-valued unidirectional cross reference is mapped to a column and a foreign key.
7. In all other cases, a cross reference is mapped to a table. Only a single table is generated for a bidirectional cross reference.
8. Cascading deletions ensure that all tuples representing an object are deleted when the tuple in the object table is deleted.
9. Furthermore, when an object is created, all tuples representing the objects have to be inserted into the respective relations. We assume that this task is performed in a database transaction (which, however, is not generated by the transformation).

By applying these rules, the Ecore model of Fig. 4 is transformed into the relational schema of Listing 1.

Backward Transformation. In the forward transformation, we have performed an *element-based translation*, i.e., the transformation essentially consists of rules for mapping individual elements of the source metamodel (packages, classes, inheritance relationships, attributes, and references). Now, we follow the same approach to design a backward transformation. This results in a simple translation scheme: A schema is mapped to a package, a non-key column is mapped to a single-valued attribute, a primary key is not mapped at all (Ecore assumes implicit unique object identifiers), and a foreign key is mapped to a single-valued unidirectional reference. Applying these rules to the schema of Listing 1 yields the Ecore model displayed in Fig. 5.

Bidirectional Transformation. Apart from a few restrictions, the forward transformation may be applied to arbitrary Ecore models; likewise, the backward transformation may work on arbitrary relational schemata. Both the forward and the backward transformations perform element-based translations. However, the backward transformation does not invert the forward transformation; rather, it produces an Ecore model which differs significantly from the model to which the forward transformation was applied.

In order to (approximately) invert the forward transformation, the backward transformation has to perform a *pattern-based translation*: The elements of Ecore models have to be simulated in the relational data model. The backward transformation has to recognize the simulation patterns and must transform them back to the original element.

If we compose an element-based forward transformation with a pattern-based backward transformation, we obtain a bidirectional transformation whose backward transformation (approximately) inverts the forward transformation. However, the overall bidirectional transformation does not operate symmetrically: The backward transformation assumes the patterns generated by the forward transformation and is much more specific than the forward transformation.

Listing 1. Relational schema generated from the Ecore model in Figure 4.

```
create table EObject (
    id int not null auto_increment, primary key (id));
create table Student (
    id int not null, studentNo int, primary key (id),
    foreign Key (id) references Person (id) on delete cascade);
create table Teacher (
    id int not null, staffId varchar(30), primary key (id),
    foreign Key (id) references Person (id) on delete cascade);
create table OrganizationalEntity (
    id int not null, containedEntities_inverse int, primary key (id),
    foreign Key (id) references EObject (id) on delete cascade,
    foreign key (containedEntities_inverse) references
        OrganizationalUnit (id) on delete cascade);
create table Person (
    id int not null, lastName varchar(30),
    birthday date, placeOfBirth varchar(30), primary key (id),
    foreign Key (id) references
        OrganizationalEntity (id) on delete cascade
);
create table OrganizationalUnit (
    id int not null, name varchar(30), primary key (id),
    foreign Key (id) references
        OrganizationalEntity (id) on delete cascade
);
create table Examination (
    id int not null, date date, grade varchar(30),
    teacher int, lecture int, student int, containingSemester int,
    primary key (id),
    foreign Key (id) references EObject (id) on delete cascade,
    foreign key (teacher) references Teacher (id) on delete set null,
    foreign key (lecture) references Lecture (id) on delete set null,
    foreign key (student) references Student (id) on delete set null,
    foreign key (containingSemester) references
        Semester (id) on delete cascade);
create table Lecture (
    id int not null, lectureNo int, title varchar(30), primary key (id),
    foreign Key (id) references EObject (id) on delete cascade);
create table Semester (
    id int not null, year int, winter boolean, primary key (id),
    foreign Key (id) references EObject (id) on delete cascade);
create table Module (
    id int not null, name varchar(30), primary key (id),
    foreign Key (id) references EObject (id) on delete cascade);
create table Person_firstNames (
    id int not null, value varchar(30) not null,
    foreign key (id) references Person (id) on delete cascade);
create table Student_lectures_Lecture (
    id int not null, lectures int not null,
    foreign key (id) references Student (id) on delete cascade,
    foreign key (lectures) references Lecture (id) on delete cascade);
create table Module_lecture_Lecture (
    source int not null unique, target int not null unique,
    foreign key (source) references Module (id) on delete cascade,
    foreign key (target) references Lecture (id) on delete cascade);
create table Teacher_lectures_Lecture (
    source int not null, target int not null, primary key (target),
    foreign key (source) references Teacher (id) on delete cascade,
    foreign key (target) references Lecture (id) on delete cascade);
create table Lecture_requiredByLectures_Lecture (
    source int not null, target int not null,
    foreign key (source) references Lecture (id) on delete cascade,
    foreign key (target) references Lecture (id) on delete cascade);
```

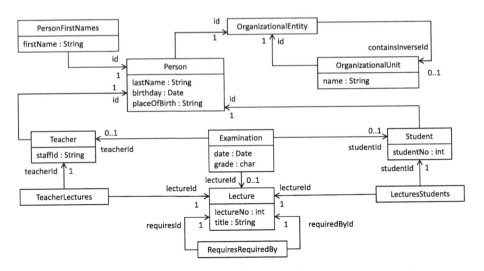

Fig. 5. Ecore model generated by the backward transformation.

5   Solution

The landscape of tools for QVT-R is populated sparsely. For our research, we used *medini QVT* [8]. medini QVT provides an integrated development environment for QVT-R, including a syntax-aided editor, an execution tool, and a debugging tool which supports breakpoints and step-wise execution.

With the help of medini QVT, we developed two versions of bidirectional transformations for object-relational mappings. These versions differ with respect to the use of *annotations*. With annotations, it is possible to augment a model with information which cannot be represented in the model itself. EMF supports annotations of elements of Ecore models (which are not needed here). To this end, the Ecore metamodel contains a class EAnnotation (not shown in Fig. 2). However, EMF does not provide generic support for annotations of model instances. Therefore, we extended the relational metamodel with an Annotation class; each model may own a set of string-valued annotations (upper right corner of Fig. 3).

Annotations constitute a well-known mechanism for reducing loss of information in model transformation; they are frequently used in model-to-code transformations to augment the generated source code. In the case of the bidirectional object-relational mapping, it turned out that the benefit of annotations is rather small; for example, they may be used to reconstruct the abstract and interface properties of classes. Therefore, the presentation below covers only the bidirectional transformation without annotations. In forward direction, the transformation creates the relational schema in Listing 1 from the Ecore model in Fig. 4. In backward direction, the Ecore model is reproduced almost exactly from the relational schema (except for some multiplicities and the enumeration type Grade).

Table 1. Rules for mapping Ecore models to relational schemas

Rule	Description
Package2Schema	Maps a package to a schema and an object table managing unique identifiers
Class2Table	Maps a class to a table with an id column (primary key)
RootClass2ForeignKey	Generates a foreign key into the object table
SubClass2ForeignKey	Generates a foreign key into the superclass table
SingleValuedAttribute2Column	Maps a single-valued attribute to a column
MultiValuedAttribute2Table	maps a multi-valued attribute to a table with id and value columns
SingleValuedUnidirectional-CrossReference2Column	Maps a single-valued unidirectional cross reference to a column and a foreign key into the table for the referenced class
MultiValuedUnidirectional-CrossReference2Table	Maps a multi-valued unidirectional cross reference to a table with id and reference columns and corresponding foreign keys
UnidirectionalContainment-Reference2Column	Maps a unidirectional containment reference to a column and a foreign key of the table for the target class
BidirectionalContainment-Reference2Column	Maps a bidirectional containment reference to a column and a foreign key of the table for the target class
BidirectionalCrossReference2Table	Maps a bidirectional cross reference to a table with source and target columns and corresponding foreign keys

Listing 2. Package2Schema.

```
top relation Package2Schema {
    name : String;
    sql_properties : OrderedSet(sql::Property);
    enforce domain ecoreModel emf_package : ecore::EPackage {
        name = name
    };
    enforce domain sqlModel sql_schema : sql::Schema {
        name = name,
        ownedTables = sql_rootTable : sql::Table {
            name = rootTableName(),
            ownedColumns = sql_idColumn : sql::Column {
                name = idName(),
                type = idType(),
                properties = sql_properties
            },
            ownedPrimaryKey = sql_primaryKey : sql::PrimaryKey {
                column = sql_idColumn
            }
        }
    };
    when {
        sql_properties = OrderedSet
            {sql::Property::NotNull, sql::Property::AutoIncrement};
    }
}
```

Listing 3. Class2Table.

```
top relation Class2Table {
    name : String;
    sql_properties : OrderedSet(sql::Property);
    enforce domain ecoreModel emf_package : ecore::EPackage {
        eClassifiers = emf_class : ecore::EClass {
            name = name
        }
    };
    enforce domain sqlModel sql_schema :sql::Schema {
        ownedTables = sql_table : sql::Table {
            name = name,
            ownedColumns = sql_idColumn : sql::Column {
                name = idName(),
                type = idType(),
                properties = sql_properties
            },
            ownedPrimaryKey = sql_primaryKey : sql::PrimaryKey {
                column = sql_idColumn
            }
        }
    };
    when {
        Package2Schema(emf_package, sql_schema);
        not (name = rootTableName());
        sql_properties = OrderedSet {sql::Property::NotNull};
    }
    where {
        AuxClass2Table(emf_class, sql_table);
    }
}
```

Since the backward transformation performs a pattern-based translation, it has to be ensured that the translation can be performed *uniquely*: Each pattern should be transformed in a unique way, i.e., there should be only one relation which may be applied to some pattern. Otherwise, patterns are inadvertently transformed multiple times. Therefore, the relations have to be checked pairwise for *conflicts*. In our bidirectional transformation, such conflicts do not occur. However, in some cases uniqueness is achieved only through naming conventions.

Table 1 summarizes the mapping rules of our bidirectional transformation; in addition, the transformation definition comprises numerous queries which will not be presented here. Below, we describe several mapping rules, each of which is realized by a QVT-R relation.

Listing 2 displays the relation for mapping a *package* to a *schema*. The source domain consists of a package with a name. The target domain is composed of a schema with the same name. In addition, it contains the object table for managing unique object identifiers. This table has a reserved name; all reserved names are defined by queries without arguments (QVT-R does not explicitly support constant definitions). In addition, the table has a single column for the object identifier (acting as primary key), which must not be null and is managed automatically (property AutoIncrement in the when clause).

The relation in Listing 3 maps a *class* to a *table*. For technical reasons, the enclosing package and the enclosing schema rather than the class and the table act as domain roots (in Ecore models, the inverses of containment links are not writable, which would be required if the class acts as domain root). By calling the relation Package2Schema in the when clause, it is demanded that the package must have already been mapped to the schema; in this way, dependencies among different relations are expressed. The class is mapped to a table with the same name. As in the object table, the table for the class gets an id column for the object identifier which serves as primary key. In the where clause, an auxiliary relation is called which establishes a relationship between the class and the table. This relationship cannot be queried by calling the top-level relation Class2Table, which relates only the package and the schema.

Listing 4. SubClass2ForeignKey.

```
top relation SubClass2ForeignKey {
    enforce domain ecoreModel emf_package : ecore::EPackage {
        eClassifiers = emf_class : ecore::EClass {
            eSuperTypes = emf_superClass : ecore::EClass {}
        }
    };
    enforce domain sqlModel sql_schema : sql::Schema {
        ownedTables = sql_table : sql::Table {
            ownedColumns = sql_idColumn : sql::Column {
                name = idName()
            },
            ownedForeignKeys = sql_foreignKey : sql::ForeignKey {
                column = sql_idColumn,
                ownedEvents = sql_event : sql::Event {
                    condition = sql::Condition::Delete,
                    action = sql::Action::Cascade
                },
                referencedTable = sql_referencedTable : sql::Table {}
            }
        }
    };
    when {
        Package2Schema(emf_package, sql_schema);
        AuxClass2Table(emf_class, sql_table);
        AuxClass2Table(emf_superClass, sql_referencedTable);
    }
}
```

For the backward transformation, it must be ensured that only appropriate tables are transformed into classes. The root table is excluded by a name constraint in the when clause. Tables for multi-valued attributes or references do have an id column, which, however, serves as a foreign rather than a primary key. This example demonstrates the conflict analysis which has to be performed to check the uniqueness of the backward transformation.

The relation in Listing 4 defines the mapping of the *inheritance hierarchy*. The when clause defines its preconditions: Package and schema, subclass and table, as well as superclass and referenced table mus correspond to each other. Thus, in a forward enforcing transformation, the package must have been transformed to a schema, and the classes must have been transformed to tables before the relation may be applied. The source pattern contains a class with a reference to its superclass. The target pattern contains a table with its id column and a foreign key referencing the superclass table. In a forward transformation, the foreign key is created, but the id column is reused: Since the column name is declared in the transformation as a key and the id column already exists, no fresh copy is created. The foreign key is decorated with an event which provides for cascading deletion if the referenced tuple is deleted; in this way, it is ensured that all tuples representing an object are deleted.

Listing 5. MultiValuedAttribute2Table.

```
top relation MultiValuedAttribute2Table {
    emf_className, emf_attributeName, sql_attributeTableName : String;
    emf_type, sql_type : String;
    sql_propertiesId, sql_propertiesValue : OrderedSet(sql::Property);
    sql_table : sql::Table;
    enforce domain ecoreModel emf_package : ecore::EPackage {
        eClassifiers = emf_class : ecore::EClass {
            name = emf_className,
            eStructuralFeatures = emf_attribute : ecore::EAttribute {
                name = emf_attributeName,
                eType = emf_dataType : ecore::EDataType {
                    name = emf_type
                },
                upperBound = −1,
                volatile = false, transient = false, derived = false
            }
        }
    };
    enforce domain sqlModel sql_schema : sql::Schema {
        ownedTables = sql_attributeTable : sql::Table {
            name = sql_attributeTableName,
            ownedColumns = sql_idColumn : sql::Column {
                name = idName(),
                type = idType(),
                properties = sql_propertiesId
            },
            ownedColumns = sql_valueColumn : sql::Column {
                name = valueName(),
                type = sql_type,
                properties = sql_propertiesValue
            },
            ownedForeignKeys = sql_foreignKey : sql::ForeignKey {
                column = sql_idColumn,
                ownedEvents = sql_event : sql::Event {
                    condition = sql::Condition::Delete,
                    action = sql::Action::Cascade
                },
                referencedTable = sql_table
            }
        }
    };
    when {
        Package2Schema(emf_package, sql_schema);
        AuxClass2Table(emf_class, sql_table);
        sql_attributeTableName =
            compose(Sequence{emf_className, emf_attributeName}); — Forward
        emf_className =
            decompose(sql_attributeTableName, 1); — Backward
        emf_attributeName =
            decompose(sql_attributeTableName, 2); — Backward
        sql_propertiesId = OrderedSet { sql::Property::NotNull };
        sql_propertiesValue = OrderedSet { sql::Property::NotNull };
        legalEcoreType(emf_type); — Forward
        sql_type = sqlType(emf_type); — Forward
        legalSqlType(sql_type);      — Backward
        emf_type = ecoreType(sql_type); — Backward
        emf_dataType = dataType(emf_type); — Backward
    }
}
```

The backward transformation is unique: For each table for a class, there is exactly one foreign key on the id column. Either the key references the object table, or it references another class table. The latter case is handled by the current relation, the former case is taken care of by the relation RootClass2ForeignKey.

The relation in Listing 5 maps a *multi-valued attribute* to a *table*. The source pattern contains a class with an attribute which is multi-valued (upperBound = -1) and neither volatile nor transient or derived. Among others, the when clause demands that the enclosing package must have been transformed to a schema and the class must have been mapped to a table. In addition, the when clause checks that the data type of the attribute is legal, and maps it to a predefined SQL type. Finally, the when clause includes an expression for calculating the name of the table to be generated. The target domain contains a table with two columns and one foreign key. The first column is an id, on which a foreign key into the owning class table is defined. The second column carries an attribute value. For both columns, null values are excluded.

Listing 6. UnidirectionalContainmentReference2Column.

```
top relation UnidirectionalContainmentReference2Column {
    name, columnName : String;
    sql_properties : OrderedSet(sql::Property);
    enforce domain ecoreModel emf_parentClass : ecore::EClass {
        eStructuralFeatures = emf_reference : ecore::EReference {
            name = name,
            containment = true,
            eType = emf_childClass : ecore::EClass {},
            volatile = false,
            transient = false,
            derived = false
        }
    };
    enforce domain sqlModel sql_childTable : sql::Table {
        ownedColumns = sql_column : sql::Column {
            name = columnName,
            type = idType(),
            properties = sql_properties
        },
        ownedForeignKeys = sql_foreignKey : sql::ForeignKey {
            column = sql_column,
            referencedTable = sql_parentTable : sql::Table {},
            ownedEvents = sql_event : sql::Event {
                condition = sql::Condition::Delete,
                action = sql::Action::Cascade
            }
        }
    };
    when {
        emf_reference.eOpposite.oclIsUndefined();  — Forward
        columnName = compose(Sequence {name, inverse()});  — Forward
        name = decompose(columnName, 1);  — Backward
        not (reservedColumnNames().includes(name));
        AuxClass2Table(emf_parentClass, sql_parentTable);
        AuxClass2Table(emf_childClass, sql_childTable);
        sql_properties = OrderedSet{};
    }
}
```

The backward transformation relies heavily on naming conventions. A table to be transformed into a multi-valued attribute is recognized with the help of columns with reserved names (idName() and valueName()). Furthermore, it assumes a specific composition of the table name, which has to be decomposed into a class name and an attribute name (see when clause). To generate an attribute in the Ecore model, it is further necessary to translate the SQL type of the value column into an Ecore data type.

Please note that the order of expressions in the when clause is not semantically significant. Rather, it is required that the expressions may be evaluated in an order which satisfies data flow constraints (e.g., in an equation $v = e$, either all variables are bound, or v is unbound and all variables in e are bound). In particular, expressions may be evaluated in different orders in forward and backward transformations. The comments Forward and Backward indicate that the respective expressions are relevant in only one transformation direction. However, they are actually evaluated in both directions, and execution must be successful in both cases.

As a last example, let us consider the mapping of a *unidirectional containment reference* to a *column* (Listing 6). The root of the source domain is the parent class, which owns a containment reference which is neither volatile nor transient or derived. Furthermore, it must not have an opposite reference (see when clause). Both the parent class and the referenced child class must have been transformed to tables. In the child table, a column is generated along with a foreign key with cascading deletion. The column name is derived from the name of the containment reference.

In the opposite direction, it has to be verified that the column name is not a reserved name. Furthermore, the name of the containment reference has to be extracted from the column name (see when clause again). Please note that the column name must be composed exactly as specified for the purpose of the forward transformation; otherwise, the equation for the column name will evaluate to false, preventing the application of the relation.

6   Discussion

The object-oriented and the relational approach to data modeling vary significantly from each other. Accordingly, a bidirectional transformation between Ecore models and relational schemata has to cope with *heterogeneous metamodels* (Fig. 1): For example, operations cannot be mapped at all to relational schemata, volatile, transient, and derived features should not be mapped because they are not stored persistently, and multi-valued features have to be simulated by tables. In the opposite direction, the concept of a primary key does not match the concept of an (implicit) unique object identifier, and it is difficult to map properties of columns and events attached to foreign keys to Ecore.

As we have shown in Subsect. 4.2, there is no unique, canonical way to derive a bidirectional transformation from the metamodels and their relationships. Rather, the transformation approach depends on *requirements* and *design decisions*. In our approach, we focused on the *forward direction*: We developed a transformation which — apart from a few restrictions — can translate any Ecore model to a relational schema. This transformation can also be executed in the opposite direction, but it works properly only on relational schemata generated by the forward transformation.

As a result, we obtained a *biased, asymmetric bidirectional transformation*: In forward direction, the transformation performs an *element-based translation*;

in contrast, the opposite transformation performs a *pattern-based translation*. As demonstrated in Subsect. 4.2, a pair of element-based translations would not constitute a bidirectional transformation based on a single relational specification.

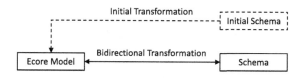

Fig. 6. Use of bidirectional transformations.

Let us discuss the implications of these observations on the way the bidirectional transformation may be used in practice (Fig. 6). We may start with an Ecore model and have it translated into a relational schema. Apart from some minor restrictions, the backward transformation may then be employed to reconstruct the Ecore model from the relational schema. However, if we try to start at the opposite end (with a relational schema), the backward transformation is useless unless the relational schema happens to satisfy the coding conventions underlying the forward transformation. In fact, migrating an arbitrary relational schema to an object-oriented class model constitutes a major database reverse engineering challenge [9].

Thus, using our bidirectional transformation, the *round-trip* has to start always with an Ecore model. Therefore, an initial *reverse engineering transformation* is required in the case that only a relational schema is available. After having improved the result of this transformation, we may start our round-trip.

Please note that the round-trip engineering scenario goes beyond the bidirectional data converter scenario inasmuch as it requires *incremental transformations*. In the most general case, both the source and the target model may be edited, and the changes have to be propagated in either direction. Using our bidirectional transformation, the Ecore modeler may freely employ the modeling concepts of Ecore. In contrast, the database designer has to stick faithfully to the coding conventions implemented in the forward transformation. This situation is not uncommon in round-trip engineering; in particular, it also applies to the well-known use case of the model-to-code round-trip.

Due to loss of information, the bidirectional transformation is _not_ *bijective*. There is no 1:1 mapping between elements of Ecore models and elements of relational schemata. While the backward transformation is controlled by the same rules as the forward transformation — executed in the opposite direction —, in general the original source model may be approximated, but it may not be reconstructed exactly. Thus, the backward transformation is not inverse to the forward transformation (this would require the guarantee of an exact reconstruction of the source model).

Annotations are used frequently for improving the functionality of transformations. In the transformation case studied in this paper, they are not vital, but they may improve the reconstruction of the original source model, e.g., by adding information about multiplicities, abstract vs. concrete classes, etc. However, the use of annotations is problematic for several reasons. First, they cannot be used if the metamodel does not provide for annotations of model elements. Second, they pollute models with tool-specific information. Third, they require the user to add annotations such that the backward transformation works properly.

All of the considerations stated above are independent of the model transformation language used for realizing a bidirectional transformation. We still have to discuss our *experiences* with *QVT-R*. As far as this case study is concerned, QVT-R was applied successfully: The relational specification behaves as expected, eliminating the need for writing separate unidirectional transformations. Since the backward transformation performs a pattern-based translation, it is crucial to check that a certain pattern does not match multiple relations. This check succeeded, but it had to be performed manually. Furthermore, for each relation is has to be verified that execution in both directions is possible. For most of the relations, this check was easy to perform. In some relations, it has to be checked carefully in which order expressions in the when clause are executed in each direction. Conceptually, some of these expressions are unidirectional. However, since QVT-R does not support *unidirectional expressions*, each expression is evaluated in each transformation direction. Therefore, it must be ensured that a conceptually unidirectional expression does not "stand in the way" if the transformation is executed in the opposite direction.

7   Related Work

The vast majority of transformation languages supports only unidirectional transformations; consider e.g. the well-known ATL language [5]. However, bidirectionality is not a unique feature of QVT-R [10]. The most prominent competitors are languages and tools based on *triple graph grammars* [11–14]. In contrast to the grammar-based approach, QVT-R follows a relational paradigm where a transformation is specified by a set of relations among patterns to be instantiated in the participating models.

QVT-R is a language which is defined only informally in the QVT standard. Not surprisingly, the informal definition suffers from lack of precision, contradictions, and ambiguities. Therefore, several authors worked on the definition of a *formal semantics* of *QVT-R*. Checking transformations are defined with the help of game theory [15], category theory [16], or the mu calculus [17]. [18,19] define enforcing transformations with the help of the mu calculus and the theory of problems, respectively.

On the practical side, a number of *applications* of *QVT-R* have been published in the scientific literature. These applications refer to a variety of domains, such as software measurement [20], model-based testing [21], pattern mining [22], translation of sequence diagrams to CSP [23], business process recovery [24], PIM to PSM transformation [25], model verification [26], model transformation verification [27], and service description models [28]. All of the cited papers focus on the provision of innovative functionality and use QVT-R to solve the problem at hand. Furthermore, with a few exceptions [25,28], all of these papers deal with unidirectional rather than bidirectional transformations.

Our work complements these efforts by exploring *case studies* for an *evaluation* of *bidirectional transformations* in QVT-R. In a predecessor paper [29], we investigated a bidirectional transformation between different languages for project scheduling (Gantt diagrams and CPM networks). We mainly focused on problems occurring in the synthesis of bidirectional transformations from unidirectional transformations, and proposed extensions to QVT-R. In contrast, the current case study of an object-relational mapping focuses on bidirectional transformations between heterogeneous metamodels (in the previous case study, the metamodels were different, but still quite closely related). In particular, we stated some observations concerning the properties of bidirectional transformations which, as we believe, are not confined to the case studied in this paper.

8   Conclusion

In this paper, we presented and investigated a bidirectional transformation between heterogeneous metamodels. To this end, we selected the well-known problem of object-relational mappings and presented a solution in QVT-R. The transformation is bidirectional, and it takes a large fraction of the Ecore metamodel into account. The concepts of Ecore models have to be simulated in relational schemata. The bidirectional transformation is not bijective; in contrast, source and target models are structured in significantly different ways. Furthermore, the transformation is not symmetric: While the forward transformation performs an element-based translation, the backward transformation realizes a pattern-based translation. Essentially, the backward transformation can be applied only to models generated by the forward transformation. QVT-R has been used successfully to solve the transformation problem at hand. However, the observations stated above are not specific to QVT-R and should apply to other bidirectional transformation languages, as well.

References

1. Schmidt, D.C.: Guest editor's introduction: model-driven engineering. IEEE Comput. **39**, 25–31 (2006)
2. Object Management Group: OMG Meta Object Facility (MOF) Core Specification Version 2.4.1, Needham, MA. formal/2013-06-01st edn. (2013)
3. Steinberg, D., Budinsky, F., Paternostro, M., Merks, E.: EMF Eclipse Modeling Framework. The Eclipse Series, 2nd edn. Addison-Wesley, Upper Saddle River (2009)
4. Object Management Group: Meta Object Facility (MOF) 2.0 Query/View/Transformation Specification Version 1.2, Needham, MA. formal/2015-02-01st edn. (2015)
5. Jouault, F., Allilaire, F., Bézivin, J., Kurtev, I.: ATL: A model transformation tool. Sci. Comput. Program. **72**, 31–39 (2008)

6. Kühne, T.: Matters of (meta-) modeling. Softw. Syst. Model. **5**, 369–385 (2006)
7. Reddy, S., Venkatesh, R., Zahid, A.: A relational approach to model transformation using QVT Relations. Technical report, Tata Research Development and Design Centre, Pune, India (2006). http://www.iist.unu.edu/vs/wiki-files/QVT-TRDCC.pdf
8. ikv++ technologies: medini QVT (2014). http://projects.ikv.de/qvt
9. Jahnke, J., Zündorf, A.: Applying graph transformations to database re-engineering. In: Ehrig, H., Engels, G., Kreowski, H.J., Rozenberg, G., (eds.) Handbook on Graph Grammars and Computing by Graph Transformation, vol. 2: Applications, Languages, and Tools. World Scientific, Singapore, pp. 267–286 (1999)
10. Czarnecki, K., Foster, J.N., Hu, Z., Lämmel, R., Schürr, A., Terwilliger, J.F.: Bidirectional transformations: a cross-discipline perspective. In: Paige, R.F. (ed.) ICMT 2009. LNCS, vol. 5563, pp. 260–283. Springer, Heidelberg (2009)
11. Schürr, A.: Specification of graph translators with triple graph grammars. In: Mayr, E.W., Schmidt, G., Tinhofer, G. (eds.) WG 1994. LNCS, vol. 903, pp. 151–163. Springer, Heidelberg (1995)
12. Königs, A., Schürr, A.: Tool integration with triple graph grammars - a survey. In: Heckel, R., (ed.) Proceedings of the School of SegraVis Research Training Network on Foundations of Visual Modelling Techniques (FoVMT 2004), vol. 148, pp. 113–150. Electronic Notes in Theoretical Computer Science, Dagstuhl, Germany, Elsevier Science (2006)
13. Schürr, A., Klar, F.: 15 years of triple graph grammars - research challenges, new contributions. In: Ehrig, H., Heckel, R., Rozenberg, G., Taentzer, G. (eds.) ICGT 2008. LNCS, vol. 5214, pp. 411–425. Springer, Heidelberg (2008)
14. Kindler, E., Wagner, R.: Triple graph grammars: Concepts, extensions, implementations, and application scenarios. Technical report tr-ri-07-284, University of Paderborn, Paderborn, Germany (2007)
15. Stevens, P.: A simple game-theoretic approach to checkonly QVT Relations. Softw. Syst. Model. **12**, 175–199 (2013)
16. Guerra, E., de Lara, J.: An algebraic semantics for QVT-Relations check-only transformations. Fundamentae Informaticae **114**, 73–101 (2012)
17. Bradfield, J., Stevens, P.: Recursive checkonly QVT-R Transformations with general *when* and *where* clauses via the modal mu calculus. In: de Lara, J., Zisman, A. (eds.) Fundamental Approaches to Software Engineering. LNCS, vol. 7212, pp. 194–208. Springer, Heidelberg (2012)
18. Bradfield, J., Stevens, P.: Enforcing QVT-R with mu-Calculus and Games. In: Cortellessa, V., Varró, D. (eds.) FASE 2013 (ETAPS 2013). LNCS, vol. 7793, pp. 282–296. Springer, Heidelberg (2013)
19. Giandini, R., Pons, C., Pérez, G.: A two-level formal semantics for the QVT language. In: Brogi, A., Araújo, J., Anaya, R. (eds.) Memorias de la XII Conferencia Iberoamericana de Software Engineering (CIbSE 2009), pp. 73–86. Medellín, Colombia (2009)
20. Mora, B., García, F., Ruiz, F., Piattini, M., Boronat, A., Gómez, A., Carsí, J.A., Ramos, I.: Software measurement by using QVT transformations in an MDA context. In: Cordeiro, J., Filipe, J., (eds.) Proceedings of the Tenth International Conference on Enterprise Information Systems (ICEIS 2008). Vol. DISI., Barcelona, Spain 117–124 (2008)

21. Lamancha, B.P., Mateo, P.R., de Guzmán, I.R., Usaola, M.P., Velthius, M.P.: Automated model-based testing using the UML testing profile and QVT. In: Proceedings of the 6th International Workshop on Model-Driven Engineering, Verification and Validation (MoDeVVa 2009), Denver, Colorado, USA, pp. 6:1–6:10. ACM (2009)

22. Kübler, J., Goldschmidt, T.: A pattern mining approach using QVT. In: Paige, R.F., Hartman, A., Rensink, A. (eds.) ECMDA-FA 2009. LNCS, vol. 5562, pp. 50–65. Springer, Heidelberg (2009)

23. Dan, L.: QVT based model transformation from sequence diagram to CSP. In: Calinescu, R., Paige, R.F., Kwiatkowska, M.Z. (eds.) Proceedings of the 15th IEEE International Conference on Engineering of Complex Computer Systems (ICECCS 2010), pp. 349–354. IEEE Computer Society, Oxford (2010)

24. Pérez-Castillo, R., García-Rodríguez de Guzmán, I., Piattini, M.: Implementing business process recovery patterns through QVT transformations. In: Tratt, L., Gogolla, M. (eds.) ICMT 2010. LNCS, vol. 6142, pp. 168–183. Springer, Heidelberg (2010)

25. Ma, K., Yang, B., Chen, Z., Abraham, A.: A relational approach to model transformation with QVT Relations supporting model synchronization. J. Univ. Comput. Sci. **17**, 1863–1883 (2011)

26. Elaasar, M., Briand, L., Labiche, Y.: Domain-specific model verification with QVT. In: France, R.B., Kuester, J.M., Bordbar, B., Paige, R.F. (eds.) ECMFA 2011. LNCS, vol. 6698, pp. 282–298. Springer, Heidelberg (2011)

27. Guerra, E., de Lara, J., Wimmer, M., Kappel, G., Kusel, A., Retschitzegger, W., Schönböck, J., Schwinger, W.: Automated verification of model transformations based on visual contracts. Autom. Softw. Eng. **20**, 5–46 (2013)

28. Schwichtenberg, S., Gerth, C., Huma, Z., Engels, G.: Normalizing heterogeneous service description models with generated QVT transformations. In: Cabot, J., Rubin, J. (eds.) ECMFA 2014. LNCS, vol. 8569, pp. 180–195. Springer, Heidelberg (2014)

29. Westfechtel, B.: A case study for evaluating bidirectional transformations in QVT Relations. In: Filipe, J., Maciaszek, L. (eds.) Proceedings of the 10th International Conference on the Evaluation of Novel Approaches to Software Engineering (ENASE 2015), pp. 141–155. Spain, INSTICC, SCITEPRESS, Barcelona (2015)

The Implementation of ISO/IEC 29110 Software Engineering Standards and Guides in Very Small Entities

Claude Y. Laporte[1], Rory V. O'Connor[2(✉)],
and Luis Hernán García Paucar[3]

[1] École de technologie supérieure, Montréal, Canada
Claude.Y.Laporte@etsmtl.ca
[2] School of Computing, Dublin City University, Dublin, Ireland
roconnor@computing.dcu.ie
[3] Universidad Peruana de Ciencias Aplicadas, Lima, Peru
luis.garcia@upc.edu.pe

Abstract. This paper outlines the details of seven case studies involving the pilot usage of the new standard ISO/IEC 29110 standard 'Lifecycle Profiles for Very Small Entities', which was specifically designed by Working Group 24 of ISO/IEC JTC1/SC7 to address the standardization needs of Very Small Entities (VSEs). The purpose of this paper is to add substantially to the body of knowledge and the literature on the rollout and implementation of this new and evolving standard and to act as guidance for other researchers in the design and implementation of ISO/IEC 29110 case studies. Furthermore it is hoped that that the lessons learnt from these case studies will help promote the adoption of this new standard in an industrial setting.

Keywords: Very small entities · ISO standards · ISO/IEC 29110 · VSE

1 Introduction

In the domain of software development, small and very small companies have the challenge of handling multiple small-scale, fast-moving projects allowing little room for unwieldy management processes, but still requiring an efficient and straightforward monitoring process [1]. Moreover due to the small number of people involved in the project and the organization, most of the management processes are performed through an informal way and less documented [2]. The perception of heavyweight processes, especially in terms of documentation, cost and nonalignment with current development process, are among the reasons why the companies did not plan to adopt a lifecycle standard in the short to medium term [3, 4].

The definition of "Small" and "Very Small" Entities is challengingly ambiguous, as there is no commonly accepted definition of the terms. The term "very small entity" (VSE) had been defined by the ISO/IEC JTC1/SC7 Working Group 24 and subsequently adopted for use in the new ISO/IEC 29110 process lifecycle standard as being "an entity (enterprise, organization, department or project) having up to 25 people" [5].

© Springer International Publishing Switzerland 2016
L.A. Maciaszek and J. Filipe (Eds.): ENASE 2015, CCIS 599, pp. 162–179, 2016.
DOI: 10.1007/978-3-319-30243-0_9

Industry recognizes the value of Very Small Entities (VSEs) in contributing valuable products and services. For example in Canada, close to 98 percent of businesses are small businesses with fewer than 50 employees. About 32 percent of these have between one and 19 employees [6].

VSEs have unique characteristics, which make their business styles different to larger organizations and therefore most of the management processes are performed through a more informal and less documented manner [7]. Furthermore there is an acknowledged lack of adoption of standards in small and very small companies, as the perception is that they have been developed for large software companies and not with the small organisation in mind [8, 43]. As smaller software companies have fewer resources in term of people and money there are many challenges [9].

There is evidence that the majority of small and very small software organizations are not adopting [54] existing standards/proven best practice models because they perceive the standards as being developed by large organizations and orientated towards large organizations, thus provoking the debate the in terms of number of employees, size does actually matter [10, 44]. Studies have shown that small firms' negative perceptions of process model standards are primarily driven by negative views of cost, documentation and bureaucracy [11]. In addition, it has been reported that SMEs find it difficult to relate standards to their business needs and to justify the application of the international standards in their operations [12]. Most SMEs cannot afford the resources for, or see a net benefit in, establishing software processes as defined by current standards and maturity models [13].

Accordingly, a new standard ISO/IEC 29110 "Lifecycle profiles for Very Small Entities" is aimed at meeting the specific needs of VSEs [14]. The overall objective of this new standard is to assist and encourage very small software organizations in assessing and improving their software process and it is predicted that this new standard could encourage and assist small software companies in assessing their software development process [50]. The approach [15] used to develop ISO/IEC 29110 started with the pre-existing international standards, such as the software life cycle standard ISO/IEC/IEEE 12207 [40, 41] and the documentation standard ISO/IEC/IEEE 15289 [42].

The working group behind the development of this standard is advocating the use of pilot projects as a mean to accelerate the adoption and utilization of ISO/IEC 29110 by VSEs [7]. Pilot projects are an important mean of reducing risks and learning more about the organizational and technical issues associated with the deployment of new software engineering practices [16]. To date a series of pilot projects for the software engineering profile standard have been completed in several countries with the results published in a variety of literature [17–20].

2 The ISO/IEC 29110 Standard for VSEs

The working group (WG24) of the ISO/IEC JTC1 SC7 mandated to develop the new set of standards for VSEs, used the concept of ISO standardized profiles (SP) to ISO/IEC/IEEE 12207 to develop the new standards for VSEs developing software. From a practical point of view, a profile is a kind of matrix, which identifies precisely the elements that are taken from existing standards from those that are not. The overall approach followed by WG24 to develop this new standard for VSE consisted of the following steps:

- develop a set of profiles for VSEs not involved in critical software development,
- select the ISO/IEC/IEEE 12207 process subsets applicable to VSEs having up to 25 people,
- select the description of the products, to be produced by a project, using ISO/IEC/IEEE 15289 standard
- develop guidelines, checklists, templates, examples to support the subsets selected.

The basic requirements of a software development process are that it should fit the needs of the project and aid project success [21, 22]. And this need should be informed by the situational context where in the project must operate and therefore, the most suitable software development process is contingent on the context [23, 24]. The core situational characteristic of the entities targeted by ISO/IEC 29110 is size.

Profile Groups are a collection of profiles. The Generic Profile Group has been defined as applicable to VSEs that do not develop critical software. This Profile Group is a collection of four profiles (Entry, Basic, Intermediate, Advanced) providing a roadmap to satisfying a vast majority of VSEs worldwide. VSEs targeted by the Entry Profile are VSEs working on small projects (e.g. at most six person-months effort) and for start-up VSEs. The Basic Profile describes software development practices of a single application by a single project team of a VSE. The Intermediate Profile is targeted at VSEs developing multiple projects with more than one project team. The Advanced Profile is target to VSEs which want to sustain and grow as a competitive software development business.

2.1   The ISO/IEC 29110 Basic Profile

At the core the Basic Profile of this standard is a Management and Engineering Guide, officially know as ISO/IEC TR 29110-5-1-2 [52], which focuses on Project Management and Software Implementation as illustrated in Fig. 1. The purpose of the Basic Profile is to define Software Implementation (SI) and Project Management (PM) processes from a subset of ISO/IEC/IEEE 12207 and ISO/IEC/IEEE 15289 [42] appropriate for VSEs, as illustrated in Fig. 1.

The main reason to include project management is that the core business of VSEs is software development and their financial success depends on successful project completion within schedule and on budget, as well as on making a profit. The high-level view and the relationships between the Software Implementation Process and the Project Management processes are illustrated in Fig. 1.

This standard defines two processes: Software Implementation and Project Management. The purpose of the Software Implementation process is the systematic performance of the analysis, design, construction, integration and tests activities for new or modified software products according to the specified requirements. The purpose of the Project Management process is to establish and carry out in a systematic way the tasks of the software implementation project, which allows complying with the project's objectives in the expected quality, time and cost.

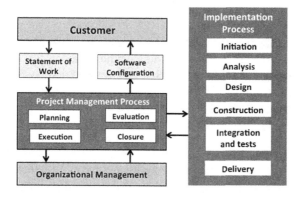

Fig. 1. Basic profile processes and activities [26].

The seven objectives of the PM process are [52]:

1. The Project Plan for the execution of the project is developed according to the Statement of Work and reviewed and accepted by the Customer.
2. Progress of the project is monitored against the Project Plan and recorded in the Progress Status Record.
3. The Change Requests are addressed through their reception and analysis. Changes to software requirements are evaluated for cost, schedule and technical imp
4. Review meetings with the Work Team and the Customer are held. Agreements are registered and tracked.
5. Risks are identified as they develop and during the conduct of the project.
6. A software Version Control Strategy is developed. Items of Software Configuration are identified, defined and baselined.
7. Software Quality Assurance is performed to provide assurance that work products and processes comply with the Project Plan and Requirements Specification.

The four activities of the Project Management Process are [52]:

- The Project Planning activity documents the planning details needed to manage the project.
- The Project Plan Execution activity implements the documented plan on the project.
- The Project Assessment and Control activity evaluates the performance of the plan against documented commitments.
- The Project Closure activity provides the project's documentation and products in accordance with contract requirements.

The purpose of the Software Implementation process is to achieve systematic performance of the analysis, design, construction, integration, and test activities for new or modified software products according to the specified requirements. The seven objectives of the SI process are [52]:

1. Tasks of the activities are performed through the accomplishment of the current Project Plan.
2. Software requirements are defined, analyzed for correctness and testability, approved by the Customer, baselined and communicated.
3. Software architectural and detailed design is developed and baselined. It describes the Software Components and internal and external interfaces of them.
4. Software Components defined by the design are produced. Unit test are defined and performed to verify the consistency with requirements and the design.
5. Software is produced performing integration of Software Components and verified using Test Cases and Test Procedures. Results are recorded at the Test Report.
6. A Software Configuration, that meets the Requirements Specification as agreed to with the Customer, which includes user, operation and maintenance documentations, is integrated, baselined and stored at the Project Repository.
7. Verification and Validation Tasks of all required work products are performed using the defined criteria to achieve consistency among output and input products in each activity.

The activities of the Software Implementation Process are [52]:

- Software Implementation Initiation: Ensures that the Project Plan established in Project Planning activity is committed to by the Work Team.
- Software Requirements Analysis: Analyzes the agreed Customer's requirements and establishes the validated project requirements.
- Software Architectural and Detailed Design: Transforms the software requirements to the system software architecture and software detailed design.
- Software Construction: Develops the software code and data from the Software Design.
- Software Integration and Tests: Ensures that the integrated Software Components satisfy the software requirements.
- Product Delivery: Provides the integrated software product to the Customer.

As illustrated in Fig. 1, the customer's statement of work (SOW) is used to initiate the PM process. The project plan will be used to guide the execution of the software requirements analysis, software architectural and detailed design, software construction, and software integration and test, and product delivery activities. The PM process closure activity will deliver the Software Configuration (i.e. a set of software products such as documentation, code and tests) and will obtain the customer's acceptance to formalize the end of the project.

2.2 ISO/IEC 29110 Deployment Assistance

A novel approach was taken to assist VSEs with the deployment of ISO/IEC 29110 and to provide guidance on the actual implementation this standard. A set of Deployment Packages (DPs) have been developed to define guidelines and explain in more detail the processes defined in the ISO/IEC 29110 profiles [26]. A deployment package is not a complete process reference model. Deployment packages are not intended to preclude or discourage the use of additional guidelines that VSEs find useful. The elements of a typical DP are: description of processes, activities, tasks, steps, roles, products, templates, checklists, examples, references and mapping to standards and models, and a list of tools.

DPs were designed such that a VSE can implement its content, without having to implement the complete ISO/IEC 29110 framework, i.e. all the management and engineering activities, at the same time. A set of nine DPs have been developed and are freely available from [27].

3 ISO/IEC 29110 Industry Trial

In this section we will present 7 trial implementations of ISO/IEC 29110. The purpose of these trials is to illustrate the usage of this standard in an industrial context and to provide feedback to standards authors. Whilst not a detailed methodological approach to validation of this standard and whilst acknowledging the validation limitations, we believe that these high level results are useful to researchers and practitioners alike.

3.1 Case 1: A Peruvian IT Start-up

Over 98 % of Perú are micro, small and medium enterprises (MSMEs) having fewer than 10 workers. About 7,6 million people work in companies having fewer than 10 workers. About 14,000 Peruvian companies are associated with the Information Technology and Communications (ITC) industry [28].

An implementation of ISO/IEC 29110 has been conducted in a four-people start-up VSE created in 2012 [29]. During its two years of existence, the VSE has been involved in over 80 projects, most of which have lasted less than two months. The VSE used agile practices to implement software solutions such as Web 2.0 responsive design systems and mobile applications. After completing the implementation of the Basic profile of ISO/IEC 29110, the VSE executed in 2014 a project under contract. The product developed was a software solution that facilitates communication between clients and legal consultants at one of the largest insurance companies in Peru. The solution had to be implemented on a web platform and deployed into a cloud environment.

Since the VSE was using agile methods to implement its software projects, customer requirements were expressed as user stories. For this project, the VSE had determined that the duration of a sprint would be one week. The project had 6 sprints. All software components, test cases, test procedures and user stories were linked through a traceability matrix. As illustrated inn Table 1, the total effort to implement the project was 882 h. The effort devoted to prevention activities such as installation of the environment (servers, tools, etc.) was 14 h, task execution took 585 h, reviews took 124 h and effort to correct defects identified in reviews and in testing took 159 h. The start-up wasted only 18 % of the total project effort (i.e. 159 h/882 h) on rework. Since it was the first time the VSE had executed the new ISO/IEC 29110 processes in a real project, so there was a learning curve that resulted in additional hours spent on rework

Table 1. Effort to execute, detect and correct errors [29].

Title of task	Prevention (hours)	Execution (Hours)	Review (Hours)	Rework (Hours)
Environment installation	14			
Project plan development		15	3	7
Plan execution, project assessment & control		108		
Specification development		107	28	58
Architecture development		35	10	14
Test plan development		45	8	11
Code development and testing		253	70	62
Develop user guide & maintenance document		14	5	7
Product deployment		6		
Project closure		2		
Total hours	**14**	**585**	**124**	**159**

for different project tasks. Despite this situation, the result was close to the percentage of rework (i.e. about 15 % to 25 %) of an organization that has implemented the Capability Maturity Model and is at maturity level 3.

For the first stage of the audit process, the Peruvian VSE invested about 22 h and 500 $ for the auditor. For the initial certification stage, the VSE invested about 63 h. The cost of the auditor, excluding the travel expenses, was 1,500$. The total effort and cost of an ISO/IEC 29110 audit is very small compared to a typical CMMI official assessment. This start-up became the first Peruvian VSE to obtain an ISO/IEC 29110 certification. The third stage of a certification cycle involves the completion of two surveillance audits one and two years after obtaining the initial certification. Finally, the fourth stage is the recertification of the VSE; once the 3-year certification cycle has elapsed.

In order to promote the recognition of qualifications between countries, there are international organizations such as the International Accreditation Forum (IAF). The IAF is the world association of conformity assessment accreditation bodies in the fields of management systems, products and services, and to date, it has more than 60 member countries. The Peruvian and the Brazilian accreditation bodies are members of this organization. An ISO/IEC 29110 certificate of conformity issued by an accreditation body member of the IAF is recognized by all members of IAF. The conformity certificate has become a major differentiator with regard to the main competitors of the VSE. The Peruvian start-up VSE has gained access to larger software development projects and increased its customer base. The VSE has increased its number of workers to date, from 4 to 23 employees.

3.2   Case 2: A Canadian IT Start-up

An implementation project has been conducted in an IT start-up VSE by a team of two developers [25]. Their web application allows users to collaborate, share and plan their trips simply and accessible to all. The use of the Basic profile of ISO/IEC 29110 has guided the start-up to develop an application of high quality while using proven practices of ISO 29110. The total effort of this project was nearly 1000 h. The two members of the team were assigned roles and activities of ISO 29110. The management and engineering guide of the Basic profile lists the documents that have to be developed during a project as well as their typical content.

During the software development, a traceability matrix was developed between the software requirements, defined in the requirements specification document, and the software components. Since, in most projects requirements, defined in the requirements activity, are never finalized at the end of this activity, a traceability matrix is very useful. One advantage of such a matrix is the possibility of rapidly identifying the impacted software components when modifications, additions, deletions, of soft ware requirements are done during a project.

Verification tasks, such as peer reviews, were performed on documents such as the requirement specifications and the architecture. The team used the desk-check to review their documents which is inexpensive and easy to implement in any organization and can be used to detect anomalies, omissions, improve a document or present and discuss alternative solutions.

As defined in ISO/IEC 29110, the software integration and tests activity ensures that the integrated Software Components satisfy the software requirements. This activity provides [30] work team review of the project plan to determine task assignment:

- Understanding of test cases and procedures and the integration environment.
- Integrated software components, corrected defects and documented results.
- Traceability of requirements and design to the integrated software product.
- Documented and verified operational and software user documentations.
- Verified software baseline.

To manage the defects detected, a tracking tool was used. Such software allowed the team to do an inventory of problems found during the integration and testing activity, to track problems and to classify them, and to determine a priority for each defect found. In this project, the open source Bugzilla software tool had been used to manage the defects.

The members of the start-up have recorded the effort, in person-hours, spent on tasks of the project to the nearest 30 min. For each major task, the effort to execute the task, the effort required to review a document, such as the software specification document, in order to detect errors and, the effort required to correct the errors (i.e. the rework). As an example, for the development of the software architecture document, it took 42.5 h to develop, an additional 1.5 h to conduct a review and an additional 3.5 h to correct the errors.

For this start-up project, about 8.9 % (i.e. 89 h/990.5 h) of the total project effort has been spent in prevention tasks such as the installation of the server, the workstations and the software tools; and only 12.6 % has been spent on rework (i.e. 125 h/990.5 h). This indicates that the use of appropriate standards, in this case for a start-up company, can guide all the phases of the development of a product such that the wasted effort (i.e. rework) is about the same as a more mature organization (i.e. about level 3 of CMM).

In most start-ups, the wasted effort, for a project similar to this one, would have added about 90 h (i.e. 30 % of 716 or 215 h– 125 h). This also implies, that for a net effort of about 6 h per member per day (if we subtract from an 8 h day interruptions (e.g. phone call), answering emails, discussions in corridors, etc.), the product would have been ready for delivery to a customer about 15 days, of 6 h, later than with a project with only 12.6 % of waste.

These two projects have demonstrated that, by using ISO/IEC 29110, it was possible to properly plan the project and develop the software product using proven software practices documented in standards as well as not interfering with the creativity during the development of their web site. People who think that standards are a burden, an unnecessary overhead and a treat to creativity should look at this start-up project and revisit their results.

3.3   Case 3: A Canadian/Tunisian IT Start-up

Metam is a company founded in 2013 by a software engineering graduate student of ÉTS. The company has one site in Canada and one site in Tunisia. Its business domains are software development services, web solutions, mobile applications as well as consulting services to implement ERP solutions. The Basic profile of ISO/IEC 29110 was used as the framework for the company's software processes. It was also used as a foundation to implement CMMI DEV level 2 practices because it was requested by some military contracts. In 2015, the VSE has 12 employees.

3.4   Case 4: A Large Canadian Financial Institution

The Cash Management IT department, of a large Canadian financial institution, is responsible for the development and maintenance of software tools used by traders. The software team is composed of 6 people. Each year, the division is faced with an increase in the numbers of requests to add, correct or modify features related to supported applications. Before the implementation of the ISO 29110-agile process, customers had the following complaints:

- Very difficult to know the status of specific requests
- Very often, there is an incident when a change is put in production.
- There is a large number of faults detected by the quality assurance department
- The development process is painful and the documentation produced is not very useful.

In response to this problem, the process was evaluated by comparing the tasks of the maintenance process in use to those of the Basic profile of the ISO/IEC 29110. Some shortcomings were found in the project management process and in the software implementation process.

The project management process has been adapted to the context of the division, by injecting a few tasks of the SCRUM methodology. The new agile process, using the Basic profile of the ISO/IEC 29110, has been tested on three pilot projects. The new process helped to significantly reduce the number of major incidents caused by changes to the tools of the traders. The users are delighted with the new agile planning and control approach, which allows them to better manage their priorities and to always know the status of their requests. The maintenance team was also very pleased to see an improvement in the quality of the change requests, resulting in a noticeable decrease in the number of defects when handed to traders.

The adoption of this agile approach, however, requires a higher availability from the users. Initially, this new approach presented a challenge. In some cases, a few users appointed a representative to play the role of head of product backlog. But, that person did not have adequate knowledge of the business domain. Also, the head of product backlog was not able to respond quickly to questions from developers about the requirements, and user stories were not sufficiently documented in advance to maintain the velocity of the team. Finally, representatives of the Project Office and the Audit Group required a few modifications to the new ISO 29110-agile process.

A survey has been conducted to measure the satisfaction level of traders after the deployment of the new ISO 29110-agile process. The following ten questions were asked to traders (on a 0 to 10 scale):

- How do you qualify the quality of our software upgrades (e.g. number of incidents recorded in production)?
- Are you well informed about the content of the next software upgrade?
- Is the frequency of delivery right for you?
- How do you trust the new process?
- How would you describe the ability of the new process to respond to your needs?
- How easy is it to consult the status of a change request?
- How much the new process prioritizes the added value for you as a trader?
- What is the quality level of upgrades?
- Are you satisfied with the productivity of the team in response to your needs?
- What is your overall level of satisfaction about the new process (e.g. quality, cost, return on investment)?

The new ISO 29110-agile process has been tested on three pilot projects. The new process helped to significantly reduce the number of major incidents caused by changes to the tools of the traders. The users are delighted with the new agile planning and control approach, which allows them to better manage their priorities and to always know the status of their requests. The maintenance team was also very pleased to see an improvement in the quality of the change requests, resulting in a noticeable decrease in the number of defects in the software tools handed to traders.

3.5   Case 5: A Canadian Company in the Automotive Field

TM4 is a Canadian company of more than 140 people, of whom 14 are directly employed as software engineers, the meeting the criteria of being a VSE. The company designs and sells electric powertrain systems in the automotive field. Their products are embedded software that controls the operation of engines in real time and software that controls the interactions between the components of a vehicle.

The company planned to increase its production systems in the coming years. Before this increase in production, and for the sake of improvement and compliance with standards, the company wanted to review and improve its software development processes.

The Basic Profile of ISO/IEC 29110 was used in this effort to improve its processes. A compliance study was conducted to establish the difference between the processes in place and those proposed by the ISO/IEC 29110. A pilot project has been successfully completed in May 2015. New software projects will use the ISO/IEC 29110-based processes.

An analysis of differences between ISO/IEC 29110 and ISO 26262, a standard for the automotive industry, was conducted and an economic impact assessment was conducted using the methodology developed by ISO [31].

3.6   Case 6: A Canadian Transportation Enterprise

A project was created to define and implement project management and engineering processes at CSinTrans Inc. (CSiT), a Canadian company, established in 2011 [32]. The company specializes in the integration of interactive systems, communication and security in the field of public transport such as trains, subways and buses and railway stations, and stations bus stops. Some customers in this domain are requiring from their suppliers to be assessed at CMMI Level 2. Implementing the practices of CMMI Level 2 was too demanding for a start-up. Instead, ISO/IEC 29110 standards and guides for systems engineering, developed from a subset of ISO/IEC/IEEE 15288 [53] and ISO/IEC/IEEE 15289 appropriate for VSEs, have been used as the main reference for the development of the processes of CSiT [37].

To avoid additional process and produce too many documents, participants gave themselves the 2 sets of guidelines:

- Regarding processes, the guideline was to add tasks not described in the Basic profile only if they add value to the context and projects of the company or provided an alignment with CMMI level 2.
- For the document templates, the guidelines wer
  - Group different documents into one where this is possible;
  - Each section of a template must be relevant and applicable. If a section does not provide added value, it is not included.

The ISO 29110 standard has helped raise the maturity of this young organization by implementing proven practices and developing uniform work products. ISO/IEC 29110 was a good starting point to align processes with selected level 2 and 3 practices of the CMMI model. Compliance with the ISO standard allowed CSiT to be recognized as producing quality products. ISO/IEC 29110 has also helped in developing lightweight processes allowing the small company to remain flexible as well as its ability to react quickly to its customers. CSiT performed an external audit of the management and engineering processes, mainly based on ISO 29110.

3.7   Case 7: The Implementation in a Division of an Engineering Enterprise

A Canadian division of a large American engineering company, the Transmission & Distribution of electricity division, has implemented a program to define and implement project management processes for their small-scale and medium-scale projects [51]. The firm already had a robust and proven process to manage their large-scale projects. The objectives of this process improvement project were to reduce cost overruns and project delays, standardize practices to facilitate the integration of new managers, increase the level of customer satisfaction and to reduce risk-related planning deviations. Their projects are classified into three categories as illustrated in Table 2. As illustrated in the table, over 95 % of the projects fall in the small- and medium-scale categories.

Pilot projects have been conducted to test the project management processes and associated support tools (e.g. templates, checklists). The pilot projects consisted of running three different projects where project managers implemented the process and the associated tools. Managers then evaluated the proposed processes, identified problems and potential improvements.

Table 2.   Classification of projects by the engineering firm [51].

	Small project	Medium project	Large project
Duration	< 2 months	> 2 and < 8 months	> 8 months
Team size	<= 4 people	4-8 people	> 8 people
No. of engineering specialties	1	>1	Many
Engineering fees	$5,000 - $70,000	$50,000 - $350,000	> $350,000
Percentage of projects	70 %	25 %	5 %

The project management practices used by the company's managers were assessed against the ISO standard's Basic Profile. The division used the project management process of the Entry Profile of ISO 29110 [52] to document their small-scale project management process and they used the project management process of the Basic profile to document their medium-scale project management process.

Three pilot projects have been conducted to test the project management processes and associated support tools (e.g. templates, checklists). The pilot projects consisted of running three different projects where project managers implemented the process and the associated tools. Managers then evaluated the proposed processes, identified problems and potential improvements. The lessons learned sessions conducted at the end of the pilot projects have identified minor adjustments to the processes and tools.

A section of the intranet, dedicated to project management, was created and served as a main access to project management documents such as project management process guides, checklists, forms and templates. Project managers were trained in the new processes and support tools.

The tools developed to support the project management processes proved very useful and helped the project managers rapidly integrate the knowledge required to execute the processes. The improvement program was so successful that managers of the company's other divisions have shown an interest in learning this approach in order to implement it within their respective divisions.

ISO has developed a methodology to assess and communicate the economic benefits of standards (ISO 2010), which was used, by the engineering firm, to estimate the anticipated costs and benefits over a period of three years. The key objectives of the ISO methodology are to provide:

The sponsors of this process definition project made the estimates. The improvement program project sponsors made an estimate of anticipated costs and benefits over a period of three years. Table 3 shows the results for the first three years.

Table 3. Costs and benefits estimations [51].

	Year 1	Year 2	Year 3	Total
Implement & maintain	59 600$	50 100$	50 100$	159 800$
Net Benefits	255 500$	265 000$	265 000$	785 500$

The engineering firm is planning to document and implement their systems engineering processes for the small-scale and medium scale projects using the Entry and Basic Profiles of the ISO 29110 systems engineering standard and guides.

4 Discussion and Future Work

This section will present some discussion on the pilot case study implementation and well as describe future work in relation for the continued development of ISO/IEC 29110 set of standards.

4.1 Discussion

The seven pilot case studies presented in this paper have demonstrated that by using ISO/IEC 29110, it was possible to properly plan and execute projects and develop products or conduct projects using proven system or software engineering practices without interfering with the creativity of developers. The relationship between the success of a software company and the software process it utilized has been investigated [33, 34] showing the need for all organizations, not just VSEs to pay attention to software process practices such as ISO standards.

4.2 Planned Standard Development

As ISO/IEC 29110 is an emerging standard there is much work yet to be completed. The main remaining work item is to finalize the development of the remaining two software profiles of the Generic Profile Group: (a) Intermediate - management of more than one project and (b) Advanced - business management and portfolio management practices.

Working Group 24 of ISO/IEC JTC1/SC7 who was initially authorized to develop the ISO/IEC 29110 for software, was also assigned to develop a similar approach for VSEs involved in the domain of systems engineering [35, 36]. Recently the ISO published the systems engineering and management guide of the Basic profile ISO/IEC TR 29110-5-6-2:2014 [37] and Entry profile ISO/IEC TR 29110-5-6-1:2015 [38].

Work currently underway on an assessment mechanism for ISO/IEC 29110 [39], a clear niche market need is emerging which may force the process assessment community to change their views on how process assessments are carried out for VSEs. It is clear that the process assessment community will have to rethink process assessment, new methods and ideas for assessing processes in VSEs.

4.3 Standards Education

In 2009, it was proposed to establish an informal interest group about education. Its main objective is to develop a set of courses for software undergraduate and graduate students such that students learn about the ISO standards for Very Small Entities before they graduate.

One way to develop standards professionals is by having professional graduate students involved in the application and improvement of international standards. At the École de technologie supérieure (ÉTS), a 10,000-student engineering school of Montréal, International Software Engineering Standards are introduced and used in Software Quality Assurance and Software Process Improvement courses and industrial projects conducted by graduate professional software engineering and IT students [55].

The role of education [45–47] is a significant issue in ensuring that the next generation of software project managers and software process engineers are both familiar with the benefits of standards, specifically in VSEs and the role of ISO/IEC 29110 in particular. Such education programmes may assist with addressing the perceived issues with standards adoption and the lack of managerial commitment [48, 49] in adopting VSE standards.

5 Additional Information

The following web site provides more information about ISO/IEC 29110: http://profs. logti.etsmtl.ca/claporte/English/VSE/index.html

References

1. Coleman, G., O'Connor, R.V.: An investigation into software development process formation in software start-ups. J. Enterp. Inf. Manage. **21**(6), 633–648 (2008)
2. O'Connor, R.V., Laporte, C.Y.: Software project management in very small entities with ISO/IEC 29110. In: Winkler, D., O'Connor, R.V., Messnarz, R. (eds.) EuroSPI 2012. CCIS, vol. 301, pp. 330–341. Springer, Heidelberg (2012)

3. Basri, S., O'Connor, R.V.: Evaluation on knowledge management process in very small software companies: a survey. In: 5th Knowledge Management International Conference, Terengganu, Malaysia, May 2010

4. Mora, M., O'Connor, R., Raisinghani, M., Macías-Luévano, J.: An IT service engineering and management framework (ITS-EMF). Int. J. Serv. Sci. Manage. Eng. Technol. 2(2), 1–15 (2011)

5. Laporte, C.Y., Alexandre, S., O'Connor, R.: A software engineering lifecycle standard for very small enterprises. In: O'Connor, R.V., et al. (eds.) Software Process Improvement. CCIS, vol. 16, pp. 129–141. Springer, Heidelberg (2008)

6. Statistics Canada (2008). http://www.ic.gc.ca/sbstatistics

7. O'Connor, R., Laporte, C.Y.: Towards the provision of assistance for very small entities in deploying software lifecycle standards. In: Proceedings of the 11th International Conference on Product Focused Software (PROFES 2010). ACM (2010)

8. O'Connor, R., Coleman, G.: Ignoring 'Best Practice': Why Irish Software SMEs are rejecting CMMI and ISO 9000. Australas. J. Inf. Syst. 16(1) (2009)

9. Basri, S., O'Connor, R.V.: A study of software development team dynamics in SPI. In: O'Connor, R.V., Pries-Heje, J., Messnarz, R. (eds.) EuroSPI 2011. CCIS, vol. 172, pp. 143–154. Springer, Heidelberg (2011)

10. Coleman, G., O'Connor, R.: Software process in practice: a grounded theory of the Irish software industry. In: Richardson, I., Runeson, P., Messnarz, R. (eds.) EuroSPI 2006. LNCS, vol. 4257, pp. 28–39. Springer, Heidelberg (2006)

11. Petkov, D., Edgar-Nevill, D., Madachy, R., O'Connor, R.: Information systems, software engineering, and systems thinking: Challenges and opportunities. Int. J. Inf. Technol. Syst. Approach (IJITSA) 1(1), 62–78 (2008)

12. O'Connor, R., Basri, S.: The effect of team dynamics on software development process improvement. Int. J. Hum. Capital Inf. Technol. Prof. 3(3), 13–26 (2012)

13. O'Connor, R.V., Coleman, G.: An investigation of barriers to the adoption of software process best practice models. In: ACIS 2007 Proceedings, vol. 35 (2007)

14. O'Connor, R.V., Laporte, C.Y.: Deploying lifecycle profiles for very small entities: an early stage industry view. In: O'Connor, R.V., Rout, T., McCaffery, F., Dorling, A. (eds.) SPICE 2011. CCIS, vol. 155, pp. 227–230. Springer, Heidelberg (2011)

15. O'Connor, R.V., Laporte, C.Y.: Using ISO/IEC 29110 to harness process improvement in very small entities. In: O'Connor, R.V., Pries-Heje, J., Messnarz, R. (eds.) EuroSPI 2011. CCIS, vol. 172, pp. 225–235. Springer, Heidelberg (2011)

16. Laporte, C.Y., O'Connor, R., Fanmuy, G.: International systems and software engineering standards for very small entities. CrossTalk J. Defense Softw. Eng. 26(3), 28–33 (2013)

17. Laporte, C.Y., Séguin, N., Boas, G.V.: Seizing the benefits of software and systems engineering standards. ISO Focus +, International Organization for Standardization, pp. 32–36, February 2013

18. O'Connor, R.V.: Evaluating management sentiment towards ISO/IEC 29110 in very small software development companies. In: Mas, A., Mesquida, A., Rout, T., O'Connor, R.V., Dorling, A. (eds.) SPICE 2012. CCIS, vol. 290, pp. 277–281. Springer, Heidelberg (2012)

19. Ribaud, V., Saliou, P., O'Connor, R.V., Laporte, C.Y.: Software engineering support activities for very small entities. In: Riel, A., O'Connor, R., Tichkiewitch, S., Messnarz, R. (eds.) EuroSPI 2010. CCIS, vol. 99, pp. 165–176. Springer, Heidelberg (2010)

20. Galvan, S., Mora, M., O'Connor, R.V., Acosta, F., Alvarez, F.: A compliance analysis of agile methodologies with the ISO/IEC 29110 project management process. Procedia Comput. Sci. 64, 188–195 (2015)

21. Clarke, P., O'Connor, R.V.: The meaning of success for software SMEs: an holistic scorecard based approach. In: O`Connor, R.V., Pries-Heje, J., Messnarz, R. (eds.) EuroSPI 2011. CCIS, vol. 172, pp. 72–83. Springer, Heidelberg (2011)
22. O'Connor, R., Clarke, P.: Software process reflexivity and business performance: initial results from an empirical study. In: International Conference on Software and System Process (ICSSP 2015), 24–26 Aug 2015
23. Jeners, S., Clarke, P., O'Connor, R.V., Buglione, L., Lepmets, M.: Harmonizing software development processes with software development settings – a systematic approach. In: McCaffery, F., O'Connor, R.V., Messnarz, R. (eds.) EuroSPI 2013. CCIS, vol. 364, pp. 167–178. Springer, Heidelberg (2013)
24. Clarke, P., O'Connor, R.: The situational factors that affect the software development process: Towards a comprehensive reference framework. J. Inf. Softw. Technol. **54**(5), 433–447 (2012)
25. Laporte, C.Y., Hébert, C., Mineau, C.: Development of a social network website using the new ISO/IEC 29110 standard developed specifically for very small entities. Softw. Qual. Prof. J. **16**(4), 4–25 (2014). ASQ
26. O'Connor, R.V., Laporte, C.Y.: An innovative approach to the development of an international software process lifecycle standard for very small entities. Int. J. Inf. Technol. Syst. Approach **7**(1), 1–22 (2014)
27. Deployment Packages repository. http://profs.logti.etsmtl.ca/claporte/English/VSE/index.html
28. Krasner, H.: Using the cost of quality approach for software. Crosstalk J. Defense Softw. Eng. **11**, 6–11 (1998)
29. Garcia, L., Laporte, C.Y., Arteaga, J., Bruggmann, M.: Implementation and certification of ISO/IEC 29110 in an IT startup in Peru. Softw. Qual. Prof. J. **17**(2), 16–29 (2015). ASQ
30. ISO/IEC TR 29110–1:2011, "Software Engineering - Lifecycle Profiles for Very Small Entities (VSEs) - Part 1: Overview". Geneva: International Organization for Standardization (ISO), (2011). Available at no cost from ISO. http://standards.iso.org/ittf/PubliclyAvailableStandards/c051150_ISO_IEC_TR_29110-1_2011.zip
31. ISO, Economic Benefits of Standards, Methodology guide » Version 2.0. International Organization for Standardization, Geneva, Switzerland 2013
32. Tremblay, N., Menaceur, J., Poliquin, D., Laporte, C.Y.: Mise en place de processus de gestion de projets et d'ingénierie système chez CSiT, une entreprise canadienne dans le domaine du transport collectif. Revue Génie Logiciel **114**, 11–27 (2015)
33. Laporte, C.Y., O'Connor, R.V.: A systems process lifecycle standard for very small entities: development and pilot trials. In: Barafort, B., O'Connor, R.V., Poth, A., Messnarz, R. (eds.) EuroSPI 2014. CCIS, vol. 425, pp. 13–24. Springer, Heidelberg (2014)
34. O'Connor, R.V., Basri, S.: Understanding the role of knowledge management in software development: a case study in very small companies. Int. J. Syst. Serv. Oriented Engineering **4**(1), 39–52 (2014)
35. Laporte, C.Y., O'Connor, R,V.: Systems and software engineering standards for very small entities: implementation and initial results. In: 9th International Conference on the Quality of Information and Communications Technology (QUATIC), pp.38–47, 23–26 September 2014
36. O'Connor, R.V., Sanders, M.: Lessons from a pilot implementation of ISO/IEC 29110 in a group of very small Irish companies. In: Woronowicz, T., Rout, T., O'Connor, R.V., Dorling, A. (eds.) SPICE 2013. CCIS, vol. 349, pp. 243–246. Springer, Heidelberg (2013)

37. ISO/IEC TR 29110-5-6-2:2014 - Systems Engineering – Lifecycle Profiles for Very Small Entities (VSEs) – Part 5-6-2: Systems engineering - Management and engineering guide: Generic profile group: Basic profile, International Organization for Standardization/Interna tional Electrotechnical Commission: Geneva, Switzerland. Available at no cost from ISO. http://standards.iso.org/ittf/PubliclyAvailableStandards/c063371_ISO_IEC_29110-5-6_2_2014.zip

38. ISO/IEC TR 29110-5-6-1:2015 - Systems and software engineering – Lifecycle Profiles for Very Small Entities (VSEs) –Part 5-6-1: System engineering Management and engineering guide: Generic profile group: Entry profile, International Organization for Standardization/International Electrotechnical Commission: Geneva, Switzerland. Available at no cost from ISO. http://standards.iso.org/ittf/PubliclyAvailableStandards/index.html

39. ISO/IEC 29110-4-1:2011, Software Engineering – Lifecycle Profiles for Very Small Entities (VSEs) - Part 4-1: Profile specifications: Generic profile group. Geneva: International Organization for Standardization (ISO) (2011)

40. ISO/IEC/IEEE 12207, Systems and software engineering– Software life cycle processes. International Organization for Standardization/International Electrotechnical Commission: Geneva, Switzerland

41. Clarke, P., O'Connor, R.: Harnessing ISO/IEC 12207 to examine the extent of SPI activity in an organisation. In: Riel, A., O'Connor, R., Tichkiewitch, S., Messnarz, R. (eds.) EuroSPI 2010. CCIS, vol. 99, pp. 25–36. Springer, Heidelberg (2010)

42. ISO/IEC/IEEE 15289, Systems and software engineering - Content of systems and software life cycle process information products (Documentation), International Organization for Standardization/International Electrotechnical Commission: Geneva, Switzerland

43. O'Connor, R.V., Basri, S., Coleman, G.: Exploring managerial commitment towards SPI in small and very small enterprises. In: Riel, A., O'Connor, R., Tichkiewitch, S., Messnarz, R. (eds.) EuroSPI 2010. CCIS, vol. 99, pp. 268–279. Springer, Heidelberg (2010)

44. Basri, S., O'Connor, R.: A study of knowledge management process practices in very small software companies. Am. J. Econ. Bus. Adm. 3(4), 636–644 (2012)

45. Laporte, C.Y., O'Connor, R.: Software process improvement in graduate software engineering programs. In: O'Connor, R.V., Mitasiunas, A., Ross, M. (eds.) Proceeding of the 1st International Workshop on Software Process Education, Training and Professionalism (SPETP 2015). CEUR Electronic Workshop Proceedings, vol. 1368, pp. 18–24 (2015)

46. Laporte, C.Y., O'Connor, R.V., Software process improvement in graduate software engineering programs. In: Proceedings 1st International Workshop Software Process Education, Training and Professionalism (SPEPT 2015). CEUR Workshop Proceedings, pp. 18–24 (2015)

47. Ribaud, V., Matthieu, A.B., O'Connor, R.V.: Process Assessment Issues in a Bachelor Capstone Project. In: Proceedings 1st International Workshop Software Process Education, Training and Professionalism (SPEPT 2015), pp. 25 – 33, CEUR Workshop Proceedings, 2015

48. Sanchez-Gordon, M.-L., O'Connor, R.V., Colomo-Palacios, R.: Evaluating VSEs viewpoint and sentiment towards the ISO/IEC 29110 standard: a two country grounded theory study. In: Rout, T., O'Connor, R.V., Dorling, A. (eds.) SPICE 2015. CCIS, vol. 526, pp. 114–127. Springer, Heidelberg (2015)

49. Basri, S., O'Connor, R.: Organizational commitment towards software process improvement an Irish software VSEs case study. In: 4th International Symposium on Information Technology 2010 (ITSim 2010), Kuala Lumpur, Malaysia, June 2010

50. Ribaud, V., O'Connor, R.V.: Blending process assessment and employees competencies assessment in very small entities. In: O'Connor, R.V., Akkaya, M.U., Kemaneci, K., Yilmaz, M., Poth, A., Messnarz, R., (eds.) EuroSPI 2015. CCIS, vol. 543, pp. 206–219. Springer, Heidelberg (2015). doi:10.1007/978-3-319-24647-5_17

51. Laporte, C.Y., Chevalier, F.: An innovative approach to the development of project management processes for small-scale projects in a large engineering company. In: 25th Annual International Symposium of INCOSE (International Council on Systems Engineering), Seattle, US, 13–16 July 2015

52. ISO/IEC TR 29110-5-1-1:2011 – Software engineering – Lifecycle Profiles for Very Small Entities (VSEs) –Part 5-2-1: Management and engineering guide: Generic profile group: Entry profile, International Organization for Standardization/International Electrotechnical Commission: Geneva, Switzerland. Available at no cost from ISO. http://standards.iso.org/ittf/PubliclyAvailableStandards/c051153_ISO_IEC_TR_29110-5-1_2011.zip ISO/IEC TR 29110-5-1-1:2011

53. ISO/IEC/IEEE 15288, Systems and software engineering– System life cycle processes. International Organization for Standardization/International Electrotechnical Commission: Geneva, Switzerland

54. Clarke, P., O'Connor, R.V.: An approach to evaluating software process adaptation. In: O'Connor, R.V., Rout, T., McCaffery, F., Dorling, A. (eds.) SPICE 2011. CCIS, vol. 155, pp. 28–41. Springer, Heidelberg (2011)

55. Laporte, C., O'Connor, R., Garcia Paucar, L., Gerancon, B.: An innovative approach in developing standard professionals by involving software engineering students in implementing and improving international standards. Stand. Eng. J. SES (The Society for Standards Professionals) **67**(2), 2–9 (2015)

Improving Mobile Banking Usability Based on Sentiments

Lalit Mohan[✉], Neeraj Mathur, and Y. Raghu Reddy

Software Engineering Research Center,
International Institute of Information Technology,
Hyderabad (IIIT-H), Hyderabad, India
{lalit.mohan,neeraj.mathur,raghu.reddy}@students.iiit.ac.in
http://www.iiit.ac.in

Abstract. India has 868+ million active subscribers with 160+ smartphone users. However,the number of mobile banking transactions on smartphones is less than 1/6th of the smartphone users and 1/5th of the other digital transactions excluding ATM channel. Though adoption of mobile (feature/smartphone) has been in the increasing trend, concerns of security, availability of sustained data connectivity and usability will be the key factors for improving usage. We suggest a Mobile App Usability Index (MAUI) metric for improving usability based on various usability parameters. The parameters were formulated from sentiment analysis of user comments posted in Google play store on the mobile banking apps of banks. The proposed index has been validated by mobile banking channel managers and chief information security officers.

Keywords: Mobile app usability · Mobile banking in India · Usability · Error handling

1 Introduction

With increasing penetration of 3G and the launch of 4G connections, adoption of smart phones (growth rate of 44 % as per International Data Corporation, 2015 reports) and internet (expected adoption to be 300+ million in next 2 years as per India on the Go, 2015 report) on mobile phones is expected to grow significantly. In the next 2 years, the number of internet users in India is expected to be more than the population of major countries like USA. From a general market perspective, decreasing smart-phone prices, younger population in India and improving technology awareness are some of the reasons for the growth of smart-phone [3].

The increasing usage of Internet on smart phones provides opportunities to banks for improved adoption of mobile banking. In India, about 120 banks (50 % increase from 2014) provide mobile app banking services to their customers [15]. Also, Reserve Bank of India (RBI), India's central banking institution, has granted license for another 23 (Payment and Small Finance) in anticipation

© Springer International Publishing Switzerland 2016
L.A. Maciaszek and J. Filipe (Eds.): ENASE 2015, CCIS 599, pp. 180–194, 2016.
DOI: 10.1007/978-3-319-30243-0_10

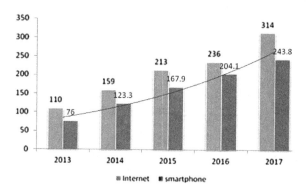

Fig. 1. Smartphone and internet usage in India ([19] and KPMG).

of improving Financial Inclusion using disruptive technologies including Mobile Banking between Aug–Sep'15. A report published by RBI suggests that a mobile banking transaction costs just 2 % of the cost of a branch transaction, one-tenth of the cost of an ATM transaction and half the cost of Internet banking transaction. In other words, the transaction cost of mobile banking is much lower than any other delivery channel in the bank [14]. This indicates that there are huge opportunities for improved adoption and increasing the operation efficiency of banks in India. Customers perform mobile banking using mobile apps, browsers on the mobile devices, Unstructured Supplementary Service Data (USSD), Short Message Service (SMS), Near Field Communication (NFC), Mobile wallets, etc. Mobile banking using apps compared to m-websites is relatively easy for frequent and repeated transaction and interactivity. The mobile transaction data shown in Fig. 1 shares insights into the rapid adoption of mobile banking. The number of mobile banking transactions in Jan'13 was about 9.5 million with an average transaction amount of INR 2,758 whereas the number of transactions in Jul'15 was about 25+ million with an average transaction amount of INR 8,574 [16].

Although there is an increase in the average transaction amount, there are opportunities for improving the adoption of mobile app banking. Considering that an average customer would perform a minimum of 3 transactions (for paying utility bills, mobile top-ups, card payments and other regular monthly usage needs) in a month, the potential for mobile banking transactions would be 500+ million transactions in a month and should grow to 1+ Billion transactions in next couple of years (Fig. 2).

This increase in adoption would decrease the transaction cost for banks, thereby aiding banks in redirecting investments in other requisite areas. Also, the small cooperative banks [16], eager to expand business are directly adopting mobile banking instead of starting with traditional Internet banking portals for desktops.

In our previous work [20], we conducted a survey to analyse the major reasons for lesser adoption of mobile banking apps. Information security, Network connectivity and Usability were the three most common reasons inhibiting adoption of mobile banking apps. With improving data connectivity (3G connection is growing

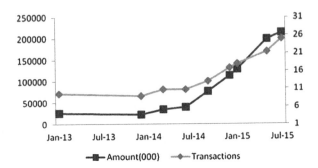

Fig. 2. Improved adoption.

at a CAGR of 61.3 % from 2013–17 and 4G is expected to grow at a CAGR of 103 % from 2013–18), and with banking security guidelines issued by RBI, Network connectivity and Information Security are currently being addressed at various levels. However, usability parameters for mobile app based banking is not available from the RBI or by the Bureau of Indian Standards (BIS). BIS is the national standards body of the government of India and responsible for standardization efforts.

In this paper, we propose usability parameters specific to mobile banking applications. We performed a thorough study of the various issues concerning the usability aspects and proposed parameters that can potentially be adopted by the standards body.

The major contributions of this paper are:

- An index named Mobile App Usability Index (MAUI) that can guide banks to improve usability of their mobile banking apps thereby increasing adoption rates.
- Fine-grained parameters based on the broad factors like time taken to complete a task, user interface display, and error handling.
- Validation of the proposed parameters and index with mobile banking channel managers (business and IT), chief information security officers and also with the mobile app customer base.

2   Mobile Banking App Usability Challenges

A survey with a sample of 1434 participants with diverse backgrounds (Chief Information Security Officers of the banks, Mobile Banking Channel Managers and smartphone users - working women and men from Information Technology (IT) and Non-IT companies, homemakers, retired staff of public sector firms, etc.) was conducted using WhatsApp, Facebook, LinkedIn, emails and face-to-face interactions to understand the usability related challenges of mobile banking [20]. The participants of the survey were aware that the authors were involved in banking technology research and hence gave feedback with an expectation for improvement of mobile banking adoption. Additionally, a total of 303,694 comments posted on 51 mobile banking apps on Google play store since Jan

2015 were analysed. We used Google playstores public API to fetch comments. The comments reflected the sentiments of users of various mobile banking apps. A sentiment analysis based on the user comments was done using RapidMiner tool. Figure 3 provides a segmentation of the positive, negative and neutral comments extracted using the tool.

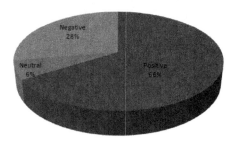

Fig. 3. Sentiment analysis of postings on app stores.

Fig. 4. Positive word cloud of banks.

We analysed the positive comments further by extracting the words from the comments. We correlated the words with usability related taxonomy to understand the positive impact of usability on mobile banking app adoption. Figure 4 shows the word cloud for the positive comments. Majority of the positive comments on Mobile Banking are on features availability such as transfer of money, ability to make card payments, getting account summary, ease of access, etc. They also reiterate the importance of simplicity, friendly, ease of use, etc. as the reasons for positive sentiment.

An analysis of negative words was done to further understand the reasons behind the negative sentiments. Figure 5 shows the word cloud from the extracted negative comments.

Fig. 5. Negative word cloud of banks.

The typical usability challenges in mobile banking apps can be summarized by some of the comments received during the survey:

1. *Gives msg 'mobile no. Not found'. Although my mobile number is registered.*
2. *Problem in installing & generating OTP. Again doesn't work on redmi 1 s with miui 6*
3. *Why should we pay RS.1 to open the application. ...coz many banks like XXXX, their application is more user friendly. ..they don't need any charge to open...*
4. *Simplify apps with inbuilt tamper free security rather answering questions start use of digital signatures assigned to individuals*
5. *Screen flickering and UI goes blank sometime*
6. *Application tends to take much more time then compared to other competitive bank, on 2G it tends to hang does not show proper error messages.*
7. *Taking least and only required inputs.. For any operation on mobile banking app.. Building trust in users to adopt mobile banking/marketing providing security pin generator token/device..even to farmers..and rest of the banking should be carried out with dtmf/sms based inputs..as these are the easiest to use.. any person can easily adopt it.. Separate/dedicated communication channels via service providers should be opened with highest security measures*

The survey results and the comments concur with our hypothesis that better usability leads to better adoption and in turn better revenues for the banks.

3   Usability Measurement

Usability is captured as a set of non-functional requirements in software engineering practices. The user interface designer develops wire frames and mock-ups based on the requirements and available organization standards. In our interaction with the Indian banks mobile banking teams, realized that most of them do not have specific personnel playing the role of user interface designers. Business Analyst or technology teams develop mock-ups or screen designs. In some cases, the interfaces were developed directly without business team/user involvement.

To understand the usability requirements and factors to measure usability, some of the widely adopted mobile banking apps of major banks (Wells Fargo, Bank of America, Barclays Bank, Citi Bank, and JP Morgan Chase Bank) and Mobile Wallets (Square, Starbucks, PayPal, mPay, etc.) were installed and the usability factors were studied.

As there are no BIS guidelines or assessment factors on usability of mobile applications, the Human Computer Interface and the User experience guidelines for mobile devices available from Apple for iOS [4], Google for Android [5] and Microsoft for Windows Mobile [11] were studied. Majority of banking apps run on these platforms, hence it covered the entire gamut of mobile banking apps. Also, the usability models suggested by Nielsen and Norman group [13] (Mobile website and application usability) and, People at the Centre of Mobile Application Development (PACMAD) model [2,9,18] were studied. In addition, the five human computer interface laws were analysed:

– Zipf law [1]
– Fitts' Law [8]
– Miller's law of STM (short term memory) [10]
– Power law of practice [12]
– Hick Hyman Law [17]

The main reason to study these laws was to correlate the human aspects of remembrance, time taken to make a decision based on the available choices and user expectations on keeping most frequently used as the first option as they have an impact on user perception on usability.

The ISO 9241 manual on Ergonomics of Human System Interaction Guidance on World Wide User Interfaces [7] was studied to assess the conformance of user interfaces of the mobile apps. However, the guidelines proposed in the manual were generic to web applications rather than mobile apps interfaces.

Like most other non-functional requirements, measuring usability is challenging. In our work, usability is measured based on the following factors:

1. Time taken to complete task: Intuitively this can be a measure as the number of clicks.
2. User interface display parameters: This refers to the font, colours, etc.
3. Error handling: This focuses on the error messages and the techniques to handle them.

The primary author is associated with banking technology arm of RBI and has a working relationship with several mobile banking channel managers and information security officers of the banks. The suggested parameters and index has been validated via a survey of the mobile banking channel managers, information security officers of the banks, some user interface designers and importantly mobile app banking users.

A thorough validation of the parameters can be done after the mobile banking apps are developed using the proposed parameters. This can be done via usability testing of the developed mobile banking apps. Instead of waiting for the development of the apps, we chose heuristic approach in this paper to validate the proposed parameters. Our thought stems from the recommendations provided by the Nielsen Norman group (NN/g) (*Mobile Website and Application Usability*), a leading organization that specializes in usability research on heuristics based approach for validating the usability parameters.

4   Recommendations for Improving Usability

Several researchers and organizations have provided usability recommendations for web applications. Some of the banks analysed in our study seemed to use these recommendations for developing their mobile banking applications. It is imperative that banks not develop the user interface of mobile banking apps similar to internet banking sites as the display screens, network connection and user attention span are all different from a desktop/laptop usage. The form factor of smart-phones vary from "2 to 6". This adds to the challenges of developing user interfaces for consistent usability experience.

As the saying goes, "what gets measured gets managed". After the adoption of the proposed parameters, a lab can be set-up for testing of mobile apps using Userzoom, Loop, Magitest, etc. for measuring the usability of the app. Additionally, focus groups can be formed to perform other types of usability testing.

We recommend a heuristic based evaluation method that computes an index score called MAUI (Mobile App Usability Index). MAUI can be used for measuring the effectiveness of implementation of Usability parameters for banks mobile app. The parameters mentioned in this paper are for the following factors:

1. Time taken to complete task
2. User interface display
3. Error handling

The parameters are given a priority rating for measuring the Index value. Priority rating values are given based on the quantum of themes emerging from the Google play store comments for the mobile banking apps and the relation it has on for improving usability. A priority of 1, 2 and 3 can be given for each of the parameters.

4.1   Time Taken to Complete Task

Table 1 mentions the usability parameters for time taken to complete a specific task. A task is considered as specific action that needs to be completed to satisfy

Table 1. Time taken to complete task.

A1 -	Account summary (using SIM, IMEI and other device information without disclosing any Personally identifiable information), nearest ATM/Branch, and contact information of call centre (with option of click to call) should be available without login using account number and password (P1)
A2 -	Maximum five fields should be sought from the customers while completing a form in the screen (P2)
A3 -	Screen navigation should start with more familiar fields (amount to transfer/deposit, deposit period, beneficiary name, account number, IFSC code, etc.) (P1)
A4 -	Based on users previous actions, there should be an option to set user/default favorites (P2)
A5-	Breadcrumbs should be available to keep users informed, on the navigation (P1)
A6 -	Labels of the fields should be in layman language and unambiguous for customer rather using bank specific terminology (P1)
A7 -	The option for Select All or Delete All should be removed (P3)
A8 -	Banking operation that started on a desktop, branch or ATM should continue over the mobile app without keying in data again (P2)
A9 -	Mobile app registration should not require going to bank branch and can be loaded from authorized app stores. The registration should be free of any SMS charges (P1)
A10 -	Sensitive information as date of birth, customer, account number that are already known should not be requested in the app (P1)
A11 -	Related fields should be grouped together (for example, beneficiary, user account details, etc.). Also, known fields should, be pre-populated (P1)

certain set of requirements. For example, adding beneficiary account, performing money transfer, making chequebook request, navigating through the screens, etc. are tasks that need to be completed. The time taken to complete the task is measured using specific number of clicks needed on the mobile phone from the start of the task to the end of that task.

4.2 User Interface Display Parameters

The font size/type, display colours, controls size and labels can change the user perception on the app. Though each individual has their own liking for a colour, font and other display parameters, the implementation of suggested parameters can enrich user experience with respect to the interface of the mobile banking app. Table 2 provides the parameters for user interface display.

Table 2. User interface display parameters.

B1 -	Colour combination in foreground and background should be consistent across screens and contrasting without any gradient/progressing colours (P1)
B2 -	Text information should be in mixed/sentence case instead of upper case (P2)
B3 -	Avoid pagination, vertical scrolling and horizontal scrolling (P1)
B4 -	Text in text boxes should be in single line and not spread across multiple lines (P2)
B5 -	Measures for size of button, textbox and other controls relative to screen size instead of pixels (P1)
B6 -	There should be bank logo, title page and frame, on every screen (P2)
B7 -	White spacing between fields should be, sufficient to view labels without overlapping (P3)
B8 -	Language used should be simple and consistent, with no long sentences and paragraphs in the screens. Having local languages,based on user preference would be highly beneficial for users (P2)
B9 -	There should be clear character spacing avoiding, any overlaps (P2)
B10 -	Bold text should be used sparingly (P2)
B11 -	The alignment of fields (left for text fields and, right for numbers) should be consistent (P2)
B12 -	There should be left, navigation available for moving between menu options (P2)
B13 -	There should not be any drag, and drop based features (P2)
B14 -	The image icons should be tested for varying resolutions (ldpi, mdpi, etc.) and different OS, (P1)
B15 -	Apps should be built using HTML5 for consistent look (P1)

4.3   Error Handling

As the mobile phone screens are smaller in size than desktops/laptops, the user attention for detail on such screens is difficult. It is important that apps are more thoroughly tested for various screens and device types and performance for various connectivity options. It is important that appropriate error messages are informed early rather than later and thus influencing user's perception of the usability of the app.

For example, if a PIN is entered incorrectly, an app developer may design the app in such a way that the error is handled immediately rather than wait for all information to be input before actually displaying the error.

4.4   Evaluating Usability Parameters Implementation

Some of the usability parameters listed are applicable for web banking applications as well. Parameters A2-A6 and A11 suggested for "time taken to complete

Table 3. Error handling.

C1 -	System messages should be classified as Information (with text in Green/Blue color), Warning (with text in Yellow color) and Error (with text in Red color) (P1)
C2 -	If a particular mobile device is not supported, an, error message should be displayed instead of allowing the user to install and, then showing an error message (P1)
C3 -	Error messages while filling a form should be, displayed next to the fields and button (P2)
C4 -	The message should provide the reason for error and, suggests the next possible action (P2)
C5 -	Application should maintain user action persistence, and recovery from abrupt exits (network connection lost, session timeout, battery, down, memory shortage, etc.) (P1)
C6 -	System messages should be configurable values rather, hardcoded for change at a later point of time (P3)
C7 -	Language of the error message should be in layman, language and easy to understand and avoid displaying any bank specific error, messages (P1)
C8 -	Error messages while loading a page should be at the, top of the screen (P2)
C9 -	The help icon should always be available and contextual to the screen (P2)
C10 -	App should be tested for varying network bandwidth, device models (make and screen size), flip/bump, back button and other buttons on the device, stylus, swipe operations, screen rotation, mobile keys, battery consumption and memory usage (P1)
C11 -	The app should have an option for user to report the error (P2)
C12 -	The version updates should be done on regular basis and ensured to keep past favorites intact (P1)

task", B2 suggested for "user interface display" and C1, C3, C4 and C6-C9 suggested for "error handling" are more relevant for mobile banking interfaces.

Based on the response to the recommendations, the banks should scale the implementation of usability parameters using the spider diagram as shown in Fig. 6. In the figure the darker line represents a reference benchmark and grey line is the MAUI values of a banking app. MAUI value can be computed as:

$$MAUI = \left(\sum Pc / \sum Pn \right) * 10 \tag{1}$$

where Pc is the sum of priority of conformed parameters, Pn is the total sum of priority of the parameters for each of the factors (Time to Complete Task, User Display Parameters and Error Handling) for assessing usability. In our paper, for sake of simplicity, MAUI is measured on a scale of 1–10, 10 being the highest and 1 being the least. Since the goal is to provide a basis for standardizing usability rather than measure the relative importance of one parameter over another, each recommendation parameter is treated equally by assigning one point each (at times this may be context driven and relative weights may be assigned to each parameter) and measured against a scaling factor. The metric can further be revised by assigning weights to the various parameters if necessary.

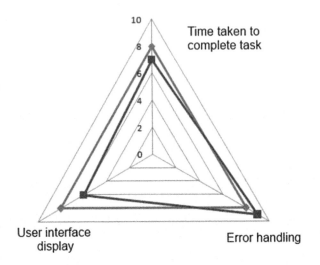

Fig. 6. MAUI parameters.

For example, if there are 15 parameters and the summation of 11 parameters met by the bank is 15 and the total of the priority of parameters is 20, the index can be calculated as (15/20) * 10 giving a value of 7.5. The score on time taken to complete task, user interface display parameters and error handling are plotted on a spider diagram shown in Fig. 6.

The figure shows a benchmark/desirable score for each of the axis as 8.0. We believe that a threshold value of 8.0 provides a reasonable assurance that the mobile banking app provides good to very good user experience. Precise benchmark values and assessment agencies/organizations to assess the conformance can be established once the rate of adoption of mobile banking apps shows a steady increase. In addition, conformance of parameters can also be further broken down into multiple levels rather than the binary value of Yes or No shown in this paper.

4.5   Mock-Ups

Once the parameters are taken into consideration, the User interfaces of various banking apps can be designed to best achieve the set threshold values. Figure 7(a)–(d) are mockup screens for the Landing page, Account details, Account statement and Fund transfer of a banking app that conforms to the usability parameters. The mockups can be used as a reference by banks for creating their mobile banking apps.

(a) Landing Page.

(b) Account Details.

(c) Account Statement.

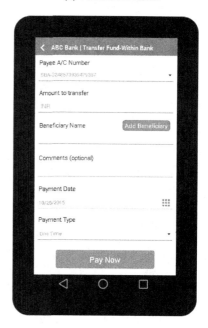

(d) Fund Transfer.

Fig. 7. Mockups.

5   Applicability of Recommendations

The applicability of MAUI is validated through a survey conducted (Google report on the Mobile App Usability survey, 2014) with Chief Information Security officers to ensure that the suggested usability parameters have reasonable security. Mobile banking channel managers having responsibility of running mobile banking business, technology managers from the banks and IT services industry involved in the development of mobile apps for the banks also participated in the survey. As the survey participants consisted of senior decision-making personnel in the banks and other relevant organizations, a detailed survey could have taken away their interest to participate. Hence a short survey for first five key parameters from Tables 1, 2 and 3 for each of the focus areas (time taken to complete task, display parameters and error handling) was conducted. There were 51 respondents in total. The responses of the survey are shown in Fig. 8.

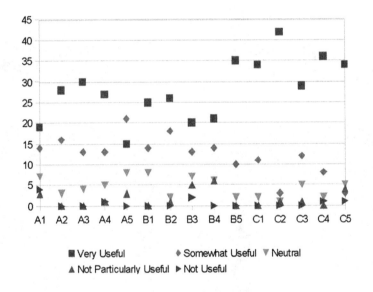

Fig. 8. Responses to MAUI survey.

We used Likert scale (Very Useful - 5, Somewhat Useful - 4, Neutral - 3, Not Particularly Useful - 2 and Not Useful - 1) to capture the response on the various parameters. The average score is 4.39/5, the lowest scores are 3.87 and 3.94 and the highest are 4.83 and 4.7. The summary of responses is shown in Fig. 8 and the detailed view of results is available at (Google report on the Mobile App Usability survey, 2014) [6].

Following were some of the comments from respondents:

– *It will be really helpful as some of the banks have really good mobile banking apps, while others don't have that good apps. So if it is standardized then user experience will be good*

- *These will definitely increase the user experience. Consistency in colors and font will increase usability.*
- *This Mobile Banking App Usability parameters if adopted, it will be very useful for the users. All these parameters are really very useful & helpful for mobile banking users in terms of saving time and ease of operations.*
- *Yes these would be very useful. Especially some sort of intelligence from the app with regards to error handling and saving the favourite activities of the user.*
- *These features may provide ease of operation to customers. Uniformity across all banks would also be helpful for customers.*
- *Good initiative to improve mobile banking*

Some additional comments to enhance/modify the suggested parameters were also provided:

- "Vertical scrolling is good but not the horizontal scrolling"
- "The first question: 'Account summary without login' may not be good idea"

Overall, the survey respondents seemed to agree the need for such parameters. Some of the comments specifically seemed to point out that the parameters can in fact be applied to most Human Computer Interfaces. Also, there were some comments from respondents to ensure security was not compromised while improving mobile banking app usability.

6 Conclusion

MAUI guides banks to improve usability and thereby increase adoption rates. Banks could use MAUI for baselining the currently deployed app and increase the adoption with an improved MAUI and perform the cost benefit analysis. These parameters are shared with IDRBT(Institute for Development and Research in Banking Technology, an organization established by RBI) and can be shared with BIS for establishing usability standards for mobile apps. A semi-automated tool may be built for measuring MAUI.

The accessibility requirements for different age groups and differently abled people can be researched for further improving mobile banking apps adoption. Improving usability is a constant journey with changing customer experiences and technology innovation. Hence, it is recommended for banks to review the usability requirements on a regular basis monitoring the feedback on app stores and the customer queries being handled by bank operations team. Also, along with standards body, the banks can form a consortium to standardize some of the interfaces of the banking applications. The MAUI metric can be extended to apps that banks are planning to deploy for internal stakeholders and also for non-banking organization building mobile apps for enterprise needs. Better usability of mobile apps improves customer loyalty and hence customer stickiness.

Acknowledgements. We thank Mobile Banking users, the mobile channel managers and chief information security officers for responding to the survey and providing their views on the usability parameters.

References

1. Apitz, G., Guimbretire, F., Zhai, S.: Foundations for designing and evaluating user interfaces based on the crossing paradigm. ACM Trans. Comp. Hum. Interact. (TOCHI), 17(9) (2010)
2. Bostrm, F., Nurmi, P.; Floren, P., Liu, T., Oikarinen, T.-K., Vetek, A., Boda, P.: Capricorn - an intelligent user interface for mobile widgets. In: Proceedings of the 10th International Conference on Human Computer Interaction with Mobile Devices and Services, pp. 327–330. ACM (2008)
3. Conn, B.: The evolution of mobile marketing in india: current trends and best practices. In: IAMAI Mobile Marketing Summit report (2014)
4. iOS Human Interface Guidelines: Designing for iOS. https://developer.apple.com/library/ios/documentation/userexperience/conceptual/mobilehig
5. Mobile App Design from Android. https://developer.android.com/design/material/index.html
6. Google report on the Mobile App Usability survey. https://docs.google.com/forms/d/1ZYAOQF2sAAEwYR26bbp8B3_vCZaJMtaKVUaWQK3ULZU/viewanalytics
7. Ergonomics of Human System Interaction Guidance on World Wide User Interfaces, ISO 9241-151: ISO/TC 159/SC (2011)
8. Fitts, P.: The information capacity of the human motor system in controlling the amplitude of movement. J. Exp. Psychol. **47**, 381–391 (1954)
9. Harrison, R., Flood, D., Duce, D.: Usability of mobile applications: literature review and rationale for a new usability model. J. Interact. Sci. **1**, 1–16 (2013)
10. Miller, G.: The magical number seven, plus or minus two. Psychol. Rev. **63**(2), 81–97 (1956)
11. Usability Guidelines. http://msdn.microsoft.com/en-us/library/bb158578.aspx
12. Newell, A., Rosenbloom, P.S.: Mechanisms of skill acquisition and the law of practice. In: Anderson, J.R. (ed.) Cognitive Skills and Their Acquisition, pp. 1–55. Erlbaum, Hillsdale (1993)
13. Nielsen Norman Group. Mobile Website and Application Usability – Nielsen Norman Group report
14. Khan, H.R.: Customizing mobile banking in India: issues & challenges. In: FICCI-IBA (FIBAC) 2012 Conference on - Sustainable Excellence Through Customer Engagement, Employee Engagement and Right Use of Technology
15. List of Banks permitted to provide Mobile Banking Service in India - Report from Reserve Bank of India (2014). http://www.rbi.org.in/scripts/bs_viewcontent.aspx?Id=2463
16. Banks wise volumes in ECS/NEFT/RTGS/MobileTransaction- Report from Reserve Bank of India (2014). http://www.rbi.org.in/scripts/NEFTView.aspx
17. Rosati, L.: How to design interfaces for choice: Hick- Hyman law and classification for information architecture. In: Slavic, A., Salah, A., Davies, C. (eds.) Classification and Visualization: Interfaces to Knowledge: Proceedings of the International UDC Seminar The Hague, The Netherlands, pp. 125–138, (2013)
18. Seongil, L.: Mobile internet services from consumers perspectives. Int. J. Hum. Comput. Interact. **25**(5), 390–413 (2009)
19. Mobile phone internet user penetration 2012-2018 - Statistic. http://www.statista.com/statistics/309019/india-mobile-phone-internet-user-penetration/
20. Mohan, L., Neeraj Mathur, Y., Reddy, R.: Mobile App Usability Index (MAUI) for Improving Mobile Banking Adoption. In: ENASE, pp. 313–320 (2015)

Author Index

Printed in the United States
By Bookmasters